THE
ARTFUL
D·O·D·G·E·R

OTHER BOOKS BY DAVID FISHER

The Umpire Strikes Back (WITH RON LUCIANO)
Strike Two (WITH RON LUCIANO)
What's What
The War Magician
Killer (WITH "JOEY")
The Pack
Louie's Widow

THE
ARTFUL
D·O·D·G·E·R

TOMMY LASORDA
and David Fisher

illustrated with photographs

ARBOR HOUSE
NEW YORK

Manufactured in the United States of America

10 9 8 7 6 5 4 3 2 1

This book is printed on acid free paper. The paper in this book meets
the guidelines for permanence and durability of the Committee on
Production Guidelines for Book Longevity of the Council on Library
Resources.

Designed by Richard Oriolo

Library of Congress Cataloging in Publication Data

Lasorda, Tommy.
The artful Dodger.

1. Lasorda, Tommy. 2. Baseball—United States—
Managers—Biography. 3. Los Angeles (Dodgers Baseball team)
I. Fisher, David, 1946-   . II. Title
GV865.L33A32 1985   796.357'092' [B]   85-3890
ISBN 0-87795-716-9

All photos courtesy of the Lasorda family.

I would like to dedicate this book to my lovely wife, Jo, who for thirty-five years has been my inspiration and love, and to my children, Laura and Tom, Jr. (Spunky), for all their love and support.

I would also like to dedicate this book to the late Mr. Walter O'Malley, for giving me the opportunity to work for the greatest organization in baseball, and to his wonderful wife, the late Kay O'Malley, for the inspiration and love she always had time to extend to me.

And I would also like to dedicate this book to Al Campanis, the man who taught me so much about the game of baseball, and for believing in me when others didn't.

And I would also like to dedicate this book to Bert Welles and John Carey, two of the greatest friends I could have ever asked for. Two of the greatest Dodgers of them all. My family and I love them both very much.

CONTENTS

•

Preface   xi

ONE

Only in This Great Country of Ours . . .   1

TWO

Herein I Become a Dodger,
I Get Married and Join the Royal Family   23

THREE

I Make My Pitch for the Big Leagues,
a Curveball, and Become a Minor Star   45

FOUR

Only in This Great Country of Theirs . . .   73

FIVE

I Join the Scouts   97

SIX

I Manage to Prosper in Utah   121

SEVEN

I Do Pennants   145

EIGHT

My Blue Heaven   173

NINE

Blue Seasoning 203

TEN

I Manage to Get to the Top 239

Acknowledgments 257

Photographs follow page 144

Preface

Sometimes, when I think about how fortunate I've been in life, I think that I'm suddenly going to hear my mother calling to wake me up so that I won't be late for school, and I'll realize that it has all been a dream.

But, in fact, my life has been better than my most outstanding dreams. It's my dreams come true. I believe I am the happiest man in the world. I found and married the most wonderful woman in the world, and we've raised two tremendous children. I have fulfilled my greatest ambition and pitched in the major leagues. I am the manager of the Los Angeles Dodgers. I have made good friends from all walks of life in practically every city in the country.

I am writing this book because I want to share the lessons I've learned, and the joy I've experienced, with youngsters and oldsters alike. I want this book to be a message to everyone, a reminder that we are living in the greatest country in the world. A land of opportunity. When I was growing up in Norristown, Pennsylvania, for example, in order for my cousin, Vince Piazza, and I to be able to afford to go out for a small lunch, we had to wait until he sold a hubcap from his small auto repair shop. Today, Vince owns twenty-five new car dealerships.

In this country anyone can be anything they want to be, no matter what their race, creed, color, or economic background. All they have to do is want it bad enough to pay the price. There is only one route to success, and that is the avenue of hard work.

I want to encourage youngsters to set their goals in life and go after them with all the drive and determination and self-confidence they possess. But I want to emphasize how important it is that they get their education. Education will open the door to success.

If I can communicate that message, as well as make you smile a few times, this book will be a success.

TOMMY LASORDA
Fullerton, California
January, 1985

ONE

•

Only in This
Great Country of Ours . . .

Recently, I attended an Old-Timers' Day reunion honoring the world champion 1955 Brooklyn Dodgers. Although many people aren't aware of it, before becoming Dodger manager I served a thirty-year apprenticeship as an extremely active player, a minor league and major league coach, a traveling secretary, a scout, and a minor league manager. In 1955, I was a semi–hard-throwing left-handed pitcher and cheerleader for Walter Alston's champions, although many baseball record books continue to misspell my name. Instead of the correct spelling, *Lasorda, Thomas Charles,* they often abbreviate it to *Others.* I pitched four memorable innings for that ball club—if you have a really exceptional memory.

At that reunion, as I was standing in the sunlight between our great captain, Harold "Pee Wee" Reese, and our slugging centerfielder, Edwin "Duke" Snider, I couldn't help thinking how incredible it was that, on a team that included such remarkable men as Reese and Snider, Jackie Robinson, Gil Hodges, Roy Campanella, Jim Gilliam, Don Zimmer, Carl Furillo, Carl Erskine, and Don Newcombe, I was the one who had become manager of the Dodgers.

"Can you believe this, Pee Wee?" I said. "Let me ask you, if someone had asked you back then, which player, out of all these great players, will eventually manage the ball club, wouldn't you have put me dead last?"

Pee Wee looked me right in the eye. "No, Tommy," he said, "I would've put you next to last."

Next to last! I was stunned. "What are you talking about?" I said.

"Who could you've possibly put behind me?"

"Sandy Amoros," he answered without hesitation. "He didn't speak English."

Me, Tommy Lasorda, manager of the Los Angeles Dodgers, the Big Blue, the greatest franchise in the history of our national pastime. It's an amazing story. For only in this great country of ours, this land of opportunity, could the son of an Italian immigrant, a runny-nosed little left-handed pitcher with a decent curveball, a player good enough only to be the third-string pitcher on his high school baseball team, a boy from a family so poor that the soles of our shoes were so thin we could tell if a coin was heads or tails when we stepped on it, grow up to become manager of a great baseball team, be invited to lunch *and* dinner at the White House, be asked to address the corps of cadets at both West Point and the Air Force Academy, be honored with a scholarship fund named after him at a major university, become close friends with some of the most celebrated entertainers of our time, and make television commercials for products ranging from frozen pizza to antacid.

I was born in Norristown, Pennsylvania, the second of the five sons of Sabatino and Carmella Lasorda. Norristown was a small town outside Philadelphia, and my father drove a truck in the quarry. The people there were poor, but proud. There was a big billboard at the city limits proclaiming "See America—But See Norristown First!" And no one was prouder, or poorer, than the Lasordas.

I learned growing up that there were two very important things that money couldn't buy—love and poverty. And my family had as much of both as no money could buy. I remember, every Sunday morning when we went to church, my father would give me two pennies to put in the collection basket. Two pennies. On a number of occasions I figured I would split it even-up with the Lord. So, when Father Pasto, our parish priest, held the basket in front of me, I'd drop one penny in and palm the other one. And then Father Pasto would hit me on the head with the basket and I'd drop the other penny in.

It was tough feeding five growing boys on my father's salary, so we grew a lot of our own food. We had a small vegetable patch about four miles from our house, and we raised tomatoes, cucumbers, peppers, anything that would grow. We'd eat them all summer, then my mother would jar the rest of our crop and we'd eat that all winter. We also raised one or two scrawny hogs that we'd slaughter for sausage and meat. My mother baked bread, but we'd also buy sacks of stale donuts and bread from the Spalding's Bakery for a nickel. If you dunked them in hot cocoa long enough they became edible.

I often say that I never missed a meal, and I didn't—but I did postpone a few. There were days when we'd eat "wish" sandwiches—that's when you'd put two pieces of bread together and wish there was some meat between them. Somehow we got by, though, and the two things there were never a shortage of in that house were love and affection. The house was always filled with people and laughter and singing. On Friday nights, when my father knew he didn't have to get up at dawn to go to work the next morning, my parents' friends would come over and my father would pull out his accordion and we'd sing Italian songs and dance all night.

We lived in a small three-story workingman's house that was air-conditioned whenever the wind was blowing and was heated by a pot-bellied stove in the kitchen that sent up heat through stovepipes to the rest of the house. We slept on the third floor, so by the time the heat got up there from the kitchen, it was the next day.

At night, after dinner, we'd lay down on the congoleum, wrap ourselves in old coats, and listen to my father tell stories. His stories always took place back in Italy, and they usually concerned five strong brothers, and they always had a message. He spoke in heavily accented English and Italian, but we always got the message. Once, for example, he told us the story of the parish priest back in his hometown of Tollo who wanted a big rock removed from behind the church. There were five brothers living in that town, and they were known to be the strongest men in the entire province. He decided to invite them for dinner, and after dinner put them to work moving the rock. Soon as the brothers heard their favorite word, "dinner," they accepted. The priest cooked this big meal, spaghetti and meatballs and sausages and this and that—my father's stories always featured great Italian cooking—and finally, when everyone was done eating, he said, "You guys have a reputation for being very strong. See that big rock over there? I'd like you to move it for me."

The five brothers turned and looked at the rock. It was big, very big, and it would take a lot of hard work to move it. "So finally," my father would conclude, "one of the brothers, Tommy was his name, he spoke up. 'You're right,' he said, 'we have worked hard to earn a reputation. But it's for eating, not working!' "

His point was that his sons all loved to eat, but none of them wanted to work.

I worked. I took any job anyone would give me. I shoveled snow, I shined shoes, I sold fruits and vegetables door-to-door, I laid track for the railroad at 50 cents an hour, I worked as a presser in a military uniform factory, I hauled bushels of ashes from people's houses to the dump for 5 cents a bushel. Hammering in railroad ties was hard work, pressing pants was boring, but the worst job of all was potato delivery boy.

I was always one of the strongest and toughest kids in the neighborhood. I learned how to defend myself from my uncle Tony Covatta. He used to take me to his friends' houses and bet them a buck that I could whip their sons. Then he'd offer me a quarter to fight.

When I was fourteen, a man we called Tom Rats, mainly because he looked like a rat, came to my house and hired me to work the back of his potato truck. He sold hundred-pound sacks of potatoes door-to-door. My job was to carry the bags from the truck to the customer's cellar. On a good day, he'd sell 400 hundred-pound sacks. And I carried every one of them. His good days were my bad days.

My salary was a dollar a day, so I knew I was never going to get rich in that business. But the family needed the money, so every Saturday morning I'd meet him at his house at 6 A.M. Maybe I'd have eaten a small bowl of cereal and some soggy stale donuts for breakfast, and then I'd have to sit there at the Rats table as he devoured piles of eggs and bacon and toast. I mean, these piles were even bigger than the ones in my father's stories. I'd sit there practicing to look hungry, but he never even offered me a bite.

So I got even with him. I'd tell my brother Eddie to meet the truck at the corner of Arch and Walnut streets and, as the truck went by, somehow a sack would accidentally fall off. Then I'd tell my brother Harry there was going to be another accident at the corner of Oak and High streets and, when we got there, *thud*, I'd kick off another sack. The Lasordas never had a lot of money—but we never ran out of potatoes.

These days, from mid-October through early February, I'll make as many as a hundred speeches and appearances, sometimes five a week, all over the country. I'm often asked how I can work so hard. I tell anyone who asks the truth. After working for the railroad, the pants place, and Tom Rats, how hard a job is it to sit on an airplane watching a movie while someone brings you food?

Some of the people I grew up with ended up in difficulty, if you consider jail difficulty. The two things that kept me out of trouble were my father's right hand and baseball. If professional boxing permitted fighters to use belts, my father could've been a world champion. He believed the quickest way to a boy's mind was through his backside, and he never hesitated to smack us with his belt when he thought we did something wrong. Sometimes, in fact, he didn't even wait till we did anything wrong. One very hot day, for example, we were working in the vegetable garden. There was a cold water spring about a mile away. My father called me over, handed me an empty milk bottle, and said, "Take this and go get me a bottle of water, and don't break the bottle."

Then, *pow!* he smacked me on the side of the head hard enough to get my attention. "Hey," I screamed, "what're you hitting me for? I haven't broken the bottle."

"Yeah," he said, "but what good's it gonna do to hit you after you break it?" Now, I know a lot of people will think that was a terrible thing to do—but a lot of people didn't have me as a kid, either. He was simply trying to prevent me from making a mistake he knew I was capable of making. And I'll tell you what—when I carried that bottle back, I carried it so tightly I almost squeezed the water out of it. I figured, Hey, if he hit me before I broke it, what was he going to do after I broke it? My father was the greatest philosopher I ever met. I couldn't have asked for a better teacher.

But more than my love for my parents, or my fear, the thing that kept me out of trouble was baseball. I knew I was going to be a major league baseball player. I didn't hope I was going to make it, I knew it. I was going to pitch for the New York Yankees. And organized baseball was very different in the 1930s. Without the competition from football, basketball, golf, and tennis, every good young athlete wanted to sign a baseball contract. The scouts wouldn't even consider signing anyone with a bad background. So I never broke a law; I stayed straight or, at worst, slightly wavy.

I don't remember when, or why, I first fell in love with the great game of baseball, but I fell hard, and for life. Even today my wife of more than three decades, Jo, accuses me of loving the Dodgers and baseball more than I love her. And when she does, I look her in the eye and tell her honestly, "All right, but I love you more than I love football and basketball."

It never occurred to me that I might have to do anything else with my life except play baseball. My father felt differently. He was a skilled bocci player—a gentleman's game in which heavy balls are softly rolled—and he didn't understand my passion for baseball. He thought, for example, that my household chores were more important than any game in which one player threw the ball at another player. So we had a continuing battle, which I continued to lose. What I'd end up doing was taking my bucket and my scrub brush, my furniture polish and rags, and go upstairs as if I actually intended to scrub the floors. Then I'd squeeze outside through the bathroom window onto the kitchen roof, slide down the drainpipe to the ground, crawl on my hands and knees alongside the house so nobody would see me, and as soon as I hit the street—*ffffttttt*—I was history. I'd meet my buddies at the park and play ball all day.

Unfortunately, I couldn't sneak back into the house. My father would be waiting for me with the belt when I got home, but I always figured a few smacks were a fair trade for a full day of baseball.

Because there was no television then we never saw real major league players; that left our imaginations free to create images of our heroes. Each of us patterned ourselves after a major leaguer. The guy I tried to be like was Dodger pitcher Van Lingle Mungo. I never saw him play, I didn't even know if he threw left-handed or right-handed. But I liked his name, and in my mind he had to be a small left-hander like I was, and I was sure he kicked his right leg high into the air when he pitched, as I did. In fact, he was a 6'2" right-hander. So much for details. But whenever we played, I was Van Lingle Mungo. I don't mean I pretended to be him, I was him. If I walked a certain way, that must have been the way he walked. My nickname became Mungo, or sometimes Mung, and that was the only name my close friends called me. Anyone who doubts my devotion to baseball should remember that Van Lingle was born a Mungo, and I picked that name. But both of us had to live with it.

When I wasn't playing baseball with my friends, I'd invent my own games. I'd spend hours throwing a ball against the side of our house, or I'd take a broomstick and go into a field near my house to hit rocks. I was a big New York Yankee fan, although it didn't bother me that Mungo was a Dodger because Brooklyn never won, so whenever I played a game by myself it was always the Yankees against somebody. And whenever the Yankees were losing, they would somehow manage to load the bases, and somehow my number-one idol, Lou Gehrig, would get to bat with the game on the line. The worst hitter I ever saw was Tony Lazzeri, who struck out all the time with the bases loaded in that field, only to be saved by Gehrig hitting in the clutch.

If we weren't playing baseball, we were talking about it. Everybody hung out under the street lamp in front of the grocery store on the corner of Marshall and Walnut streets. The older guys would stand under the brighter light on one side of the street and us younger guys would stand under the light across the street. Fortunately, there was a grocery store under each light. As the older guys got married or went into the army and left the corner, the younger guys graduated to the brighter side of the street. Older guys talked about girls, sports, girls, jobs, girls, the war; we talked about baseball. No baseball players we ever heard of went out with girls. Mostly we flipped baseball cards and played the Initial Game. I knew the initials of every major league player. WMD, for example, William Malcolm Dickey. JPD, Joseph Paul Dimaggio. The easiest one of all was

FFF, Frank Francis Frisch, the fabulous Fordham Flash. I was an expert at initials. I might not have known who defeated Cornwallis at Yorktown, but I sure knew who GHR was—George Herman "Babe" Ruth—and on the corner of Marshall and Walnut that had a lot more value.

When I wasn't playing, reading about, or talking baseball, I was listening to Philadelphia Athletic games on an old Atwater-Kent radio. And when it wasn't working, which was most of the time, I'd go into the street, because people used to sit on their porches or by a window listening to the games. Often, at Dodger Stadium today, thousands of people will be listening to Vin Scully broadcasting the game they're watching, and a ghostly whisper can be heard throughout the ball park. In Norristown, entire neighborhoods would be listening to the games, and it was possible to walk for blocks without missing three pitches.

Finally, when I wasn't playing or talking baseball, or listening to a game, or reading about it, I was dreaming about it. I often dreamed I was pitching in Yankee Stadium. I saw myself standing on the pitcher's mound, or the "hill of thrills," as I eventually named it, working out of a jam by striking out Jimmie Foxx or Hank Greenberg. Actually, I'd never seen Yankee Stadium, but it didn't matter—it was the Yankee Stadium of my dreams.

The only things I could do as well as I could play baseball were spell and fight. I may very well have been the greatest left-handed speller to come out of Norristown. When I was a student at Holy Savior I was on the school's interscholastic spelling bee team and we made it all the way to the state championships. Anyone who has grown up in a house with five boys will understand why I became a good fighter. I fought all the time, for any reason. If a few days passed and I hadn't been in a fight, I'd start one, and when the person I'd picked on complained, I'd tell him, "Look, I don't have anything against you, but chances are I'm gonna be in a real fight in the next few days, and I just don't wanna be out of practice."

I did lose a few fights, but I won a lot more than I lost. I never cared who I was fighting, or even how many people I was fighting. One great brawl took place when I was fifteen years old and was working as a bellhop at the Valley Forge Hotel. The best thing about the job was that I got to wear the snazzy uniform. What could possibly be more beautiful, I thought, than my blue uniform with gold stripes and gold braids around the shoulder epaulets? One night my father told me to wait outside the hotel after work to meet my younger brothers Joey and Morris, who were at the movies. I didn't mind standing outside and waiting, I knew people were going to be mighty impressed by a young man in uniform. But as

I waited, three grown men started making fun of it. I couldn't believe their bad taste. They gave me no choice, I had to defend the colors of the Valley Forge Hotel.

The first guy went down with one punch. Then I spun around and whacked the second guy and he went down. The third guy was hanging on me from behind, so I had to twist to get him off me. But as I cocked my arm, he held up a badly smashed hand. "Hey," he said, stopping me, "you wouldn't hit a crippled guy, would you?"

I never hit crippled guys, that was a rule I lived by. No crippled guys. So I forgot about him and hit the first guy again, and then I hit the second guy again, and meanwhile this third guy has jumped me from behind again. So again I got ready to bop him and again he held up his smashed hand and again he said, "You really wouldn't hit a crippled guy, would you?"

Oh, I wanted to. I really wanted to. But, I mean, a crippled guy? So I forgot him and turned around just in time to nail the first guy again. Then I got the second guy just as he was getting up. But meanwhile the third guy was pulling me from behind again. Once more I turned around and glared at him. Once more he held up that crippled hand. Once more he pleaded, "You wouldn't hit a crippled guy, would you?"

I had had enough. "Yeah," I told him, "I think I probably would." Then I dropped him.

I became so well known as a fighter in the neighborhood that two former professional boxers, Al Coulon and Al Bartlett, came looking for me one day to spar with a pro fighter training for a big bout in Philadelphia. They got to my house right after I had finished a big pasta and bread meal, but I didn't care. I got in the ring, and the first thing the pro fighter did was hit me in the stomach. Most fighters don't like to be hit in the head, I didn't like being slugged in the spaghetti dinner. So I went after him as if it were a real fight. I got him up against the ring post and hammered him, finally forcing him between the ropes and out of the ring.

When he fell, he twisted his ankle, forcing him to cancel the bout in Philly. A few days later Coulon and Bartlett asked me if I'd like to turn pro. I was only fifteen years old, but in those days nobody asked how old you were if you could hit a baseball or throw a punch. If I hadn't wanted to play major league baseball so badly I might have accepted their offer.

Fortunately, I was able to combine two of the things I did best, pitching and fighting. There really isn't too much of a demand for pitchers who can spell. But when I was playing, baseball became a contact sport. I was willing to drop my glove and fight at any time—particularly when someone got a hit off me. I hated to give up a hit. I hated to lose. I like to think that when I was young the only thing I wasn't good at was losing. I'm no better at it today—and I've had a lot of practice.

My desire to win, my incredible drive to excel, probably allowed me to go a lot farther in baseball than just my talent would have taken me. But my temper probably held me back. If a batter got a hit off me I'd stand on the pitcher's mound seething, ready to bust—and then the umpire would give me a hard ball and let me do whatever I wanted to do with it. Are you kidding me? Whoever invented a game that allowed me to throw a baseball at a standing target when I was angry must have had some strange sense of humor. I had batters bobbing, weaving, ducking . . . The only thing that prevented me from hitting more batters than I did was that my control was never very good. Looking back, I consider myself very fortunate I never had a great fastball—if I had had a good one I really might have hurt somebody.

I didn't play in an organized league until I was in high school. Before that I never played on a team that had uniforms. Uniforms? We barely had equipment. Most families in the neighborhood were like mine, they'd spend their money on food and clothing rather than balls and bats. So we always had to scrounge to get whatever we used. We made our own bats from pick handles or pieces of wood that we would shave and scrape and sand. Our baseballs came from the city prison on Marshall Street, about eight blocks from our house. When the inmates were playing a game, we'd stand in the cemetery beyond the walls waiting for someone to hit one out. We called those balls "jailbirds" and we'd wrap black tape around them to keep them from unraveling.

I stole my first glove from a Moose when I was fourteen. Before that I either borrowed a glove or used a heavy workglove to protect my hand. In those days every town in America had very good semi-pro baseball leagues. We had the Norristown City League, which consisted of teams sponsored by the various men's clubs. Each of these clubs had slot machines in their halls, and the profits from these machines were used to pay players. As I later found out, professional players in the low minors were paid as little as $50 a month, while semi-pro players often made as much as $25 a game, so a lot of talented players chose to stay in their hometowns and play semi-pro rather than sign a professional contract.

We used to go see as many games as we could. One night we hopped the fence to see the big game between the Moose Lodge and the Italian Club—the Lodge Antonio Mucci, or LAM. Naturally, a Lasorda had a rooting interest.

At that time players would leave their gloves on the field when they went to bat, in the major leagues as well as in the Norristown City League.

The shortstop, for example, would flip his glove into the outfield when the third out was made and leave it there until he took his defensive position again. So, on this night, the Moose and the LAM got into a real fight. There were bodies flying in every direction—it was either a bad game or a great fight. Some fans leaped onto the field to help break it up. We leaped onto the field too, to collect those loose gloves. I picked up the first glove I saw and took off. We took so many gloves that when the fight was over, the game had to be canceled, probably the only time a game has been called on account of stolen gloves.

I got Joe Burns's glove. It was a right-handed mitt, and I had to wear it backwards, but I didn't care. I finally had my own glove.

The most valuable piece of baseball equipment I ever owned was my first pair of spikes. They cost three bucks. I got them in the ninth grade. Although I'd never played in school, I went out for the Rittenhouse Junior High School team. I made the junior high varsity as a pitcher-outfielder. That was the proudest moment of my life. But two days before our first real game, the coach, Kim Custer, told me I had to get a pair of baseball shoes, spikes, or I wouldn't be permitted to play. Until that time I wore sneakers, or the steel-tipped workshoes my father bought for us. I told the coach that my family couldn't possibly afford to buy me a pair of spikes. He was sympathetic, but insistent. If I didn't have spikes I wouldn't play on the varsity.

I was heartbroken. There was just no way . . . But that night I sat down with my father and told him I'd made the varsity baseball team.

"That's good," he said, "that's very good. What's a varsity?"

I explained the way the system was set up, then I told him my problem. "I gotta have a pair of baseball shoes," I said.

"What's wrong with the shoes you got on?" he wanted to know.

As far as he was concerned, the difference in shoes was that they were either brown or black. If a pair of shoes was good enough to wear to school, they were certainly good enough to use for playing. "I need special shoes for baseball."

I don't think he'd ever heard such a silly idea. "Special shoes for baseball? It's tough enough I gotta buy you shoes to wear. I can't be buying you no shoes for baseball."

I tried to emphasize that I wouldn't be allowed to play on the varsity if I didn't get a pair of spikes, but he just shook his head and repeated that he couldn't afford shoes that could only be worn on a baseball field. I began crying, and I cried for a long time. I don't remember ever wanting anything more in my entire life than I wanted those shoes.

And when I came home from school the next day there was a box sitting on the table. "Here," he said, handing it to me. Inside was a pair of baseball spikes with bright yellow shoelaces. To this day I don't think I've received a present that meant more to me. I slipped them on my feet— they slipped on easily because they were at least three sizes too big. "Pop," I said, "these are too big."

"Hey," he said, "so you grow into them. Whattya think, I'm gonna buy you a new pair of baseball shoes every year? The way your feet are growing?" So I stuffed old newspaper into the front of these shoes and flopped around the field.

A year later I made the Norristown High School team. With my right-hander's glove on the wrong hand and my floppy shoes, I was not the most elegantly outfitted player on the team, but it didn't really matter because I rarely got into a game. Basically, I carried the equipment and pitched batting practice. I was the third-string pitcher, behind Buddy Righter and Red Henning. Unfortunately, we only used two pitchers. But even that didn't bother me because I knew I was going to make the big leagues someday. I told our coach, Harvey Fishburn, "I don't know how you can pitch those two guys ahead of me, because I'm gonna pitch in the big leagues and those two guys aren't." It seemed perfectly logical to me. I don't remember if I was that naive or that confident, but it just never occurred to me that I might not make it.

I knew I was good, Fishburn aside. Although I wasn't playing in high school games, I was the starting pitcher for the famed Norristown Parks and Recreation League All-Stars. I didn't have an overpowering fastball, but I could throw a great curveball. In that league, a great curveball was any pitch that didn't come straight in. When a player did get a hit off me, I had no qualms about throwing at him the next time he got up, so few batters felt comfortable at the plate—which also helped me.

I was also becoming a good hitter. I believed I was the best pitcher in the league, so as long as I didn't have to bat against myself I shouldn't have any trouble. My theory of hitting was just to watch the ball as it came in and hit it. As I realized years later, that is still the finest theory of hitting yet devised.

I wasn't quite sure how a player got to the big leagues. As far as I knew, he was just there one day. So I pitched at every opportunity, waiting for that day. My opportunity came when the local newspaper, the *Norristown Times-Herald*, invited the Connie Mack All-Stars to town for a game with Parks and Recreation. The All-Stars had been formed by Athletics' manager Connie Mack as a means of watching the progress of the best young players in the Philadelphia area. They played any team willing to put up $100 to cover their expenses. The *Times-*

Herald put up the money—and they wanted the local team to win.

I was chosen to pitch for Parks and Recreation, the first really important game of my life. I tried to keep the game a secret from my parents, because I was afraid they would come to the park and jinx me. But there were stories about it in the paper and they found out about it. They did not come, however, and did not jinx me. I didn't sleep the night before the game. I just lay there, my arm wrapped in a blanket to keep it warm, thinking about it. I pitched that game in my mind so many times that night that the real game was easy. I beat them 5–1, pitching a complete game and driving in four of our five runs. And, after the game, Bill Hockenbury, the coach of the Connie Mack All-Stars, invited me to come to Philadelphia and try out for his team. They were going to Baltimore, he explained, to play in a national amateur tournament, and he thought I could help them win.

I was too embarrassed to tell him I didn't know how to get to Philadelphia, so I agreed. Eventually, Sonny Monastero and Red Picard, who coached a local team, borrowed a panel truck from People's Cleaners and drove me there with all the laundry still in the back of the truck. Everything went wrong. It was illegal to drive a truck on the parkway and we were stopped by the police, and we got into an argument, trying to convince the policeman that a panel truck was not a truck. Then, when we got into Philadelphia, we got lost. By the time we found the ball park, the tryout game was half over.

That was the day I first realized how much competition I would have to face to get to the big leagues. I always believed I was the best, as well as the toughest, little left-handed pitcher around. When I got to the ball park I discovered I wasn't even the smallest little left-handed pitcher around. A pitcher by the name of Bobby Shantz was on the mound, and he was at least two inches shorter than I was. And he was good—so good he eventually pitched sixteen years in the major leagues.

Because we arrived late I didn't have time to warm up properly. They told me to put on my shoes and get ready to pitch. Naturally, I had no problem getting my shoes on. I walked confidently to the mound and proceeded to throw my first three pitches over the catcher's head into the backstop. It was either a matter of bearing down or finding a taller catcher, so I took a deep breath and really concentrated.

I pitched three innings and struck out the nine batters I faced. Not only did I make the Connie Mack All-Stars, but after the tryout, Jocko Collins, a scout for the Philadelphia Phillies who had been in the stands, came down to talk to me. He liked the way I pitched, he said, and would like to come to my house to talk to my parents after I got back from Baltimore.

This was long before professional baseball, or any sport, had a draft system that gave a team exclusive rights to a young player, so any team could sign any player it wanted to. In small towns all over America, the best-known people were the major league scouts, or "bird-dogs" as they were called, the people who found players and signed them to professional contracts. The fact that Jocko Collins, a scout, was coming to my house was big news in the neighborhood. If we had had a telephone it would have never stopped ringing.

I pitched one game and played the outfield in another in Baltimore. But most of the other teams in the tournament were representing defense plants and their players were much older and more experienced. None of us played badly, but we were just too young, and lost the tournament.

As soon as I got home, Collins scheduled an appointment. I had my mother cooking all morning, figuring if she fed him enough spaghetti there was no way, no way, he could resist offering me a contract. Neither of my parents really understood what was going on, but they knew it was important to me so they went along with it. Mr. Jocko Collins, scout, came to my house and ate my mother's spaghetti and, at the conclusion of the meal, told my father, "I've seen Tom pitch and I believe he can be successful in professional baseball. I'd like to offer him a contract to play in the Phillies organization."

I didn't know what he was talking about, "organization." I didn't even know there was such a thing as the minor leagues. I thought you signed a contract and played in the majors. Jocko offered me $100 a month to play with the Utica ball club. Utica? Sounded great to me, whatever it was. Years later, when I was scouting for the Dodgers, I told Jocko that signing me was the worst job of negotiating I'd ever seen. "You made your move too soon," I explained. "If you'd have waited five minutes more, I would've offered *you* $200 a month to let me play professional baseball."

My father did not want me to sign the contract. I was still only sixteen and couldn't sign without his permission. "Look," he told me, "I've tried to tell you I want you to go to college. I was willing to work whatever jobs were necessary to make it so you could go because I know you should get a good education. You've got a good head on your shoulders, but sometimes you just don't put it in the right direction. All you're ever concerned about is baseball and boxing.

"But it's your life and you gotta live with your decisions. I don't want you coming to me later with hate and regret telling me I deprived you of something you wanted to do, so if you want to play professional baseball, I'll sign for you."

Naturally, everyone in the neighborhood was impressed. I remember my cousin, Joe Lasorda, who lived two doors down, telling my mother, "I seen Tommy play. He'll be home within a month." I mean, nobody thought I'd make it in baseball, nobody. Boxing, maybe. But baseball, there was just no way. The fact that the war was still on and most of the good young players and even the mediocre young players were in service undoubtedly helped me, and it is possible that if it weren't for World War II I might never have played professional baseball.

I was scheduled to report to the Philadelphia Phillies in March 1945 for spring training. All I knew about spring training was that it took place in Florida, which seemed about as far away to me as Europe, and it was warm and had great beaches. But because of wartime travel restrictions, the 1945 Phillies did not go to sunny, warm Florida to train. Instead they set up training camp in the garden spot of Wilmington, Delaware, maybe fifty miles from my house.

The train trip to Wilmington was the longest short trip I've ever taken. It's hard for anyone today, with inexpensive transportation, with television, to imagine how sheltered my life had been, but there were days when we would play ball in the street all day and, on a day with a lot of traffic, two cars would drive by. The trip to Baltimore was the first time in my life I'd stayed away from home overnight except at a friend's or relative's. And here I was, seventeen years old, leaving home to play professional baseball. I sat on the train wondering if Christopher Columbus had been as scared as I was when he sailed. Probably not, I decided. He wasn't going to Wilmington, Delaware, to try to make the Philadelphia Phillies.

The team was quartered at the DuPont Hotel. I went to my room and stayed there, I just didn't know what else to do. Because most of the young players were in the service, a lot of players who would have been retired were still active, among them thirty-seven-year-old Jimmie Foxx. I couldn't believe I was in the same training camp as he was, and I really had to resist asking him for his autograph. But I just didn't think us major leaguers asked each other for autographs. I worked as hard as I could in spring training and just missed making the Phillies—actually, I missed by about six classifications. At the end of camp I was optioned to Concord, North Carolina, in a Class D league, the lowest level of professional baseball.

The first game I pitched was against Landis, North Carolina. We went into the ninth inning tied. Landis got a runner to third with two outs. I broke off a tremendous curveball—it broke maybe an inch—and the batter hit a routine groundball toward our shortstop. The ball went right through the shortstop's legs, the winning run scored, and I was a losing pitcher in my first professional game. I was incredibly upset. The one thing that had been drilled into me at training camp was how tough the competition in pro baseball was. If you didn't do the job, there was someone right behind you waiting to take your job. Since we were on the lowest level, I didn't know exactly who could be behind me, but I knew there were a lot of people ahead of me. I lost a game, I wasn't sure what happened next.

I stormed into our clubhouse and saw the shortstop just sitting quietly in front of his tiny locker. I don't know what I expected him to be doing, but somehow it didn't seem right for him to just be sitting there after making that error. So I did what I had always done in that situation—I went after him. I slugged him, then jumped on top of him and started pounding. Our manager, John "Pappy" Lehman, pulled me off. "What do you think you're doing?" he screamed.

It seemed pretty obvious to me. The shortstop had made the error that cost us the game, so I was beating him up. That's what we often did at home. "He lost the game," I said.

"You can't go around fighting with your own teammates," Lehman said.

"Why not?" I'd always done it in the past.

"You'll be fighting them all the time. No one'll want to play behind you. Lemme tell you something," he continued, "you win as a team and you lose as a team, and you'd better learn that quick if you want to stay in baseball."

It was my first lesson in professional ball, and I don't think I ever learned a more important one. From that game forward, throughout my career, if a player made an error while I was pitching, I'd get over to him in the dugout and give him a few words of encouragement. "Hang in there," I'd tell him, or "We'll get 'em next time." My father had been right, I realized—it didn't make any sense to hit somebody after the bottle had been broken, or the error had been made. I never hit a teammate again, except for the time I took on the Freese brothers in the Caribbean, but I didn't start that one. There were times I wanted to hit a teammate, times it took every ounce of self-control I had to resist going over and decking someone, but I didn't.

Of course, that rule did not apply to members of the other team, and I was often able to take out my frustration with my teammates on them.

Besides pitching, I played sixty games at first base that season. Early in the year our first baseman broke his finger and I lied to the manager, telling him I'd played first base as well as pitched in high school. I don't know if he believed me, but he had to put somebody there for the infielders to throw to, and I was one of the few healthy bodies we had on the squad. So I became a first baseman.

Most of the season I hit better than I pitched, which was either encouraging or discouraging, depending on how you looked at it. Lehman was very tactful in appraising my pitching ability. "I think your ability is very limited," he said. But, he added, he was impressed by my desire and determination, and thought I had a chance to progress in baseball as an everyday player. He wrote to Phillies' farm director Joe Reardon asking permission to make me a permanent first baseman. Reardon came to North Carolina twice that season and both times I pitched strong games. I won only three or four games that year, but Reardon saw most of them, and as far as he was concerned, I was a pitcher. Since there were a limited number of 5'10" major league first baseman—that limited number being approximately none—I was pleased at that decision.

But at the end of the season I was drafted by another organization, the United States Army. This was the very last wartime draft and I caught it. I was inducted at Fort Meade, Maryland. One thing everybody knew about the army was that, whatever your civilian occupation, they turned you into something else. Bakers became electricians, for example, and electricians became mechanics, and mechanics became bakers. At least, I thought, I didn't have to worry about that. I was a professional baseball player, what could they turn me into?

A basketball player, as it turned out. A very short basketball player. While waiting for assignment to basic training after being inducted, I was standing around with other recruits shooting baskets. I hit about five shots in a row, and the next thing I knew I was asked to stay at Fort Meade and play basketball. Officially, I was enrolled in the Cooks and Bakers School, but what I really did was play basketball. That lasted a few months, until I got thrown off the team for fighting.

The big advantage I had over most recruits was that I grew up in a neighborhood in which you had to have quick wits to get by. I was street-hardened, I knew how to play the angles, and I wasn't afraid to take a gamble. For example, the big question after the war ended was how long recent draftees would be kept in the service. They offered us a deal. Anyone who enlisted for an additional year would have a guaranteed release date, everybody else would have to take their chances. I thought about it, and decided it was better to know exactly when I was going to get out. I figured I'd let everybody else worry. Ten days later all draftees were released.

Actually, once we got all the soldiers out of the army it was an extremely positive experience for me. At Fort McClellan, Alabama, I met Lieutenant Bobby Bragan, a major league player and later a manager and president of the Texas League. Bragan was my kind of man. He had confidence. Once, for example, he scheduled a baseball game between the United States Army (Fort McClellan) and the Bragan family. I mean, there were Bragans at every position, Bragans in the stands, there were more Bragans in that ball park than there were Lasordas in Norristown. Bobby made only one mistake—there were no umpire Bragans; the Bragans lost the game.

I eventually ended up running the athletic facilities and pitching for the post baseball team at Fort Jackson, South Carolina. It was a cushy job. And one day, I was sitting in the fieldhouse, thinking about working, when two civilians came in looking for me. They ran a semi-pro team up in Goldville, they explained, a mill town, and asked me if I'd like to play for their team. They'd seen me pitch a few innings against Erskine College and had been impressed.

"Sure," I told them, "I'd be interested." I assumed they wanted me to play for free, which I didn't mind doing because I wanted to play.

"Well," one of them, Rudy Prater, said somewhat sheepishly, "we can only pay you $50 a game."

Pay? Money? Fifty dollars a game? These people are crazy, I thought to myself. That was half of what the Phillies had been paying me a month. And if they were that crazy, I figured, maybe they were even a few dollars crazier. "Fifty dollars," I said, shaking my head, but watching them to make sure they didn't change their minds, "I don't know. I don't think I'd leave the base for less than . . . seventy-five bucks a game."

They watched me throw a few pitches before deciding I was worth $75 a game, but we finally reached an agreement. I had no problem with the army. My boss, Captain DeLury, told me he didn't care what I did when I wasn't playing army baseball. So I started pitching for Goldville as well as Fort Jackson, and loving every inning. Eventually I got Captain DeLury a job playing third base for Goldville, so I really had no trouble.

A month later I was sitting in the fieldhouse again and another civilian came in looking for me. He told me he was from Camden, South Carolina, where they had a semi-pro team and wondered if I might not like to pitch for *them*, too.

"How much?" I asked. I was getting smart.

He offered $50. "Fifty dollars! Are you kidding me? You expect *me* to pitch for you for $50." I paused. "Maybe, because you look like a good guy, I'd think about it for a hundred bucks a game." In reality, for $100 a game, I would've pitched, played first base, swept the infield, cleaned the uniforms, and sold hot dogs between innings.

He was hesitant so I offered him a demonstration. I'd pitch one game for Camden. If he liked my performance, I'd be paid $100. If not, we'd shake hands and walk away. He accepted.

There were between 2,500 and 3,000 people in the stands for the game. Semi-pro baseball was the major action in these small towns. I had what I'd like to consider a typical day—for Babe Ruth. I shut out the other team 11–0, I struck out 15, and I hit a grand slam home run. In addition, I got picked off first base and got caught in a rundown. The second baseman lobbed the ball toward first and it hit me in the head. I went down, and as long as I was down, I decided to put on a little act. I grabbed my head and rolled around in the infield dirt, as if I were badly hurt. The large crowd was absolutely silent until I somehow managed to struggle to my feet. Then they gave me a great ovation. The public address announcer lauded my courage, my strength, and my determination, and urged the fans to take a collection for me.

They passed the hat and collected about $45, making my salary for that one game $145, practically six weeks' pay in pro baseball. And Rudy Prater agreed to pay me $100 a game for every game I pitched.

I had some deal going. I was making $75 a game pitching for Goldville, $100 a game pitching for Camden, and I was pitching and playing first base for Fort Jackson. I never even thought about a tired arm. They gave me the baseball and I threw it.

As the day I was to be discharged got closer, the Phillies sent me a contract for the 1947 season. They offered me $200 a month to play with Rock Hill in Class C. It appeared I was going to be one of the few people having to take a pay cut to leave the army.

But before I returned that contract, the Camden team offered me $200 a week to stay in Camden and pitch twice a week. I was not as good at math as I had been at spelling, but I knew $200 a week was a lot more than $200 a month. But Camden was not Rock Hill, although the distinction was not that obvious at the time. I made them a counter offer. I wanted $200 a week to pitch two games and an additional $75 to play the outfield in the other three games the team played each week . . .

They agreed.

. . . plus all my meals and hotel living expenses . . .

They agreed.

. . . plus $10 for every inning I pitched in relief . . .

They agreed, and as long as they kept agreeing I was going to keep demanding. My mother didn't raise no fool.

. . . plus, in case it rains all week and I didn't make any money at all, a $100 guarantee in addition to everything else.

They hesitated, but agreed. If they hadn't hesitated, I might've gone for the yacht. I wrote to the Phillies, explaining that I needed time to recuperate after the rigors of army life. They had seen me pitch; they offered me all the time I needed.

I pitched for Camden through the rest of the year, leading them to the league championship, and long enough for me to send my parents almost $5,000. My father installed a heating system, knocked down a few walls, put up a banister railing, painted the place inside and outside, and bought all new beds. For the first time, I believe, my father got interested in baseball.

In the spring of 1948 I reported to the Phillies at their training camp in Kingstree, South Carolina. It wasn't Florida, but it wasn't Wilmington, Delaware, either. I was assigned to Schenectady, New York, in the Class C Canadian-American League. I was there for a month before my family knew where I was. I couldn't even pronounce Schenectady, much less spell it, so I wrote my family that I was ten miles outside Albany. They thought that was the name of the town, Ten Miles Outside Albany. Only later did I realize that they weren't too sure where Albany was either.

As far as I was concerned, as long as it had a baseball team and I could pitch there, it didn't matter where it was close to. The one place I knew it was far from was the major leagues. I was beginning to get a little more sophisticated about professional baseball. It wasn't a dream, it was a profession, a job. It was an unusual job—there weren't too many truck drivers in the quarry who had thousands of people watching them drive, and cheering when they drove well—but it required the same kind of dedication that doing any job well required. I worked at it. I always got to bed early before a game, I got my rest, and when I walked onto the playing field I gave it every ounce of Tommy Lasorda I could generate. Later in my career, as the meals got better, there were a lot more ounces to give, but I never in my life walked onto a ball field without being prepared to play, coach, or manage.

I had some great games at Schenectady. I set a league record that still stands by striking out 25 batters in a fifteen-inning game as we beat the Amsterdam Rug Makers, then followed that performance by striking out 15, then 13, in my next two starts. I am positive my Canadian-American League records for a 25-strikeout game and 53 strikeouts over three games will never be broken, particularly since the league has long been disbanded.

Those are the only playing records I hold in baseball, if you don't count my major league mark of throwing three wild pitches in one inning.

Late in that season we were in Gloversville, New York. On the day I was scheduled to pitch, I was shooting pool in a local establishment when a man approached and started a conversation. Even then, starting a conversation with me was about as difficult as finding an Italian restaurant in Italy. Eventually, the man asked me if I'd like to earn $100.

Hey, I figured, this guy's got a semi-pro team too. This guy did not have a semi-pro team. He was offering me a bribe. He would pay me $100 to lose the game. I was too upset to hit him. I glared at him and warned, "Get outta here before I kill you." And I meant it.

We scored six runs in the top of the first inning that night. I was so determined to win that I began pressing. By the end of the second inning Gloversville had tied the score, and the only player I got out was me— out of the game and on my way to the clubhouse. As I walked around the grandstand I saw the man who had made the offer sitting there smiling. "You should've taken the money," he said, and that's when I went after him. Fortunately for both of us, I didn't catch him.

One of the best things about playing in the minor leagues is that you get close to the people in the town. You usually room at someone's house, and the ball parks are small enough so that you get to recognize the fans. Because of my pitching ability in Schenectady I received a tempting offer to manage one of the largest bowling alleys in town. Who could turn down an offer like that? I took the job, but retired as soon as I found out that the bowling alley was a front, actually a ceiling, for a bookie joint operating in the basement.

I won 9 games for Schenectady, but lost 12. That was more losses in one year than I figured I'd lose in my career, and I had a difficult time dealing with it. About the only problem with success is that it does not teach you how to deal with failure. I didn't know how to lose. When things didn't go right on the pitcher's mound I'd start throwing at batters, challenging them to fight. That only made things worse. After I'd lost a game, I'd sit in the clubhouse staring into my locker, feeling as if I'd let my team, myself, and my family down. And behind it all was the constant fear that if I didn't do well I'd have to go home as a failure and buy myself a well-made lunch pail because I was going to be carrying it for a long time.

I spent time in church praying. I called my father for advice. He couldn't tell me how to pitch, but he refused to let me get down on myself. "I never taught you how to quit," he reminded me, "and if you're gonna quit on yourself you might as well come home right now."

Although I didn't realize it at the time, in fact it was the best year I could have possibly had. Every time I pitched against the Three Rivers club, the Brooklyn Dodgers' farm team, I pitched well. Three Rivers was managed by Ed Head, who had once pitched a no-hitter in the big leagues. At the end of the 1948 season the Phillies chose not to protect me by promoting me to a higher classification, but the Dodgers decided to take a chance on me. They drafted me for $4,000.

I was thrilled. It was one thing not to be good enough to play for the sixth-place Philadelphia Phillies, it was far more exciting not to be good enough to play for the Dodgers, who had won the 1947 pennant. Brooklyn's farm director, Fresco Thompson, wrote me a nice letter welcoming me to the Dodger organization and enclosed a $300-a-month contract. I knew I had had a poor season, but the Dodgers obviously thought enough of me to pay $4,000. I figured if I was worth that much, they should be willing to pay me more than $300 a month.

They figured differently. Mr. Thompson told me they would not raise their offer. I then figured that if they were smart enough to draft me after I'd gone 9 and 12 they obviously knew what they were doing. I signed the contract.

I didn't realize it at that time, but I had just married the Dodgers for life. And, except for a few brief trial separations, we've been together ever since. The following February I reported to the Dodgers spring training complex at the old Naval Air Force Base in Vero Beach, Florida. No matter what happened in my career, I thought, at least I'd made it to Florida.

TWO

•

Herein I Become a Dodger, I Get Married and Join the Royal Family

I arrived at the Brooklyn Dodgers' School of Instruction Camp in Vero Beach about 10 o'clock at night. By that time the camp had settled down and, except for the few watchmen walking the barracks floors, the place was very quiet. After being raised in an Italian household with four brothers and a phonebook of cousins, too much quiet made me very nervous. I didn't sleep well unless there was somebody shouting. But I walked softly into my room in the barracks, climbed into an upper bunk, and lay there.

Brooklyn Dodger owner Branch Rickey had brought the Dodgers to Vero Beach a year earlier. Representatives of the town had asked for something like $50,000 rent. He gave them $1. Now, what kind of chance did I have negotiating with him? But in 1949, the changes that would eventually turn this old navy base into Dodgertown, the finest training facility in professional sports as well as a year-round meeting and recreational complex, had not yet begun. We didn't even have toilet facilities in our rooms. That would have been acceptable if we had had heat. Finally, I thought, as I huddled under the one blanket they gave me, I get to Florida—and I freeze to death my first night there.

At 6 A.M. the next day the night watchman blew his whistle and the camp stretched into life. I threw some cold water on my face to warm up and went for breakfast. As I got closer to the cafeteria I heard what sounded like a low roar. I couldn't figure out what it was. Then, I turned a corner, and I saw it: ballplayers. Ballplayers everywhere. An army of ballplayers. The breakfast line snaked out of the dining room into the lobby, out of the lobby and into the street, down the block and around the corner. There were 680 players in camp, enough to fill the rosters of twenty-six minor league teams, including 206 pitchers.

The one thing I didn't have to worry about was overconfidence.

After breakfast I reported to the equipment manager for a uniform. They had so many players in camp they had run out of team names. So instead of a team name, everybody got a color. You were either brown or blue or red, orange, green . . . I was afraid they were going to run out of colors. The various managers had white satin uniforms. The daily workout was organized by colors. Every half hour we would rotate by colors to the next skill area: reds would move to bunting, greens to executing hit-and-runs, orange to sliding or base-stealing or hitting or fielding pop-ups. The biggest handicap a Dodger player could have was being color-blind.

After the Phillies' camps, in which I knew everybody by their first name, and things got done when the time came to get them done, the size and organization of this camp came as a shock. It was run like the army would have been run if the army had been run better. I figured, No way I'm going to make it here. The best thing I can do is get out real quick.

That night I found Fresco Thompson in the players' canteen, a large room where everyone was playing cards or pool or listening to the jukebox or reading, and I introduced myself. Six hundred eighty players in camp and he knew my whole background. "Glad to have you with us," he said pleasantly. "What can I do for you?"

"Trade me," I said, believing in the direct approach, "or at least give me my release."

Okay, he was probably a little surprised. "I don't understand," he said. "You just got here last night."

"I just don't think I belong here," I continued. "So I'd rather go someplace where I think I have a real shot."

That probably was not the most intelligent approach to take. "Let me tell you something," Fresco Thompson said. "Someone in this organization thought you had a lot of talent, otherwise we would not have drafted you. We have no intention of trading you and we're certainly not going to release you."

I decided to try another approach. The Dodgers had already turned down my request for more money once, so I knew I couldn't win on that one. "Okay," I told him, "then I have to tell you I'm not satisfied with the amount of money I'm being paid."

He was starting to get a little irritated. "There are six baseball fields out there," he said loudly, causing some people to look at us. "If you want more money, go earn it out there."

I realized a less direct approach might be better. I went for sympathy. "Mr. Thompson," I said softly, "I have to be honest with you. I need more money because I'm thinking of getting married."

"*Married!*" he screamed at me. "I got some good advice for you. If you want to get married and you don't have enough money—don't get married!" Then he excused himself and walked away.

All in all, I would have to say my first day in the Dodger organization was probably not a success. They certainly seemed to want me a lot more than I wanted to be there. Eventually, of course, I would turn that around.

Mr. Rickey and his instructors taught us to run after fly balls and not women, avoid alligators, stay sober, work hard, get plenty of rest, and attend church on Sunday. We were specifically warned to be very careful of the undertow in the ocean, as infielder Bobby Morgan had almost drowned a year earlier, and to stay out of the sun. "It's very deceiving," Thompson told us, "and until you've got a little tan, don't expose yourself too long or you'll get a bad burn and won't be able to play."

Hey, I was from Pennsylvania, I thought, we had sun there. The sun was 93 million miles from earth; Vero Beach was maybe a thousand miles from Norristown—how much stronger could the sun be in Florida than in Pennsylvania?

The answer is, a lot stronger. We had Sundays off, and one Sunday Gino Cimoli, Wayne Belardi, and I decided to rent a power boat and go fishing. The fact that I knew nothing about operating a power boat didn't bother me; I didn't know anything about fishing either. Besides, I was scheduled to pitch in a Class A game in camp the next day and that was all I could think about. If I pitched well, I realized, I might make the jump from Class C to A ball without serving time in B. So I was a little nervous and I hoped the fishing trip would help me relax.

The fish started biting before we even drowned the worms. After about an hour in the sun I began to feel a little warm, so I did the natural thing, I took my shirt off. It was a wonderful day, the three of us in shorts, shirts off, reeling in those fish all afternoon.

There has never been a worse case of sunburn in history. I would've been screaming, but it hurt too much to open my mouth. Parts of my body that I didn't even know *were* parts of my body were inflamed and painful. I had big red welts all over. I didn't know what to do. I couldn't go to the infirmary because I didn't want to jeopardize my chances of pitching in a high classification. I already knew I was never going to make the majors with the Dodgers, they had too many good ballplayers, what I was hoping to do was pitch well enough to impress another club. To do that I had to pitch.

On Monday morning I wrapped my entire upper body in cotton, put on a T-shirt over the cotton, a sweatshirt over the T-shirt, and a uniform jersey over the sweatshirt. I was burning up. It was one thing to look like a lobster, it was something else to feel like one. I felt so terrible I just wanted to pitch my five scheduled innings and get out of the sun. I just reared back and fired, and as soon as I got the ball back from the catcher, reared back and fired again.

I pitched five shutout innings. The next day I was officially promoted to Pueblo of the Class A Western League.

The six weeks of training camp went by as fast as you could say Jack Robinson, which, in fact, we often did. For me, it was like going to college and graduate school. I learned more about playing the game of baseball than I had in all my previous experience. Mr. Rickey—and everybody called him Mr. Rickey—was busy revolutionizing sports, and each of us were part of his experiment. Spring training had traditionally been a time for veteran players to come down to Florida, swap some yarns, and gently ease their bodies into shape for the coming season. Mr. Rickey changed that. Every minute of every day—except Sunday—was rigidly scheduled. We spent hours doing conditioning exercises, practicing fundamentals, listening to lectures, playing simulated games which were stopped for instruction, and playing endless innings of real baseball. Mr. Rickey's theories were drilled into every player on every level, so that we would all be playing Dodger baseball. I had always been a willing worker, but for the first time I was taught how to focus my energy to make my work more effective. And perhaps most important, everyone, from the minor league rookie to the major league regular, was made to believe he had an important role to play in the success of the entire organization. Mr. Rickey wasn't simply preparing the big club for the season, he was constructing a long-term system. I didn't understand it from my vantage point as a Class D pitcher, but I was being molded into a role player in the organization.

I was thrilled to have been promoted from Class C to A, but less excited about playing ball in Pueblo, Colorado. It wasn't that I didn't like Colorado, I just didn't know anything about it. It could have been a foreign country, it could have been Idaho. All I knew for sure about Colorado is that they had Indians and that it was farther away from home than Greenville, South Carolina. So, a few days before we broke camp, I went to see Fresco Thompson again. This time I told him how much I was enjoying being in the Dodger organization—he smiled—but that

I really didn't want to go to Colorado—he winced. I could see he was not enjoying our relationship as much as I had hoped he would.

Besides Pueblo, the Dodgers had Class A ball clubs in Elmira, New York, and Greenville, South Carolina. I told Mr. Thompson that I had spent two years in South Carolina, knew a lot of people there, and enjoyed playing in that area. If it could be arranged, I said, I'd much prefer to play with Greenville.

He looked at me, sighed, frowned, and nodded. It could be arranged, he said. I was reassigned to Greenville, of the Class A Sally League, managed by Clay Bryant. That was the good news and the bad news.

When camp ended we went to Greenville to play an exhibition game with the Dodgers' Rock Hill, North Carolina, team. We had just spent six weeks training with the Rock Hill players. We lived with them, ate our meals with them, drilled with them, and broke curfew with them. They were our friends. But in the top half of the first inning a Rock Hill runner got picked off second base. Our shortstop, Don Hoak, tagged the runner in the mouth with the ball. That started the first fight of the season. On the baseball diamond, Mr. Rickey had taught us all, we had no friends.

As it turned out, that was a very symbolic way of starting the season. We finished third that year, but we led the Sally League in fights. We led any two leagues in fights. Naturally, I got in my share of them. Even when I didn't want to fight, I fought. Once, for example, we were playing Charlestown, and one of their outfielders, Sal Taormini, was getting ready to bat. He was standing a few feet away from the plate watching Rube Melton, our pitcher, finish his warmup throws. Obviously, Rube thought he was standing too close, because he buried a warmup pitch in Taormini's ribs. That didn't start the riot. When play started, Melton threw at Taormini again, and this time Sal retaliated by throwing his bat toward the pitcher's mound. Both dugouts emptied. Even that didn't start the riot. I was playing peacemaker, difficult to believe but true, trying to hold back players, when Charlestown's shortstop, Eddie Samcoff, said loudly, "I've been wanting you all season, Lasorda." I was an outstanding bench jockey in those days and had been taunting him the whole year. Apparently, this had bothered him.

Later in my career, when I was a little wiser, or at least older, there are many clever things I might have said to him. "Well, you got me," for example, or "Here I am, what are you going to do about it?" Instead, I turned around and slugged him in the mouth. *That* started the riot.

The entire Charlestown ball club jumped me. As I was being thrown to the ground I grabbed something to hold on to. It turned out to be the bright red hair of Charlestown's second baseman, Red Marion. I yanked a handful of hair right out of his head. And people thought *I* could scream.

I was on the bottom of the pile for ten minutes, trying to keep my head covered. I have always believed that there is safety in numbers, and this proved it, because the only thing that prevented me from really getting hurt was that so many people were trying to hurt me that they got in each other's way. Finally, I saw daylight, and I crawled for it. As soon as I got out from under the pile I leaped back on top and started hitting people. Almost immediately, a policeman pulled me off, then waded into the fight, screaming, "Break it up, break it up!"

"Break it up?" I yelled. "Where were you when *I* was under that pile?" Six Charlestown players were eventually taken to jail.

It may seem like I got in a lot of fights as a younger player. But, looking back, it was actually worse than it seems. I was fighting everybody, including myself. I wanted to win so badly I couldn't control my temper. I'd be standing on the pitcher's mound and someone would get a hit off me. I'd get angry at him for getting that hit and throw some bad pitches to the next batter. Then I'd get angry at myself for letting myself get angry at the batter, and lose my concentration. I'd be so angry at the batter, myself, and finally the manager when he came out to try to calm me down, that I would become ineffective.

I had no qualms about trying to hit somebody with a pitched baseball, but I never threw at anybody unless I really believed he deserved it. Of course, deserving it covered a whole lot of territory. Buster Maynard, for instance, deserved it. Growing up, I idolized baseball players. I didn't think they were gods, I thought they were more important than gods. If I had met Lou Gehrig and he had put his hand on my head and said, "Son, don't ever do anything wrong," I think I probably would have become a priest. My grudge against Buster Maynard went back to eighth grade. I was at Holy Savior and I joined the safety patrol. I didn't particularly want to be on the safety patrol, but I joined because once a year, the nun in charge of the patrol took all its members to a major league baseball game. So I stood on my corner the entire year, in the rain and the snow and the cold, because I was finally going to get to see a real major league game.

The Phillies were playing the New York Giants. Before the game, I waited near the clubhouse door, hoping to see one of my heroes up close, maybe even get an autograph. Eventually, a player came out of the Giants clubhouse, a major leaguer, and came walking right toward me. I held out my program and asked him for an autograph. He didn't even slow down. He just pushed me aside and kept going. I couldn't believe it. I couldn't believe people who were better than gods could treat safety patrol members like that. I looked at the player's number and checked my program. His name was Buster Maynard. I vowed never to forget his name, and swore to myself that when I made the major leagues I would never turn down a request for an autograph.

So, here I am pitching for Greenville in the Sally League against Augusta, Georgia. I retired the first two hitters in the first inning and the third batter started walking to the plate. As he did, the public address announcer said, "Now batting for the Augusta Yankees, Buster Maynard." Like many veteran players, he was working his way down the ladder from the major leagues.

I couldn't believe it. I couldn't believe I could be so lucky. I was going to get to hit Buster Maynard. I threw my first pitch right at his head. He took a dive; his bat went flying one way, his cap the other, and he lay spread-eagled in the dirt. What a thrill it was to see him go down. I smiled happily.

He got up, dusted himself off, glared at me, and stepped into the batter's box—and then I threw at him again. This time he got up quickly and pointed a warning finger at me. "You do that again," he threatened, "and I'm coming out after you."

"I don't see any chains holding you there," I screamed right back. "If you don't like it, come on out. I'll be right here."

"You better not throw at me again if you know what's good for you."

"Just get in the batter's box." He got back in and I decked him again. This time he got up and came after me. I started moving in to meet him halfway, but other players got between us and prevented the fight.

After the game, as I was walking toward the team bus, a man came toward me. "Hey," he said, "where's Lasorda?"

"Why?" I said, "Who wants to see him?"

"I do." I should've been able to figure out that answer.

"Who are you?"

"My name is Buster Maynard."

I smiled. "I'm Lasorda," I sort of snarled. "What are you gonna do about it?" I must admit I had a pretty good idea.

He held up his hand, "Wait, wait a second, I just wanna know one thing. You couldn't have been throwing at me because I hit you good, because I never batted against you before. And you couldn't have been throwing at me because you don't like me, because we never met. So why in the world were you throwing at me?"

"You ever play for the New York Giants?" I asked, and he admitted he had. "Well, when I was in the eighth grade, I spent a whole year standing on a corner so I could go to a major league game, and when I finally got there I asked you for an autograph and you pushed me aside and kept walking. I swore that if I ever got the opportunity, I'd get even with you."

He stood there for a moment trying to take that all in. Finally, he said, "You're serious, right?"

I nodded.

"Wow," he said softly, shook his head, turned around, and walked away. "Wow."

When I became a minor league manager I always told this story to my young players, the moral of it being "When these youngsters ask for your autograph, think of me, a young safety patrol member, standing there, and sign those little slips of paper, because otherwise one of those kids might grow up to throw at your head someday."

I would also tell my players about my manager that year, Clay Bryant. Bryant might not be the worst person I ever met in baseball, but he is definitely a finalist. I always told my players about him because then I'd be free to do almost anything I wanted to do and they would feel lucky to have me. Bryant was much more than a manager to his players, he was a dictator. My father tried to teach me to look inside a person for his goodness. I am convinced a fully equipped search party working for six months couldn't have found any goodness inside Bryant. He never tried to teach us anything, or encourage us, or boost our confidence; he just ruled by fear. Before a game we weren't allowed to talk with anyone in the stands, including our families. During a game his idea of a discussion on the pitcher's mound was to grab the baseball and say "Get out." And if we lost a game, afterwards he'd make us sit in front of our lockers, staring at the floor, until he was ready to take a shower—maybe a half hour after the end of the game. He had bed check every night on the road and often at home. Even off the field, if he met one of his players in an elevator he wouldn't say hello. The man simply did not know how to communicate with ballplayers. I was amazed that the Dodger organization, which stressed teaching in the minor leagues, allowed Bryant to manage in their system. As a manager, he was the kind of man you always wanted to be managing the other team.

We got along okay, though. He liked me because I was always hustling. I was always hustling because I believed he was a man who would send me into the quarry if he didn't like me, so I hustled to stay out of his way. It turned out I was right. A decade later, when I'd slowed down, he tried to do exactly that.

I do owe him one debt of gratitude though. He taught me a very important lesson in the art of managing a baseball team. At that point in my career I never even considered the possibility that I would manage someday. I was still confident I was going to pitch in the National League for the Brooklyn Dodgers. But I remember thinking, as I watched him strut around the Greenville clubhouse one day, that if I did manage a club, I would do everything precisely the opposite of the way he did things. There were two ways of managing, Clay Bryant's way and every other way. Every other way had to be the right one.

He simply did not know how to communicate with his players and he didn't care and he didn't try. His players were so uptight and confused that they couldn't play to the best of their ability. They were afraid to be aggressive because they were terrified to make a mistake. We had some talented people on that club, but Bryant did nothing to bring out their talent. I could understand his not wanting to be there; what I couldn't understand is why he didn't want his players to be there.

In spite of him, I had a good season. I won as many games as I lost and I met Miss Joanne Miller, of the Greenville, South Carolina, Millers.

I was sitting on the dugout steps one evening and I glanced into the bleachers—and saw this beautiful girl sitting there. The reason she was at the game, I later found out, was that she was going out with a man her parents didn't like, so they brought her to the ball game. I'll tell you what, if they had known she was going to meet me that night, they would have appreciated him a lot more.

She was with her parents, Mr. and Mrs. Lee F. Miller; her sister Gladys, the real baseball fan in the family; her sister Fran and Fran's husband, Meb Redick; her brother, Lee; and her best friend, Margaret Goldsmith. Fortunately, I knew Margaret. I couldn't keep my eyes off Joanne Miller. It was difficult, because Bryant objected to his players flirting with fans during games. But Bryant had never met Joanne Miller.

Admittedly, I've always been very popular with the girls, except for the fact that I barely had the courage to speak to a girl until I was sixteen, and had had exactly one date before leaving home. But I really wanted to meet this girl.

While we were batting in the fourth inning, and Bryant was out of the dugout coaching third base, I got Margaret's attention and asked her who was sitting next to her. Margaret shouted to me, "Joanne Miller."

"Ask her if she'll go out with me," I said. Margaret turned and said something to Joanne Miller. Joanne Miller looked at me, then turned to Margaret and shook her head. Perfect. Not only was she beautiful, she had good taste. I made a motion as if I were cranking a telephone, my way of telling Margaret to get Joanne Miller's phone number. Again Margaret spoke to her friend, and again Joanne Miller shook her head. I could see she was crazy about me.

While we were at bat in the seventh I signaled Margaret to meet me behind the clubhouse. I asked her why her friend wouldn't go out with me, and Margaret told me about the other guy. "Do me one favor," I asked. "After the game, just hold her in the parking lot long enough for me to get dressed so I can talk to her myself."

"It won't do you any good," Margaret warned.

"Just hold her there."

I went back to the dugout and really started rooting. I really wanted to win that ball game. The thought of sitting in the clubhouse waiting for Bryant to take a shower while she drove out of my life almost made me sick. We won. In the ninth inning I was waiting on the dugout steps with my shoelaces untied and my shirt unbuttoned, and five minutes after the final out was made I was casually sauntering up to the Miller family in the parking lot. Margaret introduced us and I was my usual charming self. I knew Joanne Miller wouldn't be able to resist me now that she had really met me. I'll never forget her answer when I asked her to have lunch with me.

"No, thank you," she said.

I accepted her challenge, I liked a woman who played hard to get. Knowing that the quickest way to a young girl's heart is through her mother, I turned to Mrs. Miller and said, "If your daughter would go out with me, I could be a 20-game winner in any league."

That truly impressed Mrs. Miller, who asked, "What's a 20-game winner?"

I liked a mother who played hard to get. Finally, I managed to convince Joanne to give me her telephone number at work. "I'll call you," I promised.

In all honesty, she never did say she would answer the call. I called, and I called, and I called. The switchboard operator continually told me Joanne Miller wasn't there, which surprised me since Jo was the switchboard operator. On the few occasions when Jo did speak to me, she was polite, but firm: She did not want to go out with me.

The only reason I was so persistent was that I knew what she was depriving herself of, but finally even I had had enough, so I made her a very attractive offer. "Just have lunch with me once," I said, "and then, if you don't want to see me anymore, I'll never bother you again."

I knew she would not be able to resist.

We went to a small restaurant for lunch. She was even prettier than

I remembered. I wanted to be very careful not to be too aggressive, so I waited until our sandwiches came before telling her I intended to marry her. "You may think I'm crazy," I said, "but we are going to get married."

I think it was probably my sense of humor that most appealed to her. Whatever it was, she agreed to see me again. We spent a lot of afternoons just eating lunch at her home with her family. The Millers were absolutely outstanding people and, even better, Mrs. Miller was a great cook. Even if I hadn't been in love with Jo, I would've kept coming for those big meals. But I was in love with Jo, and I figured the daughter of a woman who could cook like that had to make a great wife. I am one of those people who believe that cooking is hereditary.

Jo knew nothing about baseball—the first time she came to a double-header she asked her sister Fran if they could get hot dogs at half-time —so I knew her attraction to me had nothing to do with the fact that I was a little-known $300-a-month minor league pitcher.

If I had any doubts I was in love with her, they ended when I spent $17.50 for a suit. It was the first suit I'd ever bought just so I'd look good for a woman. At that time, $17.50 was about the extent of my savings, but it was a great suit. Brown tweed. And worth every penny of that money. Next to my bellhop's uniform from the Valley Forge, it was about the most impressive piece of clothing I'd ever had on.

When the season ended I went back to Norristown, intending to return to school. Jo and I promised to write, and I made plans to return to Greenville for a visit during the Christmas holidays. But soon after I got home I received an invitation to play Winter League baseball in the Panama Canal Zone. Maybe I hadn't been so good in geography, but I knew that Panama was where the Panama Canal was, and that it was warm there in the winter, and that I would get to pitch there, and that they would pay me $400 a month. So I put on my $17.50 suit and went to play for the Cristobal team. That was the last time I saw winter for more than two decades.

It was in Panama that I decided to ask Jo to marry me. I was in the market one day and bought her a necklace and some earrings for about $20. That was even more than my suit cost. As I was walking back to my hotel, I thought to myself, Well, Tom, if you spend $20 on this girl, you must really be in love with her. So you'd better marry her.

Call me a crazy romantic. This time, Jo believed I was serious, and agreed to marry me. I was tremendously excited. I was getting a beautiful woman who could cook; that was like winning both ends of a double-header.

We decided to get married in the spring. I managed to save $200 in

Panama, which I had in my pocket when I reported to spring training in Vero Beach. I immediately hid the money in my room. I hid it so well, in fact, that it took someone maybe four minutes to find it. Now I was in a jam, broke and getting married. I couldn't even afford a wedding ring. The Dodgers were my only hope.

Naturally, I couldn't tell Fresco Thompson I was getting married and needed money because I'd told him that the year before. So I went to see Mr. Rickey. "I met this girl in Greenville, South Carolina, last year," I explained, "and we'd like to get married, but we don't have any money. So, what I'd like to do, I'd like to borrow $500 from the Dodgers." I didn't even hesitate when I said $500, but I wasn't breathing too good either.

Mr. Rickey told me that he believed married players performed better than single players because they had more stable relationships, so he agreed to loan me the money. The actual loan was made by E. J. "Buzzy" Bavasi, the general manager of the Dodgers Triple-A farm club, the Montreal Royals.

I left Vero Beach a week before camp ended and went to Greenville. On April 14, 1950, Jo and I were married. If, the night before our wedding, I had been able to make a list of everything I wanted in a woman, and everything I wanted in a marriage, I would've had that order fulfilled. When I said "I do," I really did. I've said a lot of things to a lot of people on a lot of occasions, but I've never said anything smarter than those words to that woman on that day in South Carolina.

Even before I got married, spring training had been unbelievable. When I returned from Panama, I was assigned to the Montreal club in the International League. That was one level below the big leagues, and rarely did a player make the jump from A ball to AAA in one season. What made it especially difficult was that the big club, the Dodgers, were set at every position. They had Roy Campanella catching, Gil Hodges at first, Jackie Robinson at second, Pee Wee Reese at shortstop, Billy Cox was the third baseman, and Duke Snider, Carl Furillo, Gene Hermanski, Jim Gilliam, and Sandy Amoros were in the outfield. Suppose a young catcher hit .325 with 33 homers at Montreal. Campanella was doing the same thing in Brooklyn. And that also meant that the catcher in Double A, who only hit .315, was frozen too. With almost seven hundred players on twenty-six teams, there wasn't a lot of mobility within the organization, so my promotion was a major leap.

I wasn't sure I was ready to make that jump, but Mr. Rickey convinced me I could do it. "When it comes to pitching," he used to say, "I know my onions." He enjoyed working with young pitchers at The Strings, an area in which pitchers attempted to throw the ball through a string rectangle which approximated the strike zone. I was told to report there and spent twenty minutes showing Mr. Rickey my entire pitching repertoire, which consisted of a fastball, curve, and confidence, while he questioned me at length about my background. After the workout I asked him for an honest assessment. "Do you think I can win at Montreal?" I said.

"Young man," he said, "if you don't, I'll personally be up there to investigate why."

The thing that continued to impress me about the Dodger organization was that it was so well . . . organized. Everybody, management and front office as well as the players, knew exactly what their function was, where they were supposed to be when, and what was expected of them. And the people, with the exception of a certain minor league manager I won't name—Clay Bryant—were wonderful. I grew up with the Dodgers, and many of the people I met those first few seasons grew up with me. I remember, for example, meeting a scout named Al Campanis in spring training in 1950. The Montreal club was busing up to Miami to play the Triple-A Marlins, and Campanis took the seat next to mine. "I want to tell you something," he said. "If I'm ever in a position to hire you, you're gonna work for me one day." He had been watching me, he continued, and had been impressed by my competitive spirit, desire, and willingness to work.

I didn't pay any attention. I thought the guy was just making conversation. He was a scout. The idea that he would eventually become general manager of the Dodgers was as absurd as the idea that I would eventually become manager. Besides, the man I really wanted to work for that season was the new manager of the Montreal Royals, Walter Alston.

Eventually, Walter Alston would become my friend and my teacher. I would play for him six seasons and coach for him four others, and finally succeed him as manager of the big club. But that spring, in 1950, I was desperately trying to prove that it was indeed possible, in this great country of ours, for the son of an Italian immigrant, a runny-nosed little left-handed pitcher with a decent curveball, a player good enough only to be the third-string pitcher on his high school baseball team, to pitch for the Royals of the International League, only one big step away from the major leagues.

Walt Alston and Clay Bryant were as different as Bobby Knight and Doris Day. If you couldn't play baseball for Walter Alston, you couldn't play for anybody. He was as tough as any man I've ever known, and honest and fair. In all the years I played for him and worked for him I never saw him belittle or embarrass a player or try to kill a player's confidence. He had not been a successful player himself—not only did he strike out in his only major league at bat, he booted one of two fielding chances he had at first base, making him a lifetime .000 hitter and a .500 fielder—but he knew how to motivate players, how to get along with them, how to earn their respect, how to communicate with them, and, finally, how to manage twenty-five of them on the same ball club. I played for many managers, but I learned more from Walter about running a ball club than from anyone else.

I never forgot the lessons he taught me. Once, for example, after I'd become Dodger manager, I walked slowly out to the mound to take out Bobby Welch. "I'm gonna bring in Steve Howe," I said, and started to signal the bullpen.

"Gimme a shot," Bobby asked. "I'll throw this guy a curveball and I'll get the double play."

I hesitated. As he said that, I heard myself talking to Walter. It was during a game against the Baltimore Orioles, then in the International League, and the player coming to bat was a big left-handed hitter named Babe Barna. "Leave me in, skip," I told Alston. "I'm gonna throw him a low curveball and he's gonna hit it on the ground and we're gonna turn the double play." I could see I had his attention, so I added the clincher, "If I don't get the double play, you go ahead and fine me."

Alston left me in, I left Welch in. Barna hit my first pitch over the right-field fence. Welch got out of his situation. It had taken twenty-five years to prove that Walter had made the correct decision.

Perhaps the most important thing I learned from him was that a manager could be friends with his players and still command their respect. Walter used to make lists of things in which he could beat certain players. He had his pool list, his card list, his golf and running lists, and he accepted all challenges. Naturally, everyone wanted to beat him. Don Hoak and I once worked out an elaborate set of signals for every card in the deck, then played Hearts with Walt and his partner. We weren't very subtle about it, we didn't let them win a hand. Walt was burning, which we encouraged by casually saying things like "Well, skip, maybe you should try a new game," or "I guess this just isn't your night." Finally, after four hours, he stood up, ripped the deck in half, and stormed out of the train's club car. Only later did he find out we had been cheating, by which time we were carefully out of sight.

Winning and losing these games was not Walt's goal, what he wanted to do was get close to his players. Although his image was that of a quiet, sometimes stern, man, he encouraged a loose, loud ball club. I never missed an opportunity to play a joke on him. For example, Walt loved to pitch batting practice, a habit I picked up. And when he pitched, batting practice lasted precisely one half hour, precisely. One very hot summer's day we were in Syracuse to play the Chiefs. Their ball park, MacArthur Park, had a big clock on the right-field fence. Walt was throwing and I was shagging flies—in right field. And every few pitches, when he had his back to me, I'd go over to that clock and turn its hands back a minute or two.

He was sweltering. He'd throw a few pitches, turn around to look at the clock, shake his head in disbelief, wipe the sweat from his brow, and throw some more. After forty-five minutes he walked into the dugout and plopped down on the beach. "Boy," he said to Clyde King, then a pitcher with the club, "that was the longest thirty minutes of my life."

Clyde couldn't resist. "You threw a lot longer than thirty minutes, skip. Tommy kept moving the clock back on you." It was impossible to believe that Walt was exhausted the way he shot out of the dugout after me. He chased me around the field until neither of us could run anymore.

He commanded respect much the way a volcano does. It may never explode, but the potential is always there. Walter Alston was afraid of no one. Although I wasn't there, I know he once challenged the entire Dodger ball club to a fight if they didn't like his way of running things. That Doger club included 6'7", 255-pound Frank Howard. There is no doubt in my mind that Walter would've stood up to anyone, including Frank Howard. And then he would've gotten off the ground and stood up to him again.

He was the perfect manager for the Montreal club because he knew how to win and how to teach young players how to win. There was a time, I remember, when Mr. Rickey was experimenting with a six-man infield defense against bunts. In a bunt situation, an outfielder would hold the runner on first base, allowing the first baseman to charge the plate without having to hold the runner on base. Theoretically, this robbed the runner of perhaps two or three steps. I was on the mound one night and the play worked perfectly. I picked up the bunt, whirled, and saw I could easily throw the runner out at second, and I made a perfect throw—to center field. I mean, that baseball just sailed over everyone's head. In the clubhouse after the game, Walter calmly explained that he was not satisfied with my execution by picking up a chair and smashing it down on the food table. Cold cuts splattered all over the floor. No one would be eating dinner in that clubhouse that night.

Walter always knew how to get my attention.

I wasn't sure I'd be staying with the Royals until the second game of the season. I pitched and beat Jersey City, striking out 10, and proved to myself I could win in that league. I knew by the middle of the season that it would just be a matter of time before I was pitching in the major leagues. And it was, but like I did to Walter Alston, somebody somewhere kept turning back the hands of the clock on me.

We finished second that year, losing to the Orioles in the playoffs. I won nine and lost four. I struck out 85 batters in 146 innings; unfortunately, I walked 82. I believe that no season is really successful unless you win the final game of the World Series, but that one was at least enjoyable. I was young and cocky, I was married to a wonderful woman who could cook, I was at the point in my playing career when my wildest fantasies were still possible, and I was having fun. That was a team that knew how to have fun.

The year 1950 was the year of the longest water fight in history, the whole year. Abe Cohen, who owned ABCO Drugs in Rochester, supplied us with an arsenal of water pistols. We got our own water. We used to choose up sides. First baseman Chuck Connors usually captained one team and catcher Toby Atwell the other. No place was safe. We fought in hotel lobbies, restaurants, even in two taxis racing side-by-side down the street. And when we weren't fighting each other, we dueled the rest of the human race. Carl Erskine, young Carl Erskine, with the face of a choir boy, would sit in a train station casually reading a newspaper. But there would be a small hole in that newspaper, and when someone walked by, Carl would gun them down.

For Chuck Connors it turned out to be a rehearsal. Chuck is probably the greatest first baseman ever to become a TV star, starring in the "Rifleman" series. Chuck was an individual who would do almost anything for a laugh. Actually, that's not true, Chuck *would* do anything for a laugh. But on the diamond he was as intense as I was, which was probably the reason we became close friends. Chuck was the kind of hitter who believed any pitch he didn't swing at was a ball. If an umpire called him out on strikes he'd stomp back to the dugout ready to explode. He'd sit down next to me and start screaming at the umpire. And when he finally ran out of insults, he'd turn to me and demand, "Where was that pitch?"

I was as honest as anyone would be to an irate 6'5", 200-pound batter. "Looked high to me too, Chuck," I'd agree.

"Yeah!" he'd shout at the umpire. "Even Lasorda says it was high!" This, of course, did not ingratiate me with the umpires, but given the choice between having all the umpires in the league mad at me or Chuck Connors, I picked the umpires.

Only once did I disagree with him. He watched what appeared to me to be a good pitch go by and was called out on strikes. He came back to the dugout, screamed at the umpire, then turned to me for confirmation. "Where was that pitch, Tommy?"

"Chuck," I whispered, "I gotta tell you, it looked like a good pitch."

He took it just the way I always thought he would. He grabbed me by the throat and jammed my head against the back wall of the dugout. "You blind   ," he screamed at me, "You're just as   bad as those   umpires . . ."

When Connors was suffering through a batting slump, he was a difficult man to share a continent with. Once, I remember, he was 0-for-4 games and we were playing in Rochester. His first at-bat, he hit a shot that would've gone through the first baseman if he hadn't caught it in self-defense. His second at-bat, he blasted a rocket that the right fielder didn't have to take a step to catch. His third at-bat, he hit another bullet, but right at second baseman Lou Ortiz. Ortiz caught it before Chuck had taken two steps out of the batter's box. Without missing a beat, Chuck dropped onto his knees, looked up into the heavens, and screamed, *"Why are you doing this to me? Why don't you come down here and fight me like a man!"*

Those of us who played baseball with him knew his future was as an actor. Traditionally, there is a talent show at the end of spring training. I was always too shy to perform, but Chuck loved being onstage. One year he did an outstanding impersonation of Branch Rickey negotiating a contract with Chuck Connors. "Young man," his Mr. Rickey said, "I do not want you telling anyone how much money the Dodgers are paying you this year."

"I don't blame you, Mr. Rickey," he replied as himself, "and you don't have to worry. I'm just as embarrassed about this contract as you are."

In reality, at that time none of us was really worried about money; you can't worry about what you don't have. We used to say the Dodgers paid us good money—not a lot of money, but what there was of it was good. My salary had been raised to $500 a month when I was promoted to Montreal, so Jo and I could afford all kinds of luxuries, as long as you consider food a luxury. To save money, we shared an apartment with my teammate Wally Fiala and his wife, Ruth. Besides being truly wonderful people, and good friends, they were the kind of people who had a car. And we needed that car to drive back and forth from the ball park. Whenever Jo and I dreamed about the future, the first thing we wanted was our own little, used, dented car.

It was difficult to save any money, and I couldn't forget that I had borrowed $500 from the Dodgers to get married. Mr. Bavasi had warned me that the money would be taken out of my salary, but when I got my first few paychecks no money had been deducted. I asked him about it and he said, "Don't worry about it, we'll get it at the end of the year."

I was worried about it and I didn't want it all coming out of one check. "I just want you to take out a little bit each month," I told him. I figured it wouldn't hurt quite so much that way.

But again the following month no money was deducted from my check, and again I went to see Mr. Bavasi. He put a piece of paper in front of me and told me to sign it. "Dear Mr. Rickey," it read, "I am very happy that I was able to pay you back the $500. Thank you very much for the loan." That didn't make sense to me. I knew I hadn't paid back anything. "Sign it," Buzzy Bavasi repeated. The Dodgers had simply forgiven the entire loan.

Loyalty is built on trust, honesty, understanding, and generosity. This was true generosity. In return, the Dodgers were getting themselves one loyal runny-nosed left-handed pitcher.

I played in Cuba that winter. Al Campanis, in charge of placing players on Caribbean teams, got me a contract worth $1000 a month, plus $350 expenses. That was more money than I had ever dreamed I could make throwing a baseball. It enabled Jo and me to get started in life. We bought our first car.

While we were in Cuba Mr. Rickey sold the Dodgers to Walter O'Malley. I knew I would miss Mr. Rickey, but I didn't believe the sale affected me personally. I played for a manager; the owner was the guy in the expensive suit who sat in the stands and signed the checks. I was sure Mr. O'Malley's signature was as good at the bank as Mr. Rickey's. And I knew the Brooklyn Dodger organization would not change substantially. It was too successful, and too solid throughout. I mean, what could they do? Move the Dodgers to California?

I got my first shot at making the big club the following spring. I pitched very well against our Double-A Fort Worth team in a camp game, striking out eight in three innings, so the Dodgers ordered me to report to the major league team in Miami, where they were playing an exhibition game.

Infielder Bobby Morgan and I drove down there together. That night I left the air conditioning on in our room and I woke up with a terrible cold. I felt rotten, but this was my opportunity and I certainly wasn't going to let a cold keep me out of the big leagues. We were playing the Cincinnati Redlegs, and Dodger manager Charlie Dressen put me in to start the fourth inning. This was it, pitching for the Brooklyn Dodgers. I knew that this was the moment I had been born for. I knew I wouldn't fail. I was ready, I was confident, I was a little bit wild. I walked the first batter.

I told myself not to get nervous, I'd walked hitters before. The thing I had to do was put any thoughts of failure out of my mind and concentrate on the batter. I checked the runner on first and pitched. I walked the second batter.

Now I was really starting to get angry at myself. This was my big chance, the opportunity I'd been working for, waiting for, and if I didn't settle down I was going to blow it. I gritted my teeth, checked the runners on first and second, and pitched. I walked the third batter.

I was fuming. How stupid could I be to screw up so badly? What was the matter with me? Didn't I have the guts to throw the ball over the plate? I checked the runner on first, the runner on second, the runner on third, and pitched. I walked the fourth batter.

By the time Dressen got to the mound I had tears in my eyes. Everything I'd worked for, everything I'd hoped for, all my dreams had exploded in my face. Charlie was sympathetic. "Well, son," he said softly, "you walked one man for every year you've been working to get here. Let's call it a day, there'll be better ones."

The walk to the dugout was the longest walk I'd ever taken in my life. I was a failure. I had my shot and I couldn't do the job. I've had many highs and lows in my baseball career, but none ever lower than that one.

My control was always my problem. Some pitchers are born with the ability to thread a needle with their fastball; I had days when I couldn't have even hit a haystack. Once, when I was with Brooklyn, I threw three straight balls to Willie Jones, then hit him with the next pitch. After the game Buzzy Bavasi asked me why I'd hit him. I told him the truth: "I knew I couldn't throw him three straight strikes."

Everybody in the organization tried to work with me. I remember one day at Dodgertown, the great Preacher Roe took me aside to talk with me. Preacher was one of those pitchers who could throw his fastball through the keyhole of a swinging door. "Think about this," he said. "You pitch, and the batter gets a base hit. He takes three steps out of the batter's box, falls over, and dies right there. What happens?"

I thought about it for a moment. "Well," I said, "the fielders get the ball, throw to first base, and the batter's out."

"Correct. Now, the next hitter comes up and you throw him four balls. He takes three steps out of the batter's box, falls over, and dies right there. What happens?"

"His team puts in a pinch-runner at first base."

"Right. Just let that be a lesson to you," Preacher concluded. "There is no defense against a walk."

That story did not help my pitching—control problems continued to plague me throughout my career—but I often used it when I was managing in the minor leagues to impress the importance of control on young players. I remember telling it to a youngster in Ogden, Utah, in the Pioneer League. He listened, just as I had. He gave the right answers, just as I had. But when I asked him if he understood the moral of the story, he nodded his head firmly and said he most certainly did. "If you're dead," he explained, "they have to take you out of the game."

I won 12 games for Montreal that year, helping the Royals win the International League pennant. In the playoffs, against Rochester, I collided with their playing manager, Harry "The Hat" Walker, who was trying to score from third base on my wild pitch. He got me in the back with his knee and I couldn't move. I had to be carried off the field on a stretcher. The best orthopedic surgeon in Canada diagnosed the injury as a fractured vertebra, put me in a body cast, and told me I'd probably never be able to pitch again. I refused to pay any attention to him. If he knew so much about pitching, I figured, he'd be playing baseball instead of working in a hospital. Two months later I was pitching in Puerto Rico.

My bad outing against the Reds in spring training had only temporarily damaged my confidence. I knew I would get another opportunity to pitch in the big leagues and I didn't intend to blow that one. So I worked hard, harder than ever before.

One of the things I was learning was how to think on the mound. I realized that there are throwers—players with such great ability they could overpower the hitters—and pitchers—players who understood the strategies of pitching, who knew how to confuse a batter or make him anticipate the wrong pitch. With my fastball, I had to become a pitcher to survive.

Clint Hartung, the Hondo Hurricane, taught me that lesson while he was with the Havana Sugar Kings. Hondo was a great minor league power hitter. One day I tried to get my fastball past him and he hit it as far as I had ever seen a man hit a baseball. I was so impressed with that home run I forgot to get mad. Besides, I knew it was luck. I knew he couldn't possibly do it again. And just to prove it, the next time he came to bat I decided to challenge him with my fastball on the first pitch.

That was the moment I decided I'd better become a pitcher. That second home run made the first one seem puny.

I came back from my injury to have my best season yet in 1952, winning 14, losing 5 and only walking a few more than I struck out. I was becoming a star in the minor leagues, exactly what I didn't want to happen. I still believed everything was preparation for my major league career, but I was starting to get nervous. Some of the people I was playing with were going up to the big leagues, often with other clubs, and I was staying put. Montreal was a wonderful team to pitch for, but I didn't want to spend my career there.

That was also a great year because our daughter, Laura Lee was born. I remember every moment of her birth. I had beaten Springfield on a Friday night, and after the game Walter Alston asked me how Jo was doing. I told him that she was with her family in Greenville, and the baby wasn't due for a week. "Look," he said, "we're going into Buffalo and you're not gonna pitch in that series, so why don't you just go home?"

I took his advice. I got into Greenville Saturday evening, just in time to be rushed to the hospital by my in-laws to see my baby born.

I was really becoming settled. Now I had a wife, a car, and a baby daughter.

After my good season I really believed I would get an opportunity to stay with the big club in 1953. I didn't know who I'd replace. Not Don Newcombe certainly, or Carl Erskine, or Clem Labine. Joe Black had won 15 games, he was safe. Preacher Roe had been 11–2, I wasn't going to replace him; Billy Loes, 13–8, not him; Johnny Rutherford, 7–7; Clyde King, 2–0 . . . I figured maybe I'd make it as a spot starter or a long reliever, someone who pitched when a game got out of hand early, or maybe they would just stick me in the bullpen and I'd pitch relief, as a lot of young pitchers did. I didn't care. I was willing to pitch wherever the Dodgers felt I could do them the most good.

It turned out to be with the St. Louis Browns. The Dodgers sold me to Bill Veeck's Brownies for $50,000.

THREE

•

I Make My Pitch for the Big Leagues, a Curveball, and Become a Minor Star

A ballplayer discovers whether he is an optimist or a pessimist when he is involved in a deal between two clubs. The optimist is thrilled that his new team wanted him; the pessimist is depressed that his old team did not want him. If he is traded for other players, the optimist can't believe his old team actually got *those* players for him; the pessimist can't believe his old team got *only* those players for him. If it is a cash deal, the optimist believes he was bought; the pessimist believes he was sold.

I was somewhere in the middle of the mist. I was unhappy to be leaving the Dodger organization, but I was grateful that I was going to get the opportunity to pitch in the big leagues. Although the Brownies also purchased shortstop Billy Hunter from the Dodgers for $90,000, I was very pleased that they thought I was worth $50,000.

As it turned out, they didn't. I went to spring training with the Browns in San Bernadino, California. Marty Marion was the manager. I didn't know him, but I remembered his brother from A ball. His brother was a red-headed second baseman with a hank of hair missing from the top of his head. It turned out to be a good camp, and I made the ball club. It wasn't Brooklyn, but it was the major leagues. On the train trip east to open the season, pitching coach Harry "The Cat" Brecheen told me I was in the starting rotation. But when we stopped in Phoenix, Arizona, for an exhibition game, owner Bill Veeck met the train and asked me to come to his hotel room. I had the sinking feeling he was not going to offer me a raise.

A few days earlier, he told me, the American League had turned down his application to move the Browns to Baltimore. He was heavily in debt, and struggling to keep the team in business. There was no way he could afford to keep both me and Billy Hunter. He was very sorry to have to do it, he said, but he had to return me to the Dodgers.

He was sorry? Imagine how I felt! Now, neither the club that sold me nor the club that bought me wanted me. And, having missed spring training in Vero Beach, I had no chance to make the Dodger roster. So I reported to Montreal. Again.

And again, I had a good year, winning 17 and losing 8, then winning two more in the playoffs and a game in the Little World Series, giving me 20 wins for the season. I was voted left-handed Pitcher of the Year and made the International League All-Star team. I had proven that I could win big in Triple A, and I really expected to make the big club in 1954.

Everything appeared to be breaking right for me. Charlie Dressen, after managing the Dodgers to the 1953 National League pennant, requested a multiyear contract. Brooklyn did not give multiyear contracts. Instead, they made him an interesting counter-offer. They hired Walt Alston to manage the team. That hurt Dressen's negotiating position substantially.

I figured that was the break I needed. I'd pitched four seasons for Walter, and together we had tasted the fruits of victory. I pitched well in spring training and made the squad going north to open the season. That didn't mean I was going to stay with the team—additional cuts had to be made the first few weeks of the year—but when Walt told a New York reporter, "Lasorda is tops in his desire to beat you. He gives more than 100 percent of himself every time," I knew I had a great chance.

Our first game in New York was an exhibition game against the Yankees at Yankee Stadium. Walter put me in the bullpen. When Russ Meyer struggled, loading the bases with two outs, I got the call. I remember taking that long walk in from the visitors' bullpen—this was before they had taxi service to the mound—and looking around me at the three massive decks. Yankee Stadium. The House That Ruth Built. It wasn't anything like I had imagined in my dreams. It was even better. I was so happy I almost cried. This was the field my idols had played on. Lou Gehrig had walked on the same grass I was walking on. Babe Ruth had run the same bases. Lefty Gomez had pitched from the same mound. If I could've just stood there, instead of having to pitch to Yogi Berra with the bases loaded and my career on the line, it would have been perfect.

When I reached the mound Walt said, "You know what to do. Throw strikes." He patted me on the behind and walked to the dugout. Leaving me there alone. I looked at the plate. Berra was standing there, swinging a telephone pole. He did not look particularly nervous about facing me.

That was okay, I was nervous enough for both of us. Roy Campanella signaled for a curveball. Berra swung at my first pitch and hit an easy bouncer right back to me. I threw him out to end the inning. One pitch, one out; that was a whole lot more satisfying than the last time I'd pitched against major leaguers. This time I'd done the job, and I began to believe I was going to stay with the team.

I did not stay with the team. A few days before the season opener Buzzy Bavasi told me I was going back to Montreal. Now, I loved the Dodgers. And I sincerely liked the people in the organization. But I was not going back to Montreal. I had nothing more to prove in Triple A. I was either going to pitch in the big leagues or I wasn't going to pitch at all. I went to see Mr. Bavasi to tell him exactly that. "I don't understand it," I said, "I had a great year last year. Why are you sending me out?"

"Tommy," Buzzy replied, "we believe you're going to pitch in the major leagues, but we think you need another pitch to win up here consistently."

"That's exactly what I was told last year," I complained, "and that's why I've been throwing a changeup."

"Well then," he said, "go get another pitch. It won't hurt you."

I'd finally had enough. "Look, Mr. Bavasi, I'm not going back to Montreal." He asked me if that meant I intended to quit professional baseball. "Yes, sir," I said firmly, "it does."

Buzzy was sympathetic. "You have a job lined up?"

"No. But I'll find something."

"I'll be glad to help. I've got this friend, he runs a brewery. I'll bet he can find something for you." So as I sat in his office, Buzzy called an executive at a brewery and explained the situation. I listened, sure of my decision. Finally, he put his hand over the mouthpiece and said, "He's got something that pays a hundred and a quarter a week. Want it?"

I considered it. Mathematics had not been one of my stronger subjects, but I knew $125 a week did not come out to the $9000 a year the Dodgers would be paying me to pitch in Montreal. And that didn't involved any heavy lifting. "When do I leave for Montreal?" I said.

I had just another one of those average seasons in Montreal. By mid-July I had won 14 games and lost 5, completing 13 of 21 starts. Except for the foul pop-up that had hit me in the head while I was in the dugout, and bounced thirty feet straight into the air, it had been a perfect season. A perfect *minor league* season, but still perfect. Fourteen wins by mid-

July? Are you kidding? I didn't believe any team, major league, minor league, Little League, could beat me.

Upstairs, in the National League, the hated New York Giants had got out in front, but the Dodgers were beginning to make a run at them. So it did not surprise me when I was recalled in late July.

I figured Walt would ease me into the starting rotation and I would give the Dodgers that extra push they needed to catch the Giants. Alston was happy to see me, but didn't use me in the first few games. I expected that, I knew he wanted me to feel comfortable before throwing me into the action. I pitched a lot of batting practice.

He didn't use me the next few games either. I was getting a little edgy, but it was still okay, the team was playing good ball and he was just waiting for the right situation to get me some work. I pitched a lot more batting practice.

Finally. We were getting blown out by the Reds. They were so far ahead we wouldn't have been able to catch them in a race car. Ted Kluszewski had already hit three home runs. This was the situation Alston had been waiting for. He brought me in to pitch the ninth inning. I remember thinking, as I came in from the bullpen to make my first major league appearance, Isn't it amazing that in this great country of ours, the son of an Italian immigrant, a runny-nosed little left-handed pitcher with a decent curveball, a player good enough only to be the third-string pitcher on his high school baseball team, a boy who . . .

Pitching coach Ted Lyons met me on the mound. "Take your time," he said, trying to calm me down, "just throw strikes." Just throw strikes? If I could've done that I would've been in the majors three years earlier! The batters for the Reds were shortstop Roy McMillan, second baseman Johnny Temple, and outfielder Gus Bell. Kluszewski was scheduled to follow Bell. As I rubbed up the baseball, I took a moment to look around beautiful Ebbets Field. It had taken me a long time to get there and I wanted to savor the moment. Actually, it seemed smaller than I thought it would be. A lot smaller. And I didn't realize how close the right-field wall was to the plate until I felt right fielder Carl Furillo's breath on the back of my neck.

I got McMillan and Temple out easily, and when Gus Bell hit a routine groundball toward Gil Hodges at first base I started walking to the dugout. Hodges was the best fielding first baseman in baseball. Usually. The ball went right through his legs, allowing Ted Kluszewski to come to plate swinging for his fourth home run of the game.

I immediately noticed one thing about the Big Klu. He was big. Six feet two inches tall, 225 pounds, most of it in his arms. His arms looked like legs coming out of his shoulders. Just to intimidate pitchers, he had cut the sleeves off his jersey. It worked. I didn't want to pitch to him, so I came up with a good plan. If I balked, or looked toward home plate while I threw to first base, Bell would automatically be awarded second base. That would leave first base open, and good baseball strategy dictated that I walk Klu intentionally to set up a force play, and pitch to the next hitter. I didn't know who the next hitter was, but I sure knew who it wasn't. Kluszewski.

So I looked at Kluszewski and threw to first base, balking. Umpire Bill Stewart didn't call it. I did it again, more obviously that time. Stewart didn't call it. I threw over to first base six times and Stewart simply would not call a balk. I couldn't believe it. This was Stewart's twenty-first big league season, how could he allow me to break the rules like that?

Since he wouldn't call a balk, I had two options: pitch to Kluszewski or stand there holding the ball. I pitched to him, carefully. Very carefully. Klu took a huge cut and hit a little dribbler out in front of the plate. Campy pounced on it and threw him out at first base.

As I was walking toward the dugout, I heard someone call my name. I looked up and saw Bill Stewart walking toward me. "Hey, son," he said, "lemme tell you something. You probably didn't realize it, but you were balking out there. I could've call half a dozen balks on you if I'd wanted to, but I knew this was your first game in the bigs so I decided to give you a break."

He warned me to be more careful next time. What could I say to him?

That was the only game I pitched in for a while. About all I could figure out was that Walter was saving me for winter ball. Finally, I found out why I wasn't pitching. Between games of a doubleheader in Milwaukee, Don Zimmer came over to me in the clubhouse and said, "Tommy, you're not gonna believe the conversation I just heard between Walter and Lyons. Lyons wanted to put you in the bullpen for the second game and Walt said no. He said he wanted you on the bench because you really kept things alive when you were there. He likes the way you yell at everybody."

I got sick. I went right into Walt's office and demanded, "Did I just hear right? Are you keeping me on the bench because I'm enthusiastic?" I was livid and really airing it out. Walt sat there listening. "Did you really bring me up here to be a cheerleader? Let me tell you, I wanna pitch, and if I'm not gonna pitch up here then send me back to Montreal."

Walter got up. "Now let me tell you something," he said. "I'm the manager of this ball club and you'll do what I want you to do to. We're battling for the pennant and I'm gonna sink or swim with the people who got us here. If we don't win, then you'll get your shot. But right now I'm going with the veterans."

"Then why'd you bring me up?"

Walter was always honest. "Because I've seen you make a team come alive with all your screaming and yelling on the bench. We need some life on that bench and I brought you up here to give it to us."

We argued some more, but this was an argument I couldn't win. I spent the remainder of the season pitching batting practice, cheering as loudly as I could, and hoping for a chance to pitch. Walter was absolutely right, I knew; he had to go as far as he could with proven players, the players who had got the Dodgers into pennant contention. If I were manager I would do absolutely the same thing. The only thing was, I wasn't a manager, I didn't want to be a manger, and had no plans to manage. I was a pitcher and I wanted to pitch.

Even with my cheerleading the Giants won the pennant by five games. We were scheduled to play them after they had clinched. Billy Loes was supposed to pitch, but he went home. Alston decided to pitch either me or Karl Spooner, a young left-hander recently recalled from Fort Worth. At the last moment he picked Spooner, and put me in the bullpen to relieve him if he got into trouble.

Spooner got into trouble in the first inning. He walked three batters, loading the bases for Bobby Hofman. I started warming up. Spooner threw three straight balls to Hofman. I was getting warmer. On the bench Alston told coach Billy Herman, "If Spooner walks him, go out and get him and bring in Lasorda. I was hot.

Spooner threw a fastball up around Hofman's eyes. It would've been ball four—but Hofman took a swipe at it and missed. Spooner came back to strike him out. And the next batter. Spooner was never in trouble after that, striking out 14 and shutting out the Giants. Four days later he shut out the Pirates, striking out 13, for a two-game total of 27 strikeouts, the best two-game debut in baseball history.

And I was still in the bullpen warming up.

I continued trying to be optimistic, but it was getting tougher. I was tremendously disappointed that Walter Alston, the man I helped win two pennants and a Little World Series at Montreal, did not have enough confidence in me to give me a chance to pitch in the major leagues. I just kept reminding myself that everyone suffers setbacks and heartaches in life, and a lot of doors are going to close. And I believed that every time a door closed, if I kept my faith in myself and my abilities, and in God, another door would open.

I was determined that 1955 would be a better season for me. I was really prepared to win in the big leagues. I knew the players and the parks, and while I had once been nervous, I was now determined.

The season started out as promising as I expected it to be. The 1955 Brooklyn Dodgers were one of the great teams of all time. Hall-of-Famer Roy Campanella was the catcher. Gil Hodges, who should be in the Hall of Fame, played first. Jim Gilliam was the second baseman. Hall-of-Famer Pee Wee Reese was the shortstop. Hall-of-Famer Jackie Robinson played third. Hall-of-Famer Duke Snider in center field was flanked by Carl Furillo and Sandy Amoros. Don Newcombe led a pitching staff that included Clem Labine, Billy Loes, Carl Erskine, Johnny Podres and, finally, Tom Lasorda. We won our first 10 games, 22 of our first 24.

I didn't pitch too much during that streak, if you consider not at all not too much. But finally, when we were about 10 games in front, Alston and Newcombe had a big argument. The result was that I was to get my first major league start.

I wasn't the slightest bit nervous the night before. In fact, I slept like a baby—I was up every hour. Just before I left the locker room the next afternoon to face the St. Louis Cardinals, Mr. O'Malley called to wish me luck. Since purchasing the ball club, Mr. and Mrs. O'Malley had rooted almost as hard as me and Jo for me to stick with the team. Mr. O'Malley had even gone so far as to make sure I saw a copy of every article that mentioned my name.

I felt like I had good stuff warming up, but I opened the game by walking Wally Moon. Then I threw a sharp curveball that broke about ten feet too soon and got past Campanella—a wild pitch—and Moon went to second. Bill Virdon was the next batter and I walked him too. So far, not so good; two batters, two walks and one wild pitch. It showed signs of getting a lot worse, quickly. The batter was Stan "The Man" Musial, the best hitter in baseball. I worked on him very carefully, getting ahead in the count. Campy called for a fastball, but I wanted to throw my knuckleball. I didn't have much of a knuckleball, but I didn't have much of a fastball either. I threw the knuckleball and it bounced passed Campy—my second wild pitch—allowing the runners to move up. I decided to throw the curveball to Musial.

The next pitch was the finest curveball I threw in my entire playing career. Stan Musial swung right over it. It took a moment for the feeling to sink in. I had struck out Stan Musial. Stan Musial, the best hitter in baseball, and I had struck him out. If my career ended right at that moment, I thought, I would have been satisfied. Of course, I didn't really expect it to end at that moment.

The adrenaline was surging through my body. I felt confident, strong.

Too strong. With Kenny Boyer at bat, I threw another pitch past Campanella—my third wild pitch of the inning. Campy whirled around and ran to the backstop to get the ball, I raced in to cover the plate. Wally Moon took off for home. I got the ball just before Moon got there, and I blocked the plate with my leg. I figured, If Moon wants to score, he's gonna have to go right through me.

He went right through me, ripping open my knee. Somehow, I managed to finish the inning without any more runs scoring, and hobbled to the bench. I took a seat in the corner. My kneecap was slashed and bleeding badly, so I put my glove over it to make sure nobody saw it. I'd waited too long for this opportunity to let a cut leg cost me a chance to break into the Dodger rotation.

The fact that I had just struck out the greatest hitter in baseball helped reduce the pain. Duke Snider sat next to me and said, "Hey, buddy, as I was coming in, Musial asked me who you were."

"Yeah?" That was pretty flattering.

"Yeah. He says he can hardly wait to get up against you again."

Before I could think of a clever response, Pee Wee Reese came over and lifted my glove off my knee. There was a big red blotch on my uniform. Jackie Robinson, who hated the sight of blood, almost fainted. Alston took one look and told Billy Herman, "Get Labine ready. He's coming in."

I glared at him. "There is no way I'm coming out of this game," I said.

Our trainer, Dr. Wendler, answered for Alston, telling me, "Don't be ridiculous. You're not going out there bleeding like that."

I had just struck out Stan Musial, the greatest hitter in baseball, and they thought they were going to take me out of the game? They had no chance. "Doc," I said, "don't stand in my way. When this inning is over I'm going out there. I've been waiting too many years for this game."

Next, Dr. Fette, the team doctor, examined my knee. "Go out there if you want," he said, "but I want you to know the chance you're taking. Your tendon is exposed, and if anything happens to it, the best you can hope for is that you won't ever walk again."

I told him that that was a chance I was willing to take. It seems crazy, but that's how desperately I wanted to stay in the major leagues. Finally, they called Buzzy into the dugout. "Forget it," he said, "you're not going out there."

"I am not coming out of the game," I repeated. When the third out was made I got up and started walking out of the dugout. Newcombe and Russ Meyer grabbed my arms and dragged me, fighting, into the clubhouse. Labine came in to pitch.

That was my one inning as a starting pitcher for the Dodgers. Fortunately, I had pitched my way into the record books. A lot of pitchers struck out Stan Musial in their careers—but very few threw three wild pitches in one inning.

I was rushed to the hospital where my kneecap was sewn back into place, and my leg was immobilized in a cast for a month. It's probably not too difficult to imagine how delightful it was to be with me during that time. The one positive thing it did was reinforce my marriage, because if Jo could put up with me for that month, I knew there was nothing I could possibly do that would be worse.

The cast came off on a Monday morning. Monday afternoon I pitched ninety minutes of batting practice at Ebbets Field.

Tuesday night the Pittsburgh Pirates jumped all over our pitching staff. Walt came over to me and said, "Too bad you threw so long yesterday. This would've been a good time to get some work in."

Walt knew me very well. That was like asking me if I really wanted a plate of hot linguini with clam sauce. My arm was hanging, my whole body was sore, but I wasn't going to miss a chance to get in a major league game. "I don't care about yesterday," I said. "Just gimme the ball."

Alston was very happy to see me go to the mound. So, as it turned out, were the Pirates. Preston Ward hit a home run off me. Tom Saffell hit a home run off me. I got bombed. After the game, I sat in the clubhouse in front of my locker, head down, staring at the floor, looking so completely unhappy Clay Bryant would have been proud. I would've given anything if Walter Alston had come over or given me one word of encouragement, or did anything to boost my morale or my confidence. I waited, and waited, sitting there in my uniform until the only people left in that clubhouse were me and Pee Wee Reese. Finally, Pee Wee came over to me and put his arm around my shoulders. "Tommy," he said, "I feel awful about what happened to you. You shouldn't have been in that game today after throwing yesterday. Why'd you go and volunteer for?"

"Pee Wee," I said, "I just want to get a chance to pitch. And I guess I got it, right?"

There are no schools that teach the subject "Managing a Baseball Team." A man learns how to manage by playing baseball, by experiencing the best moments and the worst, by remembering how he was treated, and how he wanted to be treated. I didn't make any vows that day that if I ever managed I'd never let a player sit alone and depressed, as I did, but I never forgot that overwhelming feeling of loneliness and failure either. As a manager, I've sat next to a lot of players after a lot of bad games. Sometimes it has taken every ounce of self-control I have to keep my hands from around their throats. Most often, they don't even feel like talking, but believe me, they knew I was sitting there.

A few days after my disastrous performance against Pittsburgh Buzzy Bavasi called me into his office. "We have a roster problem," he explained, "we've got to cut somebody. It's a tough decision, there are a lot of outstanding players on this club . . ."

I'd just completed a month on the disabled list and in my one game I'd been hit hard. Buzzy and I were the only people in that room, and I knew *he* wasn't going to get cut. I had the feeling he was trying to tell me something.

". . . lemme ask you," he continued, "if you were me, who would you cut?"

I didn't hesitate. No matter how angry I was, I wanted to see the Dodgers win. "Koufax," I said. "That kid can't win up here." The Dodgers had recently signed a left-handed pitcher out of the University of Cincinnati named Sandy Koufax. He could throw hard, but he had absolutely no control. I knew he couldn't help the team.

Buzzy shook his head. "We've gotta keep him," he said. "Tommy, we've gotta send you out. I'm sorry."

I was crushed. "I don't understand, how can you keep a kid who can't hit a barn at sixty feet and send me down?"

The Dodgers had no choice, he explained. According to baseball rules, a club that signed a player for more than a $4,000 bonus had to keep him on the major league roster for two seasons. Koufax had signed for more than $4,000. He stayed; I went. Decades later it's easy to joke that it took the greatest left-handed pitcher in the history of baseball to force me off the roster, but it wasn't funny then. And, at times, I still think the Dodgers made a mistake. I didn't believe Koufax was ready to win in the major leagues and I knew I could.

I sat there staring at Buzzy, but I knew I would be going back to Montreal. What else could I do, threaten to quit? The last time I tried that he got me a job.

When I reported back to the International League I was cockier than ever. This is my league, I thought, I own this league, and I was just going to move in and take over.

I lost my first five games. I was just so mad at the Dodgers, at Walter Alston, at my teammates, at myself, that I couldn't pitch straight. I just didn't care about baseball. In mid-August my father came up to Montreal to see me pitch and I got knocked out in the sixth inning. Afterwards, we were sitting in my hotel room, waiting for room service to deliver dinner, and I started complaining. I told him that I'd just about had it with baseball, that I wasn't going to let anyone treat me this way, that I didn't need them, that . . .

"Hey," he interrupted after listening to me moan for about fifteen minutes, "why don't you shut your mouth, I'm tired of hearing you complain. I come up to visit you, it was hotter than Hades at home, with so much humidity I couldn't breathe, and you're living in a hotel, you're in an air-conditioned room, you're making good money, you've just ordered dinner and we're eating steaks, you just called your wife long distance on the telephone and you're wearing $30 baseball shoes and still complaining. What are you talking? You got it made."

He did have a way of putting things in perspective. He was right, things only looked bad when I thought about how close I had been to staying in the major leagues. It was painful to be that close to making it, close enough to be in the dugout, and have it slip out of my grasp.

A few days later the Royals were in Buffalo. I was walking down the street with my roommate, Don Drysdale; Wally Fiala; and Johnny Bucha; and a pigeon flew over and got me smack on the top of the head. I think —*I know*—that was the lowest of all moments. I looked up at that pigeon and screamed, "Why? Why me? Why not one of these guys?" Drysdale started to laugh. "I'll show you, you'll see!" I won nine straight games. I couldn't lose. And when I wasn't pitching, I used to walk down the street looking for pigeons. You never know.

The Dodgers won the world championship for the first time that year and I was voted a half-share of the money the players received. Jo and I decided we would use this bonus to give my father the one thing he really wanted, a trip to his hometown in Italy.

He was extremely appreciative, but told us he couldn't go, he had to work. "Now I know where I get my brains," I screamed at him. "If someone wanted to give me a trip to Italy, I'd go right away."

Finally, he told us the reason. He was only entitled to three weeks' vacation and didn't want to go home for that short time. He couldn't take additional time off because he couldn't afford to lose the pay.

"Okay," I told him, "you take three more weeks off and I'll pay your salary."

He looked at me suspiciously. "You'll pay me the salary for three weeks?"

"Yep."

He nodded. "Okay, I'll go." My father drove a hard bargain.

My brothers were not as pleased as I thought they would be when they heard about the trip. "What is this?" my brother Eddie asked. "I thought we did things together in this family?"

"That's true," I said, "but I've got this extra money and I wanted to do this." I also knew that I was doing a little better than my brothers at that time, and they really couldn't afford to chip in. We had a family meeting and decided that I would pay the air fare and salary, and they would provide all his spending money. Eddie had to take a bank loan to do it, Harry and his wife, Ginny, had to give up their savings for a washing machine, but it was worth it. It was the last time my father saw his home and many members of his family.

There were many things I learned during my pitching career, but none was more important than this: Never sign a long-term lease on an apartment. A professional athlete can guarantee he will be traded, sold, or demoted simply by giving a cash advance to a landlord. Every year the Dodgers would send me from Brooklyn to Montreal, telling me I needed to get a new pitch. By 1956 I had nine pitches, I couldn't think of anything else to throw, so I knew it had to be my year. Somewhere between Schenectady and Brooklyn I had made the transition from promising youngster to grizzled veteran. If I didn't make it in 1956, I realized, I would never have a real major league career.

During spring training the Dodgers finally gave me the opportunity to pitch in the big leagues they had been promising me; they sold me to the Kansas City Athletics. "We think the world of you, Tom," Buzzy Bavasi said as he told me about the deal, "and there'll be a place for you any time you want to come back to the Dodgers. But we had this chance to sell you and we didn't want to deny you the opportunity to pitch in the majors. You've worked too hard to earn it." Buzzy was one of the few men I have ever met who can make you want to thank him for not wanting you.

Kansas City. At least it wasn't the St. Louis Browns. The season before the Brownies bought me they had finished seventh in an eight-team league, winning 64 games. The Athletics, meanwhile, had finished sixth the year before they bought me, and they had won 63 games. So I was moving up in the American League.

The A's were managed by Lou Boudreau. Spud Chandler was his pitching coach. Chandler decided I would make a good spot starter and relief pitcher, even though I'd never really pitched in relief and had a control problem. On the other hand, Jack McMahan, who they also bought, had only pitched in relief, which is probably why they decided he should be a starter. It didn't matter too much to me; Kansas City had lost 91 games the previous year, so relief pitching had to be very important.

Ironically, Bobby Shantz, who started his career at the same time I did, was a member of that pitching staff. Between the two of us we'd already won 67 big leagues games, Bobby winning 67 of them.

I intended to change that. My first American League start came against the Cleveland Indians. The Indians were a powerful team, having won the 1954 pennant and finished second in 1955. Their lineup included Vic Wertz, 1954 batting champion Bobby Avila, Rocky Colavito, and Al Rosen, and for insurance against me, they'd gotten Preston Ward from the Pirates. Among their pitchers was Herb Score, the fireballing phee-nom who set a major league record by striking out 245 batters in 227 innings his rookie year.

Boudreau told me the day before the game that I was going to start. We were playing the Indians on a Saturday afternoon and he said matter-of-factly, "You're gonna pitch one of the games in tomorrow's double-header."

That was pretty exciting news. "Which one?"

Boudreau shrugged. "Whichever game Score starts." In baseball, this is what is known as being the sacrificial lamb thrown to the wolves. Score was one of the best pitchers in baseball, on his way to a 20–9 season, I was one of the pitchers in baseball, on my way to the minor leagues. I started thinking about the game. If I was throwing well, I believed, I could beat anybody, even Herb Score. And if I wasn't, it didn't matter who was pitching against me, I couldn't beat a rug. The more I thought about it, the more nervous I became. I figured I needed as much help as I could get, so Sunday morning Johnny Groth and I went to church. We were sitting in a pew when who came in but Herb Score and Rocky Colavito. They sat three rows in front of us. This isn't so good, I thought, looking at the back of Score's head. This guy has all the ability in the world and he's still trying to get the edge? I decided I'd get the edge on him, I'd take Holy Communion.

When I got to the altar, he was three people in front of me. I was really worried. I go to church, he goes to church; I take Holy Communion, he takes Holy Communion; he's got tremendous ability, I go to Holy Com-munion.

We started the second game of the doubleheader just as the shadows stretched over the field. Neither team scored in the first six innings, Score was pitching a one-hitter and I was pitching a two-hitter. But with two outs and nobody on base in the sixth, I walked Bobby Avila. Then Sam Mele hit a little blooper over shortstop that three players dived for and missed. First and second, Al Rosen at bat. He looked at a fastball for strike one. He took another fastball for strike two. I thought, Isn't this some-thing, Al Rosen, one of the best power hitters in baseball, can't hit my fastball.

I should have realized something unusual was up. Everybody could hit my fastball. My purpose in throwing him fastballs was to set him up for my curveball. His purpose in not swinging at my fastballs was to get me to throw him my curveball. So I threw him the curveball that I had been setting him up for which he had been waiting. He hit it over the right-centerfield wall for a three-run homer.

Score shut us out to get the win, teaching me another very important lesson: Don't let the opposing pitcher get in front of you in church.

I almost won a game that year. I had the White Sox beat 3–2 in the ninth, with one out, a runner on first, and pinch-hitter Walt Dropo at bat. Dropo could not beat Ted Kluszewski in a running race. He hit a perfect double play ball to third baseman Hector Lopez. Lopez fired to second baseman Jim Finigan, who touched the bag, made his pivot, and fired to first . . . toward first . . . near first . . . somewhere in the vicinity of first, allowing Dropo to reach the base. The White Sox put in a pinch-runner. Nellie Fox hit my next pitch into the outfield gap, tying the score. Boudreau took me out of the game, bringing Moe Burtschy in to pitch. The next batter popped up Burtschy's first pitch, ending the inning. Enos Slaughter led off the bottom of the ninth by hitting the first pitch for a game-winning home run. I had pitched eight and two-thirds innings, Burtschy made one pitch. Burtschy got the win, I got to shower before all the hot water was gone.

That was as close as I ever came to winning a major league game. I pitched in 18 games for Kansas City, 13 in relief. I struck out 28 batters in 45 innings. I also walked 45, which probably hurt my performance as a relief pitcher. I lost four games that season, finishing 0–4, making my lifetime major league record 0–4. To me, that simply proves that statistics can be misleading because they don't take into account different situations. When Don Drysdale or Bob Gibson pitched, for example, the other team never scored any runs, but when *I* pitched, they always scored runs!

Of course, I didn't finish my career in Kansas City without a fight, and that fight was with the New York Yankees. In Kansas City one day, Yankee pitcher Tom Sturdivant was beating us 5–0 in the seventh. But Harry "Suitcase" Simpson and Enos Slaughter hit home runs to make the score 5–2. Obviously, we weren't supposed to catch the Yankees, because Sturdivant retaliated by throwing at our batters. He had our hitters ducking on every pitch. Nobody on our bench said a word, they just watched it happen. Boudreau, who had been a tough player and was a tough manager, was irate. He started walking up and down the bench screaming at *us*. "Those　　　　　Yankees, everybody's afraid of them. Nobody's willing to give back some of the　　　　　they've been giving us."

Talk about your challenges. "Where I come from," I said boldly, "we're not afraid of the Yankees."

"You mean that?" he asked.

"You better believe it." A half inning later I was warmed up and in the game. I decided I was going to throw at every Yankee player. Whoever came up was going down. Joe Collins was the first batter. I sent him sprawling twice, then got him out. Sturdivant was next. I knocked him down twice, and got him out. Billy Martin was the third batter. I actually threw a couple of pitches behind him before striking him out to end the inning. I was feeling great. Throwing at Yankees was even more fun than throwing at barkers in the carnival.

Hank Bauer led off the top of the ninth. I dropped him a couple of times, then struck him out. As my infielders were throwing the ball around after that out, Billy Martin stood on the top step of the dugout and screamed, "You   , I'll get you before the year's over."

Promises, promises. "Hey, Martin," I shouted at him, "you don't have to wait until the end of the year. Why don't you come on out now, let's go." He immediately came charging out of the dugout, trailed by the entire Yankee team. Martin and I traded a few harmless punches before other players got between us. Meanwhile, Hank Bauer was on the side going out of his mind. Two guys were holding his arms, and Harry Craft, one of our coaches, had him in a headlock from behind. It looked like Bauer and the three of them were in a draw, when Bauer leaned down and flipped Craft right over his back onto the ground, then started coming after me.

"Hold it, Bauer," I screamed, slowing him up enough to allow people to get between us. "Stay out of this. It's between me and Martin." Five guys grabbed him and held on. I tried to look unhappy that I didn't get one shot at him, but even that was a struggle.

As everyone was going back to their dugouts so play could be resumed, Mickey Mantle came over and put his arm around my shoulders. "Hey, Tom," he said, "don't worry about that. Billy and Hank are really good guys, but they're not going too good right now, so you can understand how they feel."

I nodded. "Yeah, sure, Mick," I said. As I walked back to the mound, I started thinking, That Mickey Mantle, he's not a bad guy at all. After all, he knew my name. He was the next hitter and, naturally, I had intended to drill him too, but when he came to bat I looked at him and changed my mind. I decided I wouldn't hit him.

Obviously, he didn't feel the same way about me. He hit my second pitch off the wall in right center for a standup double. Talk about being ungrateful. I could've fed him a dirt sandwich and he responded that way. That was it for Mr. Nice Guy Lasorda.

In mid-season, Kansas City general manager Parke Carroll traded me to the Yankees for knuckleball pitcher Wally Burnette. "We gave them a list of players to choose from," Carroll said, "and Casey Stengel wanted you."

That made me feel pretty good. "I guess he liked my curveball," I said.

"I don't think so," Carroll told me. "He said something about liking the way you fight."

He liked me so much, in fact, that the Yankees assigned me to the Denver Bears, their Triple-A farm club in the American Association. Jo, Laura, and I drove straight through from Kansas City to Denver, because I wanted to start pitching my way back to the major leagues as quickly as possible. The Bears were managed by Ralph Houk, as friendly a manager as I'd ever played for. "Gee," he said when I walked into the clubhouse, "I've seen players take one day to travel from the minors to the majors, but you're the first guy I've ever seen go from the majors to the minors in one day."

I was tempted to tell him that I'd had plenty of practice. Instead I said that I'd read he was short of pitchers and I was ready to go.

He smiled knowingly. "You can't just do that," he explained, "you've got to get used to playing at this altitude. It's different than playing anywhere else."

Was he kidding me? I'd played ball for ten seasons in the Caribbean, and that was different than anyplace else too. Besides, I owned Triple A baseball. "The mound's sixty feet six inches away, right?"

"Yeah."

"They use the same bases, right?"

"Yeah."

"Then I can pitch."

"No, you really can't," he insisted. We finally agreed that I would pitch in relief if the starting pitcher that night got into trouble. The starting pitcher got into trouble in the second inning and I started warming up. None of the Denver players had ever seen me throw, so I thought I'd put on a little exhibition while warming up. I threw a few fastballs, then signaled I was going to break off a curve. I'll break one off like they've never seen before, I thought. Their eyes are gonna pop right out of their heads. So I snapped one off—it spun twice and floated almost straight into the catcher's glove.

Um. Wait a minute, I thought, that's not right. Evidently, I hadn't gotten on top of the ball. Okay, I knew I was really gonna have to get on top of it.

I really snapped off the second pitch. It spun two or three times and sort of dropped about an inch. I knew I was in serious trouble. I took a deep breath. Apparently, it wasn't deep enough, because I felt short of breath. And a little dizzy. That's when Ralph Houk called me in to make my American Association debut.

The first hitter I faced was Bill Taylor, a left-handed hitter I'd faced in the International League. He was a dead fastball hitter, but couldn't hit a breaking pitch. As I soon discovered, that was the perfect type of hitter to be in Denver, because I couldn't throw one.

I looked in to get the signal from the catcher, and discovered that home plate had been moved back. It appeared to be at least ninety feet from the pitcher's mound. I began to believe Ralph Houk had been correct.

I attempted to throw a curveball to Taylor, he rifled it off the fence. The next batter was Jim Pendleton. I threw a fastball under his chin to move him away from the plate, then tried to throw a curveball on the outside corner. It didn't break at all and Pendleton jumped on it, doubling to right. The next batter singled, then there was another hit, and another. After each hit, I'd knock down the next batter. But each time, the batter would get up, dust himself off, and hit my next pitch. I couldn't get anybody out. The way baseballs were shooting around me, I felt like the centerpost in a pinball game. After they'd scored five runs in the first inning I figured, well, at least I got my feet on the ground.

Finally, Ralph Houk came out to talk to me. He had a smile on his face, he knew exactly what was going on. "How you feeling?" he asked.

"Uuhhhhgggggg," I said, trying to catch my breath.

"Yeah, well, the ball travels well in this thin air."

"Uuhhhhgggggg," I told him.

"Well," he said, "just hang in there, I like what I've seen so far." His pitching staff must have been in even more trouble than the papers had written. I'd given up five runs and he was telling me he liked what he saw?

Jo had spent the day moving us into a motel. When I got to our room I collapsed into a large chair. "How it'd go?" she asked.

"Uuhhhhgggggg," I explained. When I was finally able to breath again, I told her that Ralph Houk seemed like a really good guy, "but I think he's crazy. I gave up five runs in one inning and he told me he liked what he saw."

As I soon discovered, Ralph Houk was a tremendous man to play for. A former army major, he inspired players to perform at their highest capability, and then give a little more. I've never known a better "players' manager," a manager players enjoy playing for, because he treated them as men, not as names on a roster. And he knew the value of a good brawl as much as I did, which is probably why we became such close friends.

We made the American Association playoffs that season, playing Johnny Keane's Omaha Cardinals. Omaha easily won the first three games of the best-of-seven series, winning the third game 22–8. Before the fourth game, Ralph called a clubhouse meeting. He was not emotional, just sincere. "This is it," he said. "We don't win today and it's back to the lunch buckets till next season. All I'm asking is that you go out there and give your very best."

When the meeting ended he motioned me over to his locker. "Listen," he said softly, "can you start a fight?"

Could Rembrandt paint? Can Frank Sinatra sing? He certainly knew what my best talent was. "What inning?" I wanted to know.

"Any time you want," he replied. "We've just gotta do something to liven up things around here."

Because I was the most experienced player on the ball club—by this time I would have been the most experienced player on any minor league ball club—Houk often had me coaching first base. Even before the first pitch was thrown I got on the Cardinals' pitcher, Frank Barnes. I was determined to get the fight started in the first inning. I mean, I had a reputation to uphold.

Our leadoff hitter, Bob Martyn, opened the game with a home run. Tony Kubek was our next batter, and Barnes threw his first pitch at Kubek's neck. Who did Barnes think he was? Me? The day before we had gotten beat 22–8 and our pitchers didn't drop one of their hitters. We get one run and Barnes is throwing at our shortstop. I thought everybody was wrong, we should have been throwing at them, they shouldn't have been throwing at us.

Kubek decided to take care of Barnes himself. On the next pitch he pushed a bunt down the first base line, hoping Barnes would come over to field it. If he did, Kubek was going to level him. Unfortunately, the ball rolled foul. Unfortunately for Tony and Frank Barnes. Because I picked it up, examined it, and then, instead of flipping it back softly to the pitcher, I fired it at him as hard as I could. My control was no better than usual, so the ball grazed his leg and bounced toward third baseman Stan Jok. "Come on, Barnes," I shouted, "do something about it."

Barnes turned to walk away. I couldn't believe it. I'd won only three games for the Bears that season, losing four. If I couldn't even start a small riot as a favor to the manager, my baseball career was really in jeopardy.

Stan Jok saved me. He picked up the baseball and fired it right back at me. I smelled horsehide as it whizzed under my nose. That was all the excuse I needed. I raced across the diamond after Jok. Ralph Houk, coaching third base, beat me to him, so I took a hard right turn at the mound and went after Barnes, starting a free-for-all that lasted twenty minutes.

As Houk had hoped, the fight helped turn the playoff series around. We won that game, then the next three to win the league championship. For my part in the fight, I received a telegram from league president Ed Dougherty reading, "Dear Tom, The exhibition you put on last night was a disgrace to baseball. You are hereby fined $100 and, furthermore, my advice to you is, if you want to fight, join the International Boxing Congress."

Houk insisted on paying the fine for me. I sent Dougherty the check and a note. "Dear Mr. Dougherty," I wrote, "Enclosed you will find a check for $100. As far as me being a disgrace to baseball, maybe that's right, but as far as joining the IBC, a lot of those fights are fixed, the one we had last night was on the level."

I went to spring training with Denver in 1957. I may be stubborn, but after three major league trials, and nearing my thirtieth birthday, I was beginning to realize I was never going to make it. I felt cheated. I believed then, as I believe now, that if I had ever had a fair shot, if a team had put me in their rotation and let me pitch every fourth or fifth day, I could have been a winning major league pitcher. But it didn't happen. Instead, I became a Triple-A star, which was still better than being a Double-A star.

But with my career beginning to end, I had to figure out what I wanted to do. Playing baseball was about the only thing I was qualified to do. And one of the harsh realities of life as a professional athlete is that "a good curveball" has very little value on a résumé. Since I was as passionate as I'd ever been about baseball, I wanted to stay in the game. I felt I had the best chance to do this in the Brooklyn organization, so early in the 1957 season I asked Yankee general manager Lee MacPhail to try to make a deal to get me back to the Dodgers. Buzzy Bavasi traded a minor league infielder for me, and the Dodgers assigned me to the Los Angeles Angels in the Triple-A Pacific Coast League. So, I actually beat the Dodgers to California by a full year.

My old pal Clay Bryant was managing the Angels. I was pleased to see that time had not changed him at all. He was still the same warm human being I'd played for at Greenville. The Angels' second baseman that year was George "Sparky" Anderson. Me and Sparky on the same ball club?

That's like putting a match and a fuse together. You think that team didn't have some fights? We were at war with the rest of the league. My personal choice for fight of the year took place against our crosstown rivals, the Hollywood Stars. The day before I was scheduled to pitch against them, I was sitting in our dugout watching batting practice. Hollywood's second baseman, Forrest Vandergrift "Spook" Jacobs, who could hit but had no power, kept trying to pull line drives into our dugout. I had played with Spook at Montreal before the Dodgers had traded him. "What's that all about?" I asked. "Spook's never been a pull hitter."

"He's still bitter about the way the Dodgers treated him when he was in the organization," someone explained, "so he's trying to hit balls over here."

That was all I needed to hear. The man was going to eat dirt the next day. Peace lasted until the third inning. Then Hollywood pitcher Ed Waters hit a home run off me. That was like adding fire to the fire. Jacobs was the next batter. Everybody in the western United States knew he had to go down. I threw behind him. My control has always been better when I was throwing at a big target, like a batter, rather than something small, like home plate. Spook knew the game, so he simply got up, dusted himself off, and got back in the batter's box. Never said a word. But he bunted my next pitch down the first base line. If I fielded it, or covered the base while first baseman Steve Bilko fielded it, Spook was going to take a shot at me. I didn't bother with formalities, like pretending to go after the ball. Halfway to first base I threw one of the best body blocks seen in modern baseball. Both dugouts emptied like someone had pulled a plug. So many Stars came after me Spook couldn't even get close, so he went after Sparky Anderson. That could be called a mistake. This was a real back alley slugfest, not the typical baseball fight, which is mostly serious milling. This one could have been scored by boxing officials.

We didn't confine our fighting to baseball. One night in Portland, our shortstop Bobby Dolan, outfielder Big Jim Fridley, and I were cutting across a downtown square when we crossed paths with three locals. A few unpleasantries were exchanged, then one of the locals punched Dolan in the nose and he went down. Bobby looked like someone had squashed a tomato in his face. I leaned over and asked, "You okay? Listen, if you don't think you can handle this guy, I'll take him for you."

"No, that's all right," Bobby said, admittedly a bit nasally. "Just give me a few seconds to clear my head." I helped him up and he went after the guy who'd hit him.

Then the second local and Jim Fridley started. I've always known it is a mistake to get into a fight with anyone called Big Jim. So now Dolan and Fridley were going at it pretty good. I said to the third local, "I guess we're gonna have to fight."

"I don't wanna fight," he said. "I'm not looking for any trouble."

Meanwhile, Dolan and Fridley are being knocked down, standing up, knocking down the locals, then being knocked down again. "I understand," I said sympathetically, "but look at it my way. Tomorrow in the clubhouse when these two guys are telling the story, everybody's gonna ask what I was doing. What am I gonna tell 'em? I was debating?"

I think he understood I had no choice. So we got into it. The police finally broke up the fight. They broke it up by threatening to arrest us. We couldn't decide which was worse, being arrested and thrown into jail in a strange city for who knows how long, or facing Clay Bryant. We decided on Bryant, but it was not a unanimous vote. Actually, it worked out well. Bryant was so angry that he didn't speak to any of us for a month, but since he rarely spoke to us anyway, we hardly noticed.

When Mr. O'Malley moved the Dodgers to Los Angeles in 1958, the Angels moved to Spokane, Washington. Goldie Holt was named manager and Bryant took over the Montreal team. I knew Goldie well, and liked him, and was looking forward to playing for him—and then the player-coach job opened up at Montreal. That was the perfect opportunity for me to begin my post-career career.

Talk about a dilemma. Play for Goldie Holt or play and coach for Clay Bryant? It was like having to choose between a chocolate sundae and spinach. I knew one was going to be enjoyable, but that the other was probably better for me.

Jo and I talked about it, and finally decided to go after the coaching job. I spoke to John Carey, the Dodgers' East Coast supervisor of scouting, and certainly one of the finest men who ever lived, and to my friend Al Campanis about it. They went to Buzzy and convinced him to hire me. In addition to serving as player-coach, I was named traveling secretary. I assume they figured that by that time I had to know enough about traveling to handle the job. I was grateful. I was back in the Dodger organization, a place I considered home, and I had taken the first step toward remaining in baseball when my playing career ended.

Naturally, I had the best season of my life. I won 18 games and lost 6, striking out 126 and walking only 76. I had an earned run average of 2.50, fourth best in the league. I led the league in wins, innings pitched, and complete games. My five shutouts tied for the league lead, I made the All-Star Team and was named the International League's Pitcher of the Year. I was some coach.

When I signed my first contract with the Phillies, I vowed I was going to be the best player I was capable of being. I tried. When I got the player-coach-traveling secretary job, I vowed I was going to be the best player-coach-traveling secretary I was capable of being. And I tried. I spent hours at the ball park hitting grounders to infielders, throwing batting practice, doing whatever Bryant wanted me to do. At first, I was concerned I might have difficulty making the transition because I'd played with so many people on the club. So at the beginning of the year I told them, "I hope we stay friends, but I have a job to do and I can't let our friendship interfere with that. If you have as much respect for me as I have for you, you'll listen to me and do the right thing." That speech, and the fact that I handed out meal money and hotel room assignments, seemed to have worked. We won the International League championship and never missed a plane, a train, or a meal, making it a perfect season for me as player, coach, and traveling secretary.

In May, Jo gave birth to our son, Tom Lasorda, Jr. When Jo was pregnant, the baby moved around a lot. "He's got a lot of spunk," she said, and since that day we've called him Spunky. Never Tom, never Junior. Spunky. As with Laura, I'll never forget the day Spunky was born. We were playing Toronto. I was approaching the league record for consecutive scoreless innings pitched. Jo had stayed in Greenville with her family. Her sister Fran called and told me I'd better get home, because Jo had gone to the hospital. "I can't come home," I explained. "We're fighting for the pennant and I'm pitching tonight. I'll have the rest of my life to see my baby, but I only have tonight to win this game."

In the fifth inning a Toronto player hit a home run to break my scoreless inning streak. Everything else worked out perfectly; we won the game and the pennant, and I've since seen my son many, many times.

When Jo stayed in South Carolina, she kept our car. This was no problem because a close friend in Montreal, Joe Lanza, loaned me his second car when the Royals were at home. But in July, when we returned from a road trip, he explained that his car had been stolen and he needed his other car. However, Joe owned a fleet of taxicabs and offered me one of his cabs while the team was in town.

When I picked up the cab, I found a cap on the front seat. I put it on, tugged it rakishly over my eye cabdriver style, and drove to the ball park.

We had a player on that team, I won't mention his name, but he went from there to obscurity, and he was one of the cheapest people I've ever known. Usually, a group of players would share a cab from the hotel to the ball park, or back, and split the fare. This player would always try to bum a free ride. If he had to share a cab he'd never volunteer to pay his share and he refused to tip the driver.

That night, after the ball game, he asked if I was going back to the hotel. I started to tell him about my cab, then stopped. And smiled. And laughed. This was just too good an opportunity to miss. "Sure, kid," I said, "I'll be glad to take you."

When we reached my cab, I slid into the driver's seat, jammed on my official cabdriver's cap, and put down the flag, turning on the meter. "What're you doing?" he asked.

I turned around. "Whattya mean, what am I doing? I got a wife and two kids now, I can't make it on just my salary. I been driving this thing at night, I thought you knew that."

"No," he said, "I didn't." Then he cleared his throat and asked, "You're not going to charge me for the ride back to the hotel, are you?"

"Are you kidding?" I shouted at him. "Are you kidding me? You think I drive this tank for my health?" I started to get real angry. "You think I'm having a good time coaching, pitching, and driving a cab? You think it's so much fun you can just get out and walk back . . ." I yelled all the way back to the hotel. He stayed in the corner of the backseat and didn't say one word. When we reached the hotel, I turned off the meter and told him, "That's a buck and a quarter."

He had no choice but to pay the entire fare. It practically killed him. Then, as he climbed out of the cab, I shouted, "Hey! You didn't give me no tip!"

"And I'm not going to either," he said as he slammed the door. The next day he went around the entire clubhouse warning everyone, "Whatever you do, if Lasorda offers you a ride home, don't take it!"

This was my seventh season in Montreal. Occasionally, when a player spends many years with a team and is popular with the fans, they honor him with a day. August 23, 1958, was Tom Lasorda Day in Montreal. I was given a new car, a television set, and many other wonderful gifts. Of course, they couldn't give me the only thing I really needed, which was Sandy Koufax's fastball. But as I told the people of Montreal that day, "Only in this great country of ours, including Canada, can the son of an Italian immigrant, a runny-nosed little left-handed pitcher with a decent curveball, a player good enough only to . . ."

Normally, days honoring a player are held to celebrate his retirement as an active player. It didn't work with me though, I still came back to play in 1959.

Perhaps I should've taken the hint. We had a bad ball club that year and finished down in the standings. The brand-new Los Angeles Dodgers assigned most of their better prospects to Spokane, a much shorter trip to and from L.A. Although I could still pitch and I won 12 and lost 8, that was the first year I seriously considered retiring. But Branch Rickey announced the formation of a third major league, the Continental League, and I decided to try to hang on long enough to play in it. I didn't care if they did have to found a whole new league to get me into the majors, I still wanted to make it.

The Continental League died when the major leagues decided to expand. I returned to Montreal in 1960 to pitch and coach for Clay Bryant. It was a terrible situation. There was virtually no communication between Bryant and his players. I became the go-between. He would rip into someone, or humiliate him, and then I would have to try to put together the pieces of the player's ego. Bryant's favorite whipping boy was Bob Aspromonte. He had Aspromonte so depressed he was considering quitting baseball. I wouldn't let him quit. I told him that we were all in it together, and if I was going to stick it out, he had to.

My final confrontation with Bryant came over relief pitcher Bill "Hawk" Hunter. The Hawk was having a fine season, and he asked me one day if there was a chance he could get some more money. "Hawk," I told him, "the only thing I can do for you is go talk to Clay. He's the man on that one."

Bryant's response was something to the effect that if Hunter doesn't like the way things are run around here, tell him to pack his bags and go home.

"He said no," I told Hunter.

After that Bryant started acting even colder than usual to me. It took me about a week to realize it, but it reached the point where he didn't even snarl his usual "good morning" to me. Finally, I confronted him, demanding to know what was bothering him.

He glared at me. "Did you tell Hunter you could get him more money?"

"Course not."

"Well," he said, "that's not the way I heard it. He said you told him you were going to get him more money."

"That's a lie," I said softly.

"That's not what he told—"

"I don't care what he told you," I interrupted. I was burning. "I never said it because I knew I couldn't do it. What I told him was that I would talk to you."

He repeated that that was not the story he had been told.

"Fine," I said, "let's get him down here and settle this right now." I called Hunter's hotel room and asked him to meet us. A few minutes later he was standing face-to-face with Bryant. "When we spoke in Miami," I asked him, "did I tell you I was going to get you more money?"

"No."

"Did I ever tell you I was going to get you more money?" I felt like Perry Mason in the last five minutes of his show.

"No."

"Tell this man what I told you." I wanted to hear him throw Bryant's words right back in Bryant's face. Hunter told the story exactly as it happened. When he'd finished, I said, "Hawk, this man told me that you said I promised to get you more money."

Hunter looked right at Bryant and said, "Then he's a liar."

I rested my case right there, but I knew that wasn't the end of it. For a man like Bryant, the only thing worse than being wrong was being proven wrong. I knew I'd embarrassed him and I knew he would try to get even with me. I'd seen him at work too many times. The only thing I wondered about was how, and when.

The following Friday night I pitched against Buffalo. Because of the problems with Bryant I desperately wanted to win this game. Late in the game Buffalo loaded the bases with no outs. Bryant was on the top step of the dugout, ready to pull me. In my entire career, I had never prayed on the pitcher's mound, but this time, I turned my back on the hitter, looked up, and thought, Lord, I've never asked you to help me win a game. All I've ever asked was the strength to do the best I could at all times. Lord, I'm in a jam here, and any help you can give me would be greatly appreciated.

Suddenly, I heard my name being called. "Lasorda? Lasorda?" It was incredible. I turned around. It was the umpire, Billy Williams. "Come on, Lasorda," he said, "You gotta throw it sometime."

"Wait a minute," I told him, "I'm talking to God."

"Who?"

"God," I repeated.

"Oh," Billy said, as if he understood, then turned around and walked back to home plate. He probably figured I was crazy, but on the one chance I had a direct line . . .

My first pitch was an inside fastball, neither inside enough nor fast enough. The batter jerked it down the left-field line. Our third baseman, George Risley, leaped as high as he could and deflected the ball. It bounced off his glove toward the outfield grass. A base hit, I thought as I ran to back up third base, two runs'll score at least. But our shortstop,

Jerry Snyder, dived and backhanded the ball on the fly. Lying on his back, he flipped to second base for the second out, and the second baseman fired to first to complete the triple play. I'd played thirteen summers and eleven winters of professional baseball and had never before been involved in a triple play. As I walked nonchalantly off the field, I looked at Billy Williams, who was staring at me with his mouth open. Then I looked into the sky and said, "Thank you, Lord, but was it really necessary to scare me like that?"

That turned out to be the last game I ever pitched. After the game the next night, Bryant asked me to come into his office. He was there with general manager Fern DuBois. DuBois looked at me and said, "Tommy, we are hereby giving you your unconditional release. You are no longer a member of this ball club. Then he handed me a letter from Buzzy Bavasi.

"Dear Tommy," Buzzy had written, "For the love of me, I cannot understand what is wrong with you. You had a job with the Dodgers for as long as you wanted to remain in baseball, but now, after what you've done, I cannot see any other option but to give you your unconditional release. I hope you are able to hook on with another club. Good luck to you."

I could barely speak. I couldn't understand what was going on. ". . . after what you've done . . ."? What was he referring to? "What is this all about?" I asked DuBois. He responded by showing me a second letter from Bavasi. This was addressed to him, and read, "If Tommy continues to give you problems, you have the authority to release him. We cannot accept this type of behavior in this organization."

"I want to call Buzzy right now," I said. They would not give me his home phone number. I was trying desperately to control my temper, I didn't want to make things worse than they already were, although at that moment I didn't quite believe they could get any worse. Finally, I looked at Bryant and said, "You no-good rotten   . I was the only friend you had on this ball club and you didn't have sense enough to know it. Get up, I oughta   punch you full of   holes."

DuBois kept us apart. But that night my entire world collapsed. I went home and cried. It was impossible to accept what was happening to me. I had tried to be loyal to the Dodger organization, to the team, and to Bryant. This was what I got for that.

I sat up all night, trying to understand how things could have turned so bad so quickly.

First thing the next morning I called Buzzy. "I just don't understand," I said.

Buzzy was sympathetic, but professional. "Evidently you've been un-happy in this organization for some time," he replied.

"What are you talking about?"

"For the last few weeks I've been getting calls from Bryant and DuBois telling me you didn't like the way things were being run in the club, and that you were undermining the manager and—"

"That's a lie!" I shouted. I told Buzzy all about the confrontation between Hunter and Bryant. I knew it was my word against Bryant and DuBois, and tried to think of some way of convincing Buzzy I was sincere. Then I remembered. Coincidentally, one week earlier I had written a long letter to Al Campanis thanking him for everything he had done for me and telling him how proud I was to be with the Dodgers. I told Buzzy about that letter, then asked, "If I were unhappy, why would I write a letter like that?"

There was silence on the other end of the phone. "Just wait right there," Buzzy said. "I'll get back to you."

That same morning, although I was not aware of it, the Montreal players wrote a letter in my defense. Basically, it said that the players were shocked because I had "in some way taught each of us to love this organization." The only player who didn't sign it was the man Bryant named as my replacement as a coach.

I sat by the phone all morning. Move? I barely breathed. I knew my future was on the line. If I got a reputation as a troublemaker no one would hire me. Finally, the call came. Buzzy had spoken to Al Campanis, then Fern DuBois. "I see what happened," he said, "and I'm sorry about it. But look, I can't send you back there, so tomorrow morning, you begin your career as a scout." A scout? I didn't want to be a scout. On the other hand, I didn't want to be unemployed either.

"That's great," I said, and thanked him. A few minutes later Al Campanis called. "Starting right now," he said, "you're working for me."

So in July 1960, I finally hung up my spikes. I had had a long and relatively successful career. I always said I was going to play in the major leagues and I had; I never said how long I was going to play in the major leagues. And I'd set the all-time International League record for career victories with 107. But the real evidence that my career had been success-ful was easy to measure: The spikes I hung up had cost me $35.

FOUR

•

Only in This
Great Country of Theirs . . .

During the 1970s sportswriters began referring to me as Baseball's Goodwill Ambassador. Many people assumed that this was because I was always
preaching the gospel of baseball, that I was willing to talk to a crowd of
one about the great game, a game of thrills and chills that brings so much
enjoyment to so many young people and old people, a game for the fans
as well as the players, a game of complex strategy and simple luck, a game
of character and heroics, a game which allowed the son of an Italian
immigrant, a runny-nosed little left-handed pitcher with a decent curveball . . .

Maybe. But I suspect the real reason I've been called Baseball's Ambassador is that I've spent much of my baseball career outside the country.
Baseball may well be America's national pastime, but you certainly
couldn't prove that by looking at my passport. Besides the eight seasons
I spent playing in Montreal, Canada, I've played, coached, or managed
in Panama, Cuba, the Dominican Republic, Venezuela, and Puerto Rico.
I've participated in exhibitions in Mexico and Japan, and brought the
good word, "baseball," to the great nation of Italy. During those travels
I've seen two governments overthrown, I've met dictators and presidents,
I've been a hero and I've been arrested, I've started riots and run from
riots, I've pitched with soldiers in the dugout and umpires carrying six-
shooters. Now, that's baseball.

In South America, they play the game with the same baseball we use
in the States. In fact, they make the baseball in South America. The

pitcher's mound is the same sixty feet six inches from home plate as it is in Denver, the team that scores the most runs in nine innings wins, and the fans still come out to the ball park to root, root, root for the home team. But baseball in South America is very different than it is here. Instead of players wearing their last names on the backs of their uniforms, for example, they carry advertising. One year in Cuba I played for Bubbly Bubbly bubblegum. Another year I represented a tobacco company. And the fans have their own way of showing displeasure. Once I played in Cuba with Red Sox shortstop Eddie Pellagrini. He had a tough day, striking out three times. As he was walking back to the dugout after the third strikeout, the fans started whistling. Eddie sat down next to me shaking his head in admiration. "Aren't these fans great?" he said. "Here I strike out three times and they're still rooting for me."

"I think you got it wrong, Eddie," I explained. "Down here, whistling is the way they boo you." They were whistling very loudly. But I cheered him up when I added, "Just remember, as long as they're whistling, they won't be shooting."

"Shooting?" he said.

Actually, fans rarely shoot at ballplayers, but they do have subtle ways of showing their displeasure. Before a game in the Dominican one year, I saw six men parading through the stands carrying a wooden coffin. On top of the coffin was a sign in Spanish reading "Lasorda Is Dead." What bothered me most is that one of these pallbearers was my barber, and I had given him the tickets for the game.

My introduction to baseball in South America came in 1948, when Al Campanis arranged for me to play in Panama's Winter League. As I later learned, baseball in Panama is about as representative of baseball throughout South America as Devil Dogs are representative of good pasta. We played in the Canal Zone, which was mostly American. Everybody spoke English there, the fans generally remained in the stands during games, and few people carried guns. It was almost as much a paid vacation as a learning experience. I thought winter baseball was the best job in the world. While everybody I knew was freezing in Pennsylvania, I was being paid $1000 a month to pitch in the sunshine. The only pressure on me was trying to sample every South American food in a short season.

Then, in 1950, I played in Cuba. This was pre-pre-revolutionary Cuba. There were three restaurants and one casino on every block in Havana, the Cuban people liked Americans, and they took their baseball very seriously. Very, very seriously. I thought Cuba was going to be just like Panama, but I quickly learned differently. Soon after I arrived, Dick Williams, Hank Workman, and I were asked to do a radio interview.

When we got to the station, the interviewer took us into the studio and told us where to sit. Then he sat with his back to the wall, took a large gun out of his pocket, and laid it on the table.

I just stared at that gun. I couldn't believe the questions were going to be that difficult. Finally, Dick Williams asked, "What's that for?"

"Well," the interviewer said, smiling, "you never know."

You never know what? What did we never know? I was sitting there with my back to the door, I wanted to know. I was scared to death. I've done a lot of interviews since then, but none kept my attention the way that one did.

Baseball was the most important thing in many Cubans' lives. It was their escape from hard work and little money. There were four teams in the Cuban League, and all four played in the same ball park in Havana. Each team was represented by a different color. Havana was red, for example, so all Havana fans wore red clothing at the games. Cienfuegos was green, Marianao fans wore orange, and Almandaries was blue. Each team was allowed to have nine Americans, so there were thirty-six jobs for American ballplayers down there. Because baseball was a betting sport, the fans really got involved. One run could cost a man a week's wages, so you really didn't want to be responsible for that one run scoring. Cuban baseball was not a place to learn how to play; those fans expected you to win. If a player didn't do the job right away, his club simply shipped him back to the States and brought in someone to replace him.

My manager that first season was Adolfo "The Pride of Havana" Luque, who had pitched in the American big leagues for twenty years. Luque was the worst human being I have ever known. He made Bryant look like a saint. I argued with him practically every day. Once I remember telling him, "Luque, I'm a Catholic. I love Christmas. Christmas is a day when everybody is supposed to like each other, it's a time to forget bad feelings. But I'll tell you this, the way you act, if you walked down the main street of my hometown, Norristown, Pennsylvania, on Christmas Day, they'd punch your lights out."

He would do anything to win. We had a pitcher named Terry McDuffy, whose locker was right next to mine. One night, about a half hour before game time, Luque came over to Terry and said, "McDuffy, you are going to pitch tonight."

McDuffy shook his head. "No way," he said. "I pitched two nights ago. I'm not gonna pitch with two days' rest for nobody. I'll ruin my arm."

"I tell you you are going to pitch," Luque repeated, loudly.

"And I'm telling you I am not going to pitch," McDuffy shouted. They stood there screaming at each other, with Luque warning McDuffy he'd better pitch, and McDuffy insisting he was not going to pitch. Finally, Terry said, "That's it, that's enough. You feel that way about it, I quit. I'm going home right now. Tonight." He pulled his duffel bag from the top of his locker and started throwing his equipment into it. Luque disappeared into his office.

Less than a minute later, Luque came back carrying a pistol with a barrel that looked approximately a quarter-mile long. He put it against McDuffy's forehead. "You're pitching tonight," he said.

McDuffy started taking his equipment out of his duffel bag. "Gimme the ball," he said, "I'm ready to go." Terry pitched a two-hit shutout, proving the value of positive persuasion and a gun.

In my entire career, I never had a manager pull a gun on me. No way, not a manager. An umpire or an owner . . . that's a different story.

Usually, two American umpires worked Cuban games with two local umpires. One night I was pitching against Almandaries and Tom Gorman was going to work second base. We had been together in the Canadian-American League and the International League, so he knew I had an explosive temper and often screamed at the home plate umpire. The home plate umpire that night was Cuban Amando Maestri.

Before the game Gorman took me aside and said, "Tommy, listen, do yourself a favor, don't get on this guy behind the plate tonight."

I thought that was a strange thing to say, so I asked him why.

He simply repeated, "Just believe me, don't get on this guy."

And I didn't get on him until the first inning. I threw a pitch that I thought was a strike, and he screamed, "Ball-a."

Ball-a? "Hey," I shouted at him, "what the   you talking about? You blind? That was a   good pitch . . ." He stood there staring at me, not saying a word, so I figured he must not understand English.

I threw my second pitch. Again I thought it was a strike and again he called, "Ball-a."

Now I was really getting aggravated. The fans were screaming at me and I knew it was his fault. "Maestri," I yelled, "what the   is wrong with you? Don't you know a   good pitch when you see one? You gotta   bear down back there . . ."

My next pitch split the plate in half. I think. Maestri did not. "Ball-a."

That was it. I walked halfway to the plate and really let him have it. "Why you   , no-good   ! How the   can you   miss that   pitch that   badly, you   ?"

Maestri listened, then slowly walked about ten feet in front of home plate and started unbuttoning the jacket he was wearing over his chest protector. "Lasorda," he said, the only word I ever heard him speak in English. Of course, it was all he needed to say. He pulled open his jacket to show me the biggest pistol I have ever seen, tucked into his belt.

That convinced me. "Maestri," I shouted, "you are the greatest umpire I have ever seen in my life." As I turned around, slowly, the first thing I saw was Gorman standing behind second base, his arms crossed, laughing.

And once, when I was managing in the Dominican, the owner of the San Pedro team came hunting me with his gun because I'd called a game on account of rain after he'd given his team their meal money for the trip. The fact that I was very short of healthy pitchers had little to do with my decision, despite his claims, and there had been a persistent drizzle all day. Everything worked out fine, Manny Mota spoke to him, and he couldn't find me. It was that day that I learned the value of a good lock and a large hiding place.

I've always tried to learn at least a little of the local language wherever I've been. When I went to Japan, for example, I picked up a few words of Japanese. In Norristown, I learned Italian. And in South America, I gradually became fluent in Spanish. I spent considerable time sitting on the beach with jai-alai players my first year in Cuba, and they spoke about as much English as I did Spanish. So when a dog trotted by I'd point and say "dog," and they would respond "perro."

When I knew enough to make myself understood, I started exploring the city. I learned that Cuba was a great country, with a rich, historic past, and many wonderful restaurants. Because I learned their language, enjoyed their hospitality, and played good baseball, I became very popular with the Cuban fans. I even became the subject of a famous joke.

Because my name is Lasorda I was known as "El Sorda," which translates to mean "the deaf woman." Garrio and Piñero were the Abbott and Costello of Cuba. They did a movie short, which was shown in all the theaters, telling the story of a farmer who lived high in the mountains with his wife and their deaf and dumb daughter. The daughter is never permitted to leave the village, but somehow she becomes interested in baseball. She begs her father to allow her to go to Havana to see a game, but he forbids it, telling her that the sophisticated people in the city would take advantage of her. But she persists, and eventually the farmer's wife persuades him to let thier daughter go to one game.

On the day of the game the farmer sits by his radio. His wife continues to assure him that their daughter will be all right. But the very first words the farmer hears the announcer say are, "And El Sorda is heating up in the bullpen."

El Sorda? The deaf woman? With bulls? At a baseball game? The farmer screams at his wife, "And you said she would be all right!"

I played five seasons in Cuba, pitching for two pennant-winning teams, and in 1959 I pitched Cuba into the Caribbean World Series. I pitched a one-hitter, losing my no-hitter and the $1000 bonus that went with it in the eighth inning when an outfielder lost a routine fly ball in the lights. I pitched a fourteen-inning shutout to beat Bob Shaw, 1–0. I pitched a number of low-hit games, but all people who know about Cuban baseball remember is the night I picked Chiquitin Cabrera over my head and swung him around.

I was pitching for Almandaries and Cabrera was Marianao's first baseman. He was about 6'1", 220 pounds, and very strong. He was a very good hitter, with some power and great speed, similar to Pete Rose. The last time I had pitched against Marianao he had gotten three really cheap hits off me, three bleeders, and I told reporters that he was very lucky, and he would not get one hit off me the next time I faced him.

He responded by warning me that the next time he faced me he would "cut my legs off."

I assumed that meant he was going to bunt down the first-base line, which he often did, then barrel into me as I fielded the ball. When I heard that, I warned him that the next time he batted against me I was going to put him in the hospital and the first word he was going to hear from the surgeon was "scalpel" because that was what the surgeon would need to cut the baseball out of his ear.

The next time I pitched against Marianao was a Saturday night, a Ladies' Night, and it was a complete sellout, with 30,000 people in the ball park. Jo had not planned to go to the game, but changed her mind when I told her, "I'm gonna get him tonight. I guarantee you I'm going to get him."

Usually, when a baseball player leaves for the ball park his wife wishes him good luck. Jo never did that. Instead, whenever I was pitching, she'd kiss me good-bye and ask, "Please, Tommy, don't start any fights."

I retired the first two batters in the first inning, and Cabrera came to bat. Our catcher, Mike Guerra, signaled for a curveball. I shook him off. I couldn't hit Cabrera with a curveball. Guerra finally put down one finger —fastball.

I threw it right at Cabrera's neck. He went down, his bat flying one way, his hat the other. He didn't say a word, just picked up his bat and his hat, and got set to hit again.

I threw another fastball at him. He stepped back and swung as hard as he could, sailing his bat at my legs. I hopped over it as it came spinning past me. This was now getting serious. When the batboy came out to retrieve it, I said, "Tell him it's now, now's the time to be ready."

I drilled him in the ribs with the next pitch. I mean, it was my fastball, it wasn't going to really hurt him. This is when I made my mistake. I assumed he was going to go to first base and I took my eyes off him. Suddenly, the ball park erupted. I looked up just in time to see all 220 pounds of Cabrera, carrying a 38-ounce bat, coming directly toward all 175 pounds of me.

It's amazing how quickly your mind functions in a life-threatening situation. Run, I thought, because this guy has a bat and he's going to try to kill you. But before I took that first step, I thought, No way, either he kills me or I kill him, but I've never seen an Italian from Norristown run and I'm not going to be the first one. If I had a baseball I would have fired that at him, and maybe even hit him, but I didn't. So I did the next best thing. Just as he started swinging the bat at my head, I threw my glove in his face and ducked.

I heard the bat *swizz*ing over my head. I acted on instinct. I grabbed his shirt with one hand and the inside of his leg with the other. Then, and how I did this I will never know, I lifted him up and held him over my head. I swung him around and then threw him down. The crowd was roaring, this had to be one of the best baseball games they'd ever seen.

As soon as he hit the ground I leaped on top of him and squeezed his head in an armlock. I grabbed the wrist of the arm cradling his head with my free hand and held tight. He started turning purple. Other players were trying to rip us apart, but I wouldn't let him go. I screamed, "The only way he's getting loose is for his head to go through my elbow." I believe in another ten seconds he would have been in serious physical trouble, like dead. I was enraged, the man had tried to kill me with a baseball bat. Finally, they managed to break my hands apart and got him free. There had to be fifteen players standing between us. I wanted more of him. This is not how I got to be known as Baseball's Goodwill Ambassador, however.

There was a law in Cuba prohibiting assault with a deadly weapon, even on a baseball field, so the police took both of us, still in uniform, to night court. After the judge heard the facts he asked me if I wanted to press charges against Cabrera. "No," I said, "I don't want to press charges, all I want to do is pitch against him again."

The following morning, Cabrera, me, and the directors of our ball clubs met with the league president. Cabrera was suspended for the remainder of the season. I was not penalized for my part in the fight. When we left the league office I figured that was the end of it. Actually, it was just starting to get exciting.

I was lying on the beach that afternoon when four men wearing sunglasses approached me. The sunglasses didn't bother me, most people wear sunglasses on the beach, it was the ties and jackets, shoes and hats they were wearing that made me suspect they were not trying to get a tan. They stopped in my sunlight and commanded, "Get your clothes on, you come with us."

They looked like they had just walked out of a B-movie. They were the kind of people who, when they said "Get your clothes on, you come with us," you didn't argue, you got your clothes on and went with them. "Where we going?" I asked.

"Please, get your clothes on," they repeated.

I put on my pants and shirt and told Jo not to worry, that I would worry for both of us. Naturally, they were driving a black stretch limousine. I got in the backseat and we started going wherever we were going. Wherever it was, it wasn't close, because we drove for a long time. Or maybe it just seemed like a long time. No one in the car said a word to me and, since I hadn't learned to speak Spanish yet, I couldn't talk to them. I couldn't guess where we were going, but I was pretty nervous. I knew that a lot of Cubans were not happy that a Cuban star had been suspended for the season while the American who started it was not punished.

Finally, we stopped in front of a large iron gate, guarded by soldiers with machine guns. Suspension for the rest of the season began to look very good to me. We drove up a long winding driveway to a farmhouse. There was a large veranda in front and perhaps forty men there, sipping drinks. My driver ordered me out of the car. I followed them up the steps of the veranda and suddenly saw standing in front of me President Fulgenico Batista, the Cuban dictator. I had met presidents of the Elks Lodge in Norristown, presidents of teams and presidents of leagues, but this was the first dictator I had ever met.

He offered me his hand, which I shook, gently. "Mr. Lasorda," he began, "I heard the game last night and I have invited you to come here because I want to apologize to you." The Cuban dictator apologizing to me because I tried to hit a batter? This had to be a pitcher's fantasy. "I'm very disappointed with Cabrera for coming after you with a bat," he continued. "That's not right. If he wanted to fight you, that's part of baseball, but no, not with a bat."

I agreed. I was feeling pretty good right about then, now that I was breathing again, so I said, "Mr. President, he will never come after me again, because he knows he came very close to being buried last night . . ."

Batista invited me to stay and have lunch with him. Since I had no plans for the afternoon, I accepted. So we spent the afternoon sitting on the veranda, watching armed guards patrolling the lawn, talking baseball.

I received numerous threatening letters the next few weeks. I couldn't read too much Spanish, but I recognized certain words, like "gun," "shoot," and "kill," and I assumed these were not requests for autographs. Jo wanted me to tell my new friends in the government about the threats, but I refused. I didn't need anybody's help. I believed I was tough enough to take on anybody who challenged me. I would've fought King Kong back then, believe me. They might get me, I thought, but if they try, I'm gonna take at least ten of them with me.

Cuba was really not very much like Panama at all.

Cabrera was reinstated with two weeks to go in the season. Coincidentally, I was scheduled to pitch against Marianao the day he returned to action. There was not an available ticket to that game anywhere on this island. "Please, Tommy," Jo said as she kissed me good-bye that day, "don't start any fights."

The first time Cabrera came to bat I aimed at his neck and fired at him. He went down. As he was lying on the ground, I took four steps toward the plate and shouted, "You don't like it, come on out again." He didn't make a move. I struck him out four times that night, four times.

I was in Cuba in 1952 when Batista overthrew Prio, and I was there in 1959 when Fidel Castro overthrew Batista. None of the American ballplayers had paid too much attention to Castro because he seemed hopelessly outnumbered and Batista seemed to be so strong. But on New Year's Eve, 1959, Jo and I, the Art Fowlers and the Bob Allisons were leaving a party about 3 A.M. when three large planes flew low overhead. I wondered who would be flying that late at night. It turned out to have been Batista and his cabinet fleeing the country.

A general strike was called and baseball was suspended. That was fine with me; everywhere I looked people were walking around with guns. We were living at the Club Nautico, a fenced-in luxury compound, with seven or eight other American ballplayers and their families. At first we weren't worried, we figured that after a cooling-off period we would resume the season. Then we started hearing rumors that Club Nautico had been owned by one of Batista's ministers and Castro's soldiers were going to burn it down. *That's* when we started worrying.

We quickly organized a defense force to protect the compound. Since I'd spent my army career playing baseball and making sure basketballs were sufficiently inflated, I didn't know too much about being a soldier. The only combat experience I'd had was on the baseball field. Eventually, Cuban soldiers arrived to protect us from the rumors.

After nine days Castro permitted the baseball season to resume. We were scheduled to play the second game of a doubleheader. The ball park was jammed with Castro's *barbudas,* the "bearded men" who had been with him in the mountains. All of them still carried their weapons with them. Castro, we found out, was an outstanding baseball fan. Before becoming a revolutionary, he had been a pitcher. He'd even had a tryout with the Washington Senators, which he failed. So instead of becoming a Senator, he became a dictator.

In the fourth inning of the first game the *barbudas* suddenly cleared out of the ball park. Minutes later we heard machine guns firing, a sound that made it particularly hard to concentrate on the game. The firing went on for about twenty minutes, then the soldiers returned to the stadium. We found out later that about thirty of Batista's men had been hiding in a nearby building, and the *barbudas* had killed them all.

I was pitching the second game. There were *barbudas* in the clubhouse, in the dugout and on the field. Most of them looked to be fifteen or sixteen years old, all of them armed with carbines or submachine guns. When I went out to warm up, a *barbuda* was behind home plate wearing a catcher's glove. I didn't know where Dick Brown, our regular catcher, was, but I knew where I was: in a ball park in Havana, Cuba, nine days after the Castro revolution. I warmed up with that catcher.

During the game, I remember, Art Fowler and I were sitting next to each other in the dugout. A young soldier was directly in front of us. He carried his machine gun on his shoulder, and every time he cheered, he jumped up and down. Every time he went up, Art and I went down, because we didn't know if he had his machine gun safety on or off. Finally, Art said in his deep Southern accent, "Tommy, you speak Spanish. Would you please tell that young man to move out of the way?"

I looked at him and laughed. Who was he kidding? Then I told him, "I've got some news for you, buddy. I am not telling him to move. In fact, I'm going to move." I spent the rest of the game sitting against the wall outside the dugout.

I had been friends with some members of the revolution, particularly General Camilo Cienfueges. So soon after Castro marched into Havana,

Pittsburgh Pirate scout Howie Haak and I were invited to Castro's suite in the Caribbean Hilton Hotel to meet him. This was before anyone knew he was a Communist, although we had heard stories that he was long before he took over. It would not have made any difference if we had known. In Latin America you never argue with a dictator.

Castro was wearing his jungle fatigues when we entered, and smoking a cigar. We stayed about an hour talking baseball. I kept thinking, Isn't it incredible, here I am, the son of an Italian immigrant, a runny-nosed little left-handed pitcher with a decent curveball, a player good enough only to be the third-string pitcher on his high school baseball team, sitting here talking to the leader of the entire revolution. Baseball had helped me find a wife, it enabled me to afford to have a family and build a home, it provided many thrills, and now it had allowed me to meet two Cuban dictators. However, during our conversation I did not tell Castro that I'd met Batista.

Almandaries won the Cuban League pennant that year and the right to represent Cuba in the Caribbean World Series. The World Series was played in Caracas, Venezuela. In the finals we played Caracas, Venezuela. That is not a good combination. The Venezuelan fans were the toughest I had ever seen in baseball. They were the Adolfo Luque of fans. Even when Venezuela was winning they might start throwing beer bottles and rum bottles and soda bottles at the players. And when they were winning they were happy.

Our game with Venezuela was the last game of the series, no matter who won, so the American players were going to go directly to the airport after the game. Our bags were packed and in the clubhouse and we had been paid, in cash, in American dollars. I had my money pinned in one pocket of my uniform and Rocky Nelson's money pinned in my other pocket. It turned out to be a bad game for us; we were winning by two runs with two men out in the bottom of the ninth inning. When you're beating Caracas, in Caracas, with 50,000 Venezuelans in the ball park, it is a bad game. The great Camilo Pasqual was pitching for us, with Orlando Pena and Mike Cuellar warming up in the bullpen, and Norm Cash was the Caracas batter. I was sitting safely in the dugout next to Art Fowler. Hey, we figured, as long as there were no soldiers around, what could happen?

What happened is the most outstanding riot in the history of Latin American baseball. While Pena was warming up, a fan threw a rum bottle at him. Pena picked it up and fired it into the stands. With that, fans started piling out of the stands into the bullpen. Then, like a flood rising over the top of a dam, they started coming over the outfield walls. Suddenly, the soldiers who hadn't been in the dugout raced onto the field and started swinging their rifles at people. Fans were just being batted around. The other spectators, seeing what was happening, jumped onto the field to try to help the people already on the field.

Meanwhile, Norm Cash was standing at home plate. He screamed at Pasqual to throw the ball. Pasqual lobbed it in, Cash intentionally dribbled the ball a few feet in front of the plate. Dick Brown grabbed it and threw out Cash, ending the game and the series. We were champions. Now all we had to do was survive.

The dam burst when the final out was made. Our players were desperately fighting their way off the field, soldiers were swinging rifles, fans were fighting other fans, it was the first riot I'd ever seen. I started going out onto the field. Fowler grabbed me and held on. "Where you going?" he screamed.

"Out to help our players," I yelled back.

"You crazy?" He had his own money in one pocket and Bob Allison's in his other pocket. "With this money in our pockets?"

We headed for the clubhouse. This was the most incredible thing I'd ever seen. I'd been in Cuba during two revolutions and never seen anything like this. We showered as quickly as we could, got dressed, and ran for the limousine waiting outside.

Once all the American players were safely inside the car the only thing standing between us and the airport were maybe 15,000 fans. And all of them were trying to get at that limousine. They were rocking the car, trying to turn it over, they were trying to break the windows. I was thinking, Lord, get us out of here, *please* . . . I felt helpless. The only place I could think of that would have been worse than being inside that limousine was outside that limousine. Finally, I rolled down my window and started hitting people. The driver started moving forward. Allison and Fowler in the back were leaning out of their windows pushing people away. Somehow we made it out of that crowd.

It had been a rough season, with the revolution and the riot, but the most difficult time of my life was waiting for me in Norristown. In late 1958 my father had been operated on for cancer. The doctors took out one lung, but he remained in pretty bad shape. One afternoon in January I was eating lunch at the El Ranco Restaurant in the Dominican when Jo called from Norristown, telling me I'd better get home quick. I didn't even go back to my room. I borrowed whatever money everybody had and went directly to the airport.

I got to Sacred Heart Hospital at one o'clock in the morning. My mother and my four brothers were gathered around my father's bed and a priest was giving him Last Rites. He was in an oxygen tent and having difficulty breathing. The doctor told us he would live a few hours more, at most. I was relieved to have made it back in time to say thank you to him.

I went to his bedside, crying, and said, "Pop, I don't know if you can hear me, but we're all here, and we love you very much." I kept screaming, "Don't die, Pop, please don't die." And then he opened his eyes, reached up and just pulled that oxygen tent off him. The doctors couldn't understand where he had gotten the strength to do that. I spent most of the next few days with him as he got stronger. When he was out of danger I returned to the Caribbean to finish the season.

But he was really too sick to survive. By the time I got home after the riot he was just hanging on. But he was tough, and he was fighting. He was in the hospital for a year, and every day, twenty-four hours a day, either me or one of my brothers was with him. And we took care of him. We didn't let anyone else touch him. March 19 was my brother Joey's birthday and, although it wasn't his turn, he wanted to spend it sitting in that hospital room with my father. And so he was with him when he died.

We held the funeral in our house, as my mother wanted it. My father had always taught his sons to respect and love other people. "It doesn't cost you anything to smile," he would say, "so smile and say hello and say thank you." So many people came by to show their respect and love for my father that my brother Eddie had to go into the basement and reinforce the floors with jacks. People stood in line outside for hours in the bitter cold just to spend a few minutes with us. We remembered to smile and say hello to all of them.

Between revolutions in Cuba, I played three seasons in Puerto Rico. As much as I liked the Cuban people, it didn't take me long to fall in love with the Puerto Ricans. We were playing a day-night doubleheader against Ponce on a Sunday. I pitched the afternoon game, winning 4–1. I went home between games with Henry Tattler, an outstanding umpire from the States, and Jo served a big spaghetti dinner. I knew I wasn't going to play in the night game, so I ate well.

Before the second game the owner of a large jewelry store asked me if I could pitch the game and win it. "You kidding?" I asked, thinking he was kidding. "Sure I can. Why?"

He was not kidding. He apparently had placed a sizable bet on the game. "If you pitch it and win," he offered, "I'll pay you $500."

Hey, I'd gotten into the boxing ring for $10 after eating spaghetti, I could certainly pitch a game for $500. Our manager had intended to start a local pitcher, so when I asked him if I could go, he agreed. I pitched well, and going into the tenth inning we were tied, 1–1. I retired the first two hitters, then Erv Dusak, who had played for the St. Louis Cardinals, doubled. That brought a local player—I'll never forget his name, Foco Valentin—to the plate. I threw him an outstanding curveball and he chipped a looping popup just over first base to win the ball game. I'd pitched nineteen innings and given up three runs, and all I had to show for it was a win, a loss, and a tired arm.

I took it very well. I wrecked the clubhouse. Five hundred dollars was half a month's salary. I was busy heaving things around when someone told me the fans wanted to see me outside. When I went to see what they wanted, a spokesman said that they thought pitching both games of a doubleheader was such a tremendous feat that they had passed the hat for me. He handed me $562 in cash. That was a $62 bonus for losing. The people of Puerto Rico proved to me that they were outstanding baseball fans that day.

It was on the beautiful island of Puerto Rico that I had one of my very, very few fights with a teammate. This hurt me a great deal because I feel very strongly about teammates protecting each other. Of course, it hurt this teammate even more. We were playing San Juan, and on a routine groundball to our shortstop, Roy Hartsfield, baserunner Bob Cerv tried to break up a double play by splattering Hartsfield against the outfield fence. After the fight, I told my teammates I was going to throw at every San Juan batter that came to the plate. And I was dropping them pretty regularly when Gene Freese came to bat. Gene's brother George, a former football player at the University of Pittsburgh, was our left fielder. I didn't care, I decked Gene Freese twice. After the second time he shouted to me, "Do it again and I'm coming out."

After fighting Chiquitin Cabrera I wasn't going to worry about Gene Freese. "I don't see no chains holding you back," I yelled. "You better come now, 'cause this next one has your name on it."

I got him with the next pitch and we had a battle. George Freese came running in from the outfield to break it up. But in the dugout, at the end of the inning, George started screaming at me, "What are you trying to hit my brother for?"

"Hey," I told him, "where were you when Cerv creamed Hartsfield?"

"That's got nothing to do with it. Don't you throw at my brother," George warned me, "cause he's got a chance to play in the big leagues."

"What do I care about that?" I said. "He starts with me, he's got a better chance of playing in San Juan Hospital. And if you want to fight your brother's battles, let's go right now." He grabbed me and we went at it right in front of our dugout. This wasn't a reason I've been called Baseball's Goodwill Ambassador either.

One year in Puerto Rico I played for Santurce, a club that was owned by an outstanding gentleman named Pedrin Zorilla. We became very close and I learned many important lessons from him. One concerned how to treat players. I had always thought that the only fair thing for a manager to do was treat every one of his ballplayers equally, because showing favoritism would only lead to dissension. One day Pete Zorilla came by our apartment to see if we had everything we needed, and Jo mentioned that we'd forgotten to bring a radio. Pete immediately sent one of his aides out to buy us a radio.

When the wife of another player on our team heard about this, she asked Zorilla for a radio. "Buy your own radio," he told her, "because when I see one of our starting pitchers in trouble, I see Tommy going down to the bullpen to help out and I don't see your husband. When one of our players wants extra batting practice, I see Tommy throwing to him, I don't see your husband. When one of our infielders wants someone to hit him groundballs, I see Tommy hitting groundballs, I don't see your husband. So when I want to do something extra for someone, I see Tommy, I don't see your husband."

You can't treat all your players alike, Pete explained to me. If you have two players on your team and one is hustling while the other is goofing off, and you treat them equally, you'll end up with a whole team of goof-offs. I started paying attention to the way other managers worked, and inevitably I saw that Pete was right. That changed my entire way of thinking and, when I became a manager, I adopted his philosophy.

Because of the reputation I established as a player, and a fighter, I eventually had an opportunity to manage the Escogido team in the Dominican Republic. I loved the Dominican, and those people loved their baseball. They have seven daily newspapers and every one of them headlines the baseball scores every day. During the games barefoot youngsters go through the stands selling *pastelita*, fried dough filled with meat; *catinia*, an Indian potato filled with meat; peeled oranges; apples; even pints and half-pints of rum in bottles. In some countries these would be considered weapons, but not in the Dominican. Pretty girls in mini-skirts stand on top of the dugouts leading the cheering. It's just a wonderful place to play baseball and I felt very privileged to be selected to manage there. I wanted to show my appreciation for the opportunity by setting a standard of behavior for my team, by showing the same respect for the umpires that I expected them to show for me. This is why I lasted a full month as a manager before being arrested.

We were playing in Santiago. Doyle Alexander was pitching for us and we were leading 3–1 in the ninth inning. Santiago's Tom Silverio hit a long drive over Von Joshua's head in right field. The ball hit the base of the wall, and by the time Joshua threw it in, Silverio was safe at second. A routine double. But suddenly the second base umpire, a Dominican named Elias Frias, signaled it was a home run. I knew the ball had bounced off the wall, but Frias was giving Silverio a home run. Joshua came charging in to argue, Rico Carty and Jay Alou came charging in, our shortstop Tito Fuentes started arguing, Doyle Alexander was on top of him. Frias couldn't have had more people around him if he was giving away money. I ran out and pushed all my ballplayers away, then asked the reasonable question, "How could you call that a home run when the ball didn't leave the ball park?"

He said that the ball had gone over the fence.

"Okay," I said, "if the ball went out of the ball park, where did Joshua get the ball he threw in?" I knew I had him on that one.

"He took it out of his pocket," Frias replied.

That's when I started raising my voice. I finally realized I wasn't going to be able to get Frias to change his call without getting help from another umpire. So I convinced him to at least ask home plate umpire George Blanford. Blanford was an American, and I was confident he knew what had happened. Frias asked him, "Did you see the ball go out of the ball park?"

Here it comes, I thought. "Sorry," the home plate umpire said, "I don't know. I didn't see it."

There it goes. I turned on this guy and let him have it. "Why you   , gutless   -   .   ,   ,   ,   ,   ! You needle-nosed no-good   ,   . I always knew you were a lousy umpire, but I never realized you were a gutless coward. You're afraid of the fans, that's why you won't make the right call."

"You're done, Lasorda," he yelled in my face, "you're outta the game."

"I know I'm outta the game," I screamed in his face, "but I want you to know what I think of you." With that, I took off the spiked shoe on my right foot and fired it into the stands. I took the shoe off my left foot and fired it into the stands. My hat went next. I ripped off my shirt and threw that into the air. The fans were roaring. Because I had pitched batting practice that day I wasn't wearing a T-shirt, so, naked to the waist, shoeless and hatless, I marched into our clubhouse. But the home run call stood.

Alexander retired Santiago to win the game 3–2. After the game, I was singing loudly in the shower. I am fortunate enough to have an outstanding singing voice. I was singing "Quando Caluente El Sol," an outstanding song, when a platoon of soldiers carrying rifles came into our locker room. "Where's Lasorda?" their captain demanded.

I'm proud to say my team was loyal to the old skipper to the very end. "He's in the shower room," about a dozen of them shouted.

The captain leaned into the shower room. "Lasorda," he ordered, "get your clothes on. Please come with us."

I knew I'd heard that line before. I did exactly as I was told, figuring this had to be some sort of elaborate practical joke pulled by Jay Alou or Rico Carty.

The soldiers marched me out of the clubhouse. The first thing I saw when I got outside was that an area had been roped off and was being guarded by additional soldiers. I didn't see anybody laughing. I began to get a little nervous.

They put me in the back of an army truck and drove me to jail. One of the directors of the Escogido club met me there and immediately got into an argument with the commandant of the jail. I was sitting between them, like the net in a Ping-Pong game. They were shouting at each other much too fast for me to understand what they were saying, but I began to realize this was no joke. I was being arrested.

Finally, the commandant threw his hands into the air. "Silencio!" he shouted, then made a motion like a key being turned in a lock. I knew what that meant in any language. They were going to lock me up. I couldn't figure out for what. For arguing with an umpire? I could understand a suspension or a fine. But a prison sentence?

They put me in a large cell and slammed the door. It was the first time in my life I'd ever been in a cell and I hated it immediately. It was horrible, awful. The only thing in the cell was a long bench along the back wall. I sat down on it.

Suddenly, I heard a woman screaming, and an old lady with no teeth crawled out from under the bench. She was screaming and hollering and moaning. A guard finally came in and I figured he was going to help her. Instead, he slugged her, knocking her out. This whole thing was like some terrible nightmare. An hour before I'd been sitting in a dugout, now I was locked in a cold, cement-floor jail cell that smelled of fear and sweat.

I knew I was in trouble, I just didn't know what kind of trouble. I couldn't figure out what I had done and no one would tell me anything. I didn't want to sit down anymore, so I stood in a corner of the cell.

A little while later I heard a bus pull up outside and I figured it was the team bus come to pick me up to take me back to the capital city of

Santo Domingo. Then I heard Rico Carty's deep voice talking to the commandant. Rico Carty is a national hero in the Dominican and if anyone could get me out, I knew he could. I was getting ready to leave when I heard the bus pulling away from the jail. I knew one thing, that bus was leaving and I wasn't on it.

I spent the night trying to keep calm by repeating the Latin Mass. I still couldn't find out what crime I had committed. In the morning, they kept telling me, in the morning.

In the morning, I was brought into the commandant's office. "What's this all about?" I demanded.

The general had been at the game, the commandant explained, and had placed a large bet on Santiago. When we went ahead, he was upset; when I went out to argue, he was angry; and when I took off my shirt, he had ordered me arrested for indecent exposure.

Indecent exposure! I was very upset about this charge, which I felt was very unfair. But by the time I got back to Escogido I realized I had nothing to gain by blasting the umpire, the police, or the general. So I told reporters I had actually enjoyed the situation. Enjoyed being arrested and kept in jail overnight? Naturally, no one believed me. "It's true," I insisted, "I really enjoyed it. Look, in all the years I've been going into Santiago I never knew anybody. Now I know some policemen, some soldiers, and all the guards in the jail, and they're all great people."

The story was on the front page of all seven newspapers. Felipe Alou, who had his own television program, criticized me for taking my shirt off in public. I asked to appear on his show to respond to that criticism. "You said I was wrong to take off my shirt," I said to him in Spanish. "Tell me why I was wrong."

Because, he replied, I had insulted the Dominican people with my behavior.

"Yeah?" I said. "Then let me ask you, do you have boxing matches in this country?" He said they did. "And do they box with their shirts on or off?" Off, he admitted. "And let me ask you, do you have beaches in this country?" Beautiful beaches, he said. "And when a man is walking on the beach, does he have his shirt on or off?" Off, he admitted. "Okay," I concluded, "if people can go in the boxing ring with their shirts off and they're not insulting anybody, and they can walk on the beach without insulting anybody, who am I insulting when I take my shirt off?"

I received a very favorable reaction from the Dominican people. But from that game on, every time I went on the field to talk to an umpire, the fans would scream at me, "Take it off, take it off!"

Finally, on the last day of the season, I came out to argue a close call.

I started screaming at the umpire. I took the shoe off my right foot and threw it toward third base. I took the shoe off my left foot and threw it toward first base. I whipped my hat across the field. And then I undid the top button of my shirt . . .

The fans were on their feet.

And then the second button . . .

The fans were roaring, "Take it off, take it off!"

Finally, I ripped off my shirt—revealing the second shirt I was wearing beneath it! The players loved it and the fans loved it. But I never found out how the general felt about it.

Managing in the Caribbean is unlike managing in either the American minor or major leagues. The job of the minor league manager is to develop players for the major league team. Winning is important, because you want players to have a winning attitude, and it is difficult for a losing manager to progress, but the primary job is teaching and refining skills. In the major leagues winning is all that matters. No major league manager has ever been voted Teacher of the Year. Managing in the Winter Leagues is a combination of both; you have to win, but you want to develop players too.

Caribbean baseball may only be the Winter League to American players, but is it *the* league for the fans. If you don't hustle, you get out. If you don't win, you get out. Fortunately, we won. In 1970, for example, we made the eleven-game championship playoff, losing the first five before winning our only game. In 1973 our Licey team won the Caribbean World Series. But I also had the opportunity to teach. I worked with our young players every morning, every afternoon and, sometimes, we'd even take batting practice in my hotel room after the night games.

My ball clubs were a mixture of veteran Spanish players like Manny Mota and the Alous, and young players I'd had with me when I managed in A ball at Ogden, Utah, or in Triple A at Spokane, Washington, or Albuquerque, New Mexico. And after some of the games, Tom "Wimpy" Paciorek and Bill Buckner and Steve Garvey and Bobby Valentine and Joe Ferguson and Bruce Bochte would gather in my living room, and we'd take everything off the walls, put the lamps in the closets, and I'd pitch batting practice with a tennis ball. While one player was hitting, everybody else would be in other rooms, peeking through the doorways. They could really hit that tennis ball with baseball bats and there'd be balls richocheting off the walls until two, three o'clock in the morning. I was firing the ball too, not lobbing it. We all had fun, but I also believe it helped players sharpen their reflexes.

One of the most important benefits of managing in Latin America was

that it gave me the opportunity to work with and really get to know so
many of the fine young players and their families who would eventually
be with me on the Dodgers. The basis of my philosophy as a manager is
that I can be very close personally with my players and their families and
still have them produce for me on the baseball diamond. Many managers
believe they have to maintain a distance from their players in order to
command respect and be able to discipline them when necessary. But I
remember when I was growing up there were advertisements for a milk
company that said "A contented cow gives more milk." I believe a contented ballplayer produces more too, so I have always tried to get to know
my players and do everything I can to make them happy.

One player I even nicknamed Happy, in fact—the outstanding pitcher
Burt Hooton. Happy Hooton is a perfect example of what I'm talking
about. The first time I saw him pitch was in 1971 against my Spokane
club. He was the finest-looking young pitcher I'd ever seen come directly
out of college, beating us and striking out 16 batters. Three years later,
when I saw him pitching in the big leagues for the Chicago Cubs, I
couldn't believe he was the same player. He was overweight, he looked
unsure of himself, and he looked unhappy. Al Campanis and I both knew
he had great ability, but for some reason it had not been fully developed.
I thought it was a shame that such a talented young man was struggling,
and I believed I could rebuild his confidence and motivate him, so Al and
I invited him to play for our Licey team in the winter of 1974. "I don't
want to play for you," he said.

"Okay, fine," I told him, "get lost." About a week later he called back
to say he'd changed his mind. He arrived in the Dominican before I did,
but I got there in time to catch him just finishing his dessert. "What is
that thing in front of you?" I roared.

"Baked Alaska," he said.

"Well, I don't care what it is." I was really screaming at him. "I don't
wanna see a dessert in front of you again." Then I made Burt and his wife,
Ginger, walk back to the hotel, about two miles, as penance for eating
dessert. I worked him that winter as hard as I've ever worked anybody.
He lost 25 pounds. Together with my pitching coach, Red Adams, I
started rebuilding his confidence.

He became Happy Hooton on New Year's Eve. Normally, he looks
about as happy as a farmer during a drought, but when I caught him
playing solitare during a New Year's celebration, he earned his nickname,
and he's been Happy ever since.

Because he had dropped so much weight so quickly, he had lost some
zip off his fastball. When he was hit hard during his first two starts for

the Cubs in 1975, he became available and we traded for him. I knew that once he got his strength back he'd regain his fastball. He was 18–7 for us that season, a good reason for him to be happy. But if he had not come down to play for me at Licey, I doubt we would have traded for him and it is possible he would have been out of baseball. Instead, he became an outstanding major league player and an important contributor to the success of the Los Angeles Dodgers. I not only gained a great pitcher, my family and his family became very close.

I was fortunate to have worked for Pedrin Zorilla in Puerto Rico and for a truly wonderful man named Monchin Pechardo in the Dominican. Both of these men proved to me that you could be friendly with your ball-players without losing their respect. Monchin was the president of the Licey club, and we became extremely close, eating almost every meal together. Usually I would tell my players where Monchin and I were going for dinner, and when they showed up I would try to talk him into paying for their dinners. I had worked out a set of signals with my players to let them know if he intended to pick up the check. A tug on my right ear meant he was going to treat them. If I rubbed my chin that meant I didn't know yet, and if I wiped my forehead that meant no deal.

One night after a losing ball game, Monchin and I went to a nice Italian restaurant. Soon after we got there Charlie Hough, Paciorek, Valentine, Buckner, and Garvey showed up and sat down a few tables away, watching closely for my signal. "Look, Monchin," I said, "I know we lost, but those guys really played hard, why don't you pick up their check?"

"No," he answered, "not tonight. We lost and I'm just not going to do it."

I wiped my right hand across my brow and they ordered pizza. But just as their waiter was about to put in the order, Monchin said, "Okay, you're right, they played hard. I'll pay for their dinner." I quickly canceled the first signal and tugged hard on my right ear. They called their waiter back and ordered big. I can honestly say that that group of players missed many a sign on the ball field, but never missed a sign in a restaurant.

Unlike some managers, I get a great amount of pleasure spending time with my players off the field as well as at the ball park. I eat meals with them, I play golf or other sports with them, shop with them, appear at banquets with them, and Jo and I have even gone on vacation with them. I know the names of my players' wives and children and parents. I've helped Charlie Hough's wife, Sharon, pick our spaghetti dinner off the kitchen floor in the Dominican, for example, and I even ate some of it —although I would not eat the grilled cheese sandwiches she cooked without first taking the plastic wrapping off the cheese. I've been to my players' weddings and parties and at the hospital when their children were born. I taught Bill Russell's daughter Amy Lynn her first word ("Dodgers"), although I refused to change her diapers. I am a major league manager, I don't change diapers. But a few days after Bobby Valentine's son, Robert John, was born, I received a gift-wrapped package in the mail. "Dear Uncle Tom," the card read, "I wanted you to have the very first thing I ever did by myself. Love, Robert." Inside was his first dirty diaper. A lot of these relationships were fostered or strengthened in Latin America, because few of my players spoke Spanish or knew their way around these countries, so they often had to depend on me to help them find a decent meal or a doctor or, in Charlie Hough's case, a dentist.

One time he had this terrible toothache and I found this outstanding dentist for him. Charlie went to see the man, who sat him down in this old chair, stuck all sorts of strange things in his mouth, and finally put hot wax on his teeth. At the end of this examination, Charlie asked, "What do you think?"

This man replied sincerely, "You know, I think you should go see a real dentist."

Mike Strahler got very sick and we had to put him in a local hospital. After a game one night I decided to see how he was doing. Since it was long after visiting hours had ended, I had to put on a doctor's white coat and sneak around the hospital. The place was very dark, but somehow I found his room. I turned on his light and asked him how he was feeling. He grabbed me and hugged me and started crying, "Please, Tommy," he bawled, "please get me outta here, you gotta get me outta here. I'm going crazy, I can't stand it in here anymore."

I could see he was unhappy. "Okay," I promised, "first thing in the morning."

"No," he said, "now, we have to get out of here right now."

"Hey," I said, "let's go." So we snuck out of the hospital together. I'm sure they still don't know what happened to their patient.

We had a lot of problems with automobiles. Once we were scheduled to play a night game in San Pedro, about a forty-minute drive from our hotel. Valentine, Hough, Paciorek, Garvey, Von Joshua, and I decided to drive there in the team station wagon. We made one mistake, we let Valentine drive. He started taking a route I was not familiar with and I asked him if he knew where he was going. "I know a shortcut," he said.

"Bobby," I told him, "don't take no shortcut, go the way we always go."

"No," he said flatly, "I'm taking this shortcut and you'll thank me for it."

So we started weaving through these narrow cobblestone streets, driving through parts of the city I had never seen before. An hour later we found ourselves in a traffic jam exactly one block from our hotel. I was really angry, screaming at him, telling him exactly what I thought of his shortcut. Finally, he turned to me and yelled, "How do you expect me to drive with all this noise?" Then he got out of the car and started walking away.

I got out of the car and started warning him that he'd better come back. I had to wonder exactly what I was doing there, standing on a street in the middle of Santo Domingo, the Dominican Republic, in December, wearing a baseball uniform, trying to convince the man who had gotten us lost to get back in the car and drive.

We eventually got out of the city and Bobby drove us at high speed to San Pedro. The speedometer read a hundred miles per hour, but he kept telling us it registered in kilometers. Von Joshua was turning pale in the backseat and Hough kept saying, "I didn't know these Chrysler speedometers were in kilometers."

We got there at game time. San Pedro's pitcher, J. R. Richard, who was very fast and very wild, was out on the mound taking his final warmups. Joshua took one look at Richard and got sick. Valentine was our leadoff hitter—he was a great young player and later that season won the Most Valuable Player Award in the Caribbean World Series—and he literally ran up to home plate.

Just as Richard got set to throw his first pitch, all the lights in San Pedro went out. We sat on the bench for an hour and a half waiting for them to come on again, and the entire time Valentine walked up and down the dugout complaining, "I told you we didn't have to rush."

I was driving with Paciorek one afternoon when he went through two stop signs and was finally halted by a traffic policeman. The policeman was really giving him a good going over until I got out of the car and said, "Officer, I don't know what you're hollering about. He only missed two of your signs, he hasn't seen one of my signs all season." Fortunately, this policeman was a Licey fan, and settled for Wimpy's autograph.

Being fluent in Spanish enabled me to make a hero out of Billy Russell. When I was coaching the Caracas, Venezuela, team in 1971, Billy was our shortstop. One off day I convinced him to take a long walk with me to a café where many of the local sportswriters hung out. While we were eating our lunch, one of the writers said to me in Spanish, "Tomorrow Milt Wilcox will be pitching against you. He's won four games in a row and pitched a one-hit shutout in his last start. How do you think you will do?"

Before I could answer, Russell, who did not understand Spanish, said to me, "Hey, Tom, whenever you're ready to start back, I'm ready to go."

The reporter, who did not understand English, asked me what Russell had said. And I told him. "Bill Russell, the outstanding shortstop of Caracas, said to tell you that Milt Wilcox will not last five innings against us tomorrow and that he will personally knock him out of the game."

All the reporters wrote this down, and Russell was quoted in the newspapers the following morning.

In the first inning Russell came to bat with runners on second and third and singled them in. And with two men on base in the fifth inning, he hit a long home run to knock Wilcox out of the game.

Afterwards, reporters crowded around his locker to ask him how he was able to make such a tremendous prediction. And they did not believe him when he told them he didn't know what prediction they were talking about.

In the many years I spent in Cuba, Puerto Rico, Venezuela, and the Dominican, I never placed a bet in the casinos, although I would often go and watch my players. I was once asked by a casino owner why I didn't gamble. I said, "Suppose I put a chip on fourteen red and as the ball is spinning around, I look up into the sky and ask, 'Please, Lord, let that wheel come up fourteen red.' And then it comes up fourteen red and I win $8. And the next night we're playing a game and it's the bottom of the ninth and we need a run and Garvey's the hitter and I look up into the sky and say, 'Please, Lord, help us get that run.' And then he says, 'Sorry, Lasorda, you should have thought about this before you asked me to help you with that roulette wheel.'

"You only have so much luck in your body," I concluded, "and I want to use all mine up on the baseball field."

FIVE

•

I Join the Scouts

In 1960, after my run-in with Clay Bryant, Al Campanis asked me to work for him scouting a six-state area from Pennsylvania to West Virginia. "A scout!" I said. "Are you kidding me? I'm going back to the big leagues as a pitcher."

"Tommy," he told me, "I've seen you pitch. Take the job."

I didn't want to be a scout. Scouts, I believed, were old men who wore funny hats and smoked cigars, who lived out of the trunks of their cars and spent most of their time writing in little books. What I really wanted to do when I retired was manage. I felt I had learned a great deal about handling players during my playing, coaching, and traveling secretary career, and thought I could do a good job. And when Al offered me a scouting job, that's what I told him.

"No," he said, "you don't want to manage, you want to be a scout."

"I really want to manage," I insisted.

"Believe me, Tommy, you don't," Al continued, "and I'll tell you why. Say they put you on as a manager and you're the last one that they hire. When they decide to cut a club, you're the first person that they'll fire."

"I don't agree with that at all," I argued. "They're gonna keep the good men and let the bad men go."

"You really got it wrong," he insisted. "I know, they always release the last guy to be hired."

Even if that were true, I told him, scouting just didn't appeal to me.

"I know what you think," he said, "and I'm going to change things.

I'm bringing in all new people, young people like yourself, people who know baseball and love baseball. Tommy, you just can't imagine what a thrill it is to find a young player with raw talent, it's like finding a diamond. A diamond comes out of the ground and it's black and it's rough, and then someone takes it and they shape it and polish it and the result is something very beautiful . . ."

I'd never really thought of it that way.

". . . and it is just a tremendous feeling to see this young player who you discovered, shaped and polished into a major league ballplayer. I'm telling you, scouting is the most important job in baseball. It's difficult and only very special people can be good at it, but scouting is the backbone of the entire organization. A winning team depends on its scouts to discover the talent . . ."

He was beginning to make a lot of sense to me.

". . . of course, I don't have to tell you that scouts are the unsung heroes of baseball. Without scouts, there are no baseball players. Scouts never get the credit they deserve, they don't get the public recognition, but they get a tremendous amount of satisfaction from the knowledge that they are the foundation of baseball . . ."

By the time we finished speaking, I was telling Al Campanis how grateful I was to him for giving me the opportunity to become a scout for the Dodgers. He had me convinced that scouting was the one thing I had always wanted to do. I took the job.

I immediately went to New York to meet John Carey, the eastern supervisor of scouting. John Carey and Al Campanis made me a scout. They spent hours teaching me what to look for in a young player, how to evaluate his talent, how to go into his home and talk to his parents, how to fill out forms, how to follow up tips, how to fill out expense accounts.

Scouting, I began to understand as I listened to John Carey, would enable me to take advantage of my greatest talent. My success would depend on my ability to talk.

One of the most important things John Carey taught me was to never overlook the obvious. "Walter Alston would have made an excellent scout, for example," he told me. "Once we went to look at a young prospect, we watched him pitch an entire game and we liked him, but there was something about his pitching delivery that bothered us. We just couldn't figure out what it was. Finally, after the game, Walter said, 'I just realized what's wrong with that boy. He's got his spikes on the wrong feet.' From that moment on I felt Walter had been born to be a scout."

When I signed as a scout the Dodgers continued paying me the same

$6000 a year I had been earning as a Triple-A pitcher, and I supplemented that income by working three seasons as a basketball referee in the semi-professional Eastern League. I was an excellent official because I loved the job so much I was always hustling, so I was usually in position. As in baseball, I didn't take any abuse from anyone. One night, I remember, Bill Spivey, a 7' center out of Kentucky playing for Wilkes-Barre, started throwing elbows, and I threatened to throw him out of the game. This was in the first five minutes. He went right down court and did it again, so I ejected him. Wilkes-Barre was paying Spivey something like $200 a game, so the owner got very upset when I threw out Spivey. I had to throw the owner off the bench.

After the game an older woman came up to me and, without saying a word, kicked me in the leg. She was the owner's wife. And while I was rubbing my leg, Bill Spivey came toward me. Oh Lord, I thought, he's coming after me.

"What'd you throw me out of the game for?" he demanded.

"I threw you out to prevent a fight," I said. "Cause the way you were throwing elbows there was eventually going to be one, and then you were gonna be gone anyway."

He looked down at me and said, "You know, you're a little wise guy."

"So what?" I told him. I figured if I was going to get killed, I might as well get killed by a seven-footer. That's not too embarrassing. It's when the five-footers get you that it's a shame. I just turned around and walked away. Rapidly.

I was a good enough official to work two NBA exhibition games and, if Al Campanis had not asked me to move to California in 1963, I would have ended up in the NBA. I doubt there are many umpires who will believe that I have worked as an official, however.

The very first player I signed as a scout was a young third baseman from Allentown, Pennsylvania, named Dick Krotz. This was before the draft system was created, and a team could sign any player it wanted to sign. I'd seen Krotz play in high school numerous times and thought he had major league potential, so I told John Carey I wanted to offer him a contract. John asked me how much I thought he was worth. "To me," I said, "he's worth between $8,000 and $10,000, but everybody's interested in him so I think the price is going to be much higher."

"All right," John said, "if you think highly of him, go and offer him $25,000 and sign him right now. We need some power-hitting infielders in the system."

"I can't sign him now, John," I explained, "there's too much interest in him."

"You can," John insisted. "Go do it."

A state law prohibited American Legion players from signing professional contracts before September 1, so on the night of August 31, Jo and I drove to Allentown. We had intended to take the Krotz family to the Phillies game, but Hurricane Donna hit and the game was canceled. It was going to take more than a hurricane to keep me from signing him, however.

We drove through an outstanding rainstorm, we had to detour around washed out roads, but I didn't care, I was determined to sign him that night. "Jo," I said, "this is my first attempt at signing a ballplayer and I can't fail. So if you see me crying tonight, don't pay any attention to it. I want this guy bad."

We took the Krotz family out for a steak dinner. I believe his parents were named Eleanor and Edmund, and they were fine people, but very quiet. In the middle of dinner, just as Mr. Krotz was about to put a piece of meat in his mouth, I said, "Ed, I'm going to sign Richard tonight."

He put down his fork. "I'm sorry, Tommy," he said, "but Richard can't sign tonight. We're seeing Jocko Collins of the Phillies tomorrow, then Cy Morgan of Baltimore, next Thursday we're meeting with Pat Cogin of the Indians, then Friday Harry Dorish of the Red Sox is flying us into Boston for a workout. So there's just no chance we'll sign a contract tonight, I'm really sorry."

I knew I had to sign him. For the next few hours I kept talking and talking and talking and it was no deal, no deal, no deal. I just wouldn't give up. About 3 o'clock in the morning it occurred to me that maybe I was talking to the wrong person. So I stood up and I said, "Eleanor, take a good look at me. Do I look like the type of man who would lie or cheat or deceive anybody?"

"No, Tommy," she said, "you don't."

"That's right," I agreed, "I wouldn't. And I want you to picture this in your mind. Me and your son Richard down in Vero Beach, Florida, Dodgertown, U.S.A., and me leading him by the arm, taking care of him, watching over him as if he were my own son, making sure nothing happens to him.

"Do you want to know something, Eleanor, I'm like the priest, the preacher, or the rabbi who stands in front of his congregation and begs them to save their souls, when in reality the congregation should be begging *him* to save their souls. I'm begging you to allow your son to join the finest organization in baseball, while you should be begging me to let your son play for that organization . . ." And with that, I started to cry. I cried like you have never seen a grown man cry.

And that woman looked at her son and said, "Richard, I want you to sign with Tom right now."

This is what is known in the scouting business as a complete shutout. The other teams didn't even get inside to talk to him. I was so nervous as I was filling out that first contract that my hand was shaking and I kept making mistakes. I was running out of blank contract forms. Finally, I grabbed hold of my hand with my other hand and held it as I filled in the proper information. I was exhausted when I walked out of that house, but I had accomplished what I had set out to do; I was a scout.

Invariably, a scout ends up spending much of his time with other scouts. I had been wrong about scouts being old men wearing silly hats and smoking cigars; the people I met in the business were tremendous individuals who loved the game of baseball as much as I did. I liked them and respected them. But I wanted to beat them. A good scout will do almost anything to sign a player he wants. I loved signing players, and I also loved winning the competition against other scouts. When I was looking at Krotz, for example, I had two other scouts to my home for an early dinner one evening. They asked me where I was going that night and I told them I was staying home. One of them said he had to visit his wife's relatives, the other one had to go to his son's school. Two hours later we all met at Krotz's American Legion game.

As I gained more experience, I became very good at convincing those players I wanted to sign to sign with the Dodgers. As a player I believed no one could beat me on the baseball field; as a scout I believed no one could beat me in the living room. I feared no scout in the living room. Part of the reason for this was my belief that I was representing a superior product. I loved the Dodgers, so it was not difficult for me to sincerely sell the Dodger organization to young men and their families.

Every scout eventually developed a line he used to convince players to sign with his team, and every other scout had a line to counter that line. There was a player named Billy Haas, a 6'4" first baseman, who I really wanted to offer a contract. Al Campanis had seen reports from other scouts that said Haas was not a major league prospect, but I disagreed. I really wanted him. Finally, Al told me I could pay as much as $10,000 for him, although he believed Haas would never make it. Ed Liberatore, now one of my closest friends and a special assignment scout for the Dodgers, was then with the Cincinnati organization, and he wanted Haas as much as I did. He had arranged to fly Haas and his father down to the Reds spring training camp in Tampa, Florida, so Billy could work out in front of Reds manager Freddie Hutchinson and his staff. If Hutch like Billy, Ed Liberatore told the Haases, the Reds would give him a $25,000 bonus.

I had $10,000 in my pocket. "You think that's a great offer, Mr. Haas?" I asked Billy's father.

"Sure I do," he said, "If Mr. Hutchinson thinks Billy's worth it, the Reds'll give him $25,000."

"I want you to imagine this, Mr. Haas," I told him, "just picture this. You report to Tampa with your son, and how much money he gets depends on how good he looks in a tryout. The Reds are going to put him in a game, and he's going to have to hit against Jim Maloney and Jim O'Toole and Joey Jay and all those other young fastball pitchers the Reds have. And the Reds are going to tell those pitchers, Don't let this guy even foul off the ball. These are outstanding major league pitchers, Mr. Haas, do you really think they're going to let your son hit the ball? I'll tell you, they are not. Then, after the tryout, the Reds are going to be very gracious and offer you maybe $2,000. And what are you going to do when they make that offer?"

I had him angry at the entire Reds organization. "Two thousand dollars?" he said. "We'll walk right out of that camp."

"Beautiful," I continued, "and then, when the other clubs hear that the Reds let Billy walk out of camp after a tryout, they're going to figure he's not worth anything at all. But I'll tell you what I'm going to do, and I'm going to do it right now. I'm going to offer you $8,000 and I don't have to have Walter Alston look at him. What do you think about that?"

Which is how I signed Billy Haas. Two years later baseball expanded, and the New York Mets drafted Haas as a premium player. Campanis had been right, Billy never played in the major leagues. But I was right too —the Mets paid enough money for him to practically pay all the expenses of the Dodgers' scouting staff for a year.

When the draft system went into effect scouting changed. A scout was no longer able to sign anyone he pleased, and the job became more evaluation and recommendation than bargaining. Only after an organization drafted the rights to a player did contract negotiations begin.

That didn't mean the competition between scouts ended; it just required a different approach. For example, after I moved out to California, there was a high school pitcher named Alan Foster that everybody wanted. It did not take an expert to see that he was a genuine blue-chip major league prospect. Since clubs drafted in inverse order of their position in the standings at the conclusion of the previous season, it appeared certain that a second-division club like the Mets would pick him long before the Dodgers had a selection.

At a game that took place a few weeks before the draft. I made a point of sitting down next to the outstanding New York Yankee scout Deacon Jones. Deacon was a super individual who did everything possible to help me when I moved to California, but that had nothing to do with getting a player. So as I was sitting in the bleachers, I said loudly enough for all the other scouts to hear me, "Hey, Deacon, who's that guy down there with Foster? I just heard him talking, and he said something like 'I think when you get home, I'm gonna have to give you that shot.'"

I could see from the look on Deacon's face that this was an important piece of information. "He said he's gonna have to get a shot?" he asked.

"Yeah," I said. "Who is that guy?"

"That's his father."

I appeared to be confused. "That's Foster's father? What the hell is he giving him a shot for?"

"His father's a doctor," Deacon replied.

"Holy Toledo!" I said. "If he's a doctor and he's gonna give him a shot . . ." Just in case there could be any doubts, I filled in the blanks. "That must mean there's something wrong with Foster's arm."

Now, I am not claiming that anyone believed that I had overheard Alan Foster's father saying he was going to give his son a shot. All I am doing is reporting the fact that the Los Angeles Dodgers drafted Alan Foster in the *second* round, and that he eventually played ten years in the major leagues.

Since Alan Foster had been born in Pasadena and had grown up in Southern California, all we had to do was point out to him how wonderful it would be for him to stay home and pitch in front of his family and friends. We were able to sign him quickly. Of course, when I was working in the East for the West Coast Dodgers, I could not make the same strong argument about playing near home to a prospect's family. So when a mother or father told me they wanted their son to sign with Philadelphia or New York or Baltimore or Pittsburgh so they could see him play, I had to tell them the other truth, that very often it is important for a young man trying to make his way to play far away from home. "Believe me," I would say, "I know what it's like playing too close to home. Every game he'll have all his friends and relatives calling him for tickets or wanting to meet him for dinner or something. If he plays away from home he won't have all the distractions and he'll be able to concentrate on baseball."

Naturally, I didn't get every player I went after. With the quality of the men in scouting that would have been impossible. One time, for example, I found this big kid in Scranton, Pennsylvania. I thought I was the only scout in the area onto this kid, so I took him out to a deserted

ball field to pitch to him. I often threw batting practice to young players
I was interested in. This individual was hitting me pretty good and I was
starting to get excited. Then I noticed a solitary figure in a big straw hat
sitting there watching me throw. It looked suspiciously like Chick Genovese, a San Francisco Giants scout.

It was Chick Genovese of the San Francisco Giants, and *he* shut *me*
out. He signed that player before I had an opportunity to make an offer.
I got just as angry as I had when I was pitching and I gave up a home
run. I hated to lose in the living room just as much as I had on the mound.
As it turned out, this player never made it. He turned out to be a fine
hitter in the daylight, but for some reason he could not see the ball at
night. The Giants eventually released him.

No matter how often you see a young player, no matter how carefully
you check, there is often a problem that could not be anticipated. The
Baltimore Orioles, for example, once signed a pitcher with a tremendous
fastball, only to discover that he couldn't pitch in front of large crowds,
a serious flaw that would have hurt him in most major league cities.

One of the most important aspects of a scout's job is visibility. The
more people who know about a scout, the more prospects he is going to
hear about. One way a scout makes himself visible is by speaking to civic
groups. I first began speaking to organizations when I was with the
Montreal Royals. I didn't particularly enjoy it at that time, but I did it
because I felt that part of my job as a ballplayer was to help the organization succeed financially, and that meant encouraging fans to come to the
ball park.

When I started scouting, I accepted every invitation to speak I received. I spoke to schools, clubs, Scouting groups, business groups, any
organization willing to listen to me. They used to say that if two telephone
poles stood too close together I'd give them a speech. Gradually, as I
became comfortable, I began to enjoy it. I found it was much more
enjoyable to have people laugh at me as a speaker than it had been as a
player. I had a few standard stories I'd tell, mixing them up depending
on the group. My favorite story, a story that always got a laugh, was about
one of the most outstanding individuals I've ever known, Roy Campanella.

"Everybody knows that Roy Campanella's father is Italian and his
mother is black," I would begin. "In spring training at Vero Beach in 1951
we were playing an exhibition game against the Chicago White Sox. We
had an overflow crowd, because black people from all over the South had
come to see Campy and Jackie Robinson and Don Newcombe play major
league baseball. Billy Pierce was pitching for the White Sox and, as

Campy came to bat in the first inning, some leather-lunged black fan sitting behind third base hollered, 'Come on, Campy, show these white folks how you can hit. Make us proud of you.'

"With that Pierce broke off a curveball and the umpire called, 'Strike one!'

"The black fan screamed, 'What do we care about one strike, it only takes one to hit it. Come on, Roy baby, we're proud of you, show these white folks how you can hit.'

"Pierce threw another curveball and again Campy didn't swing and the umpire called, 'Strike two!' " I had everyone listening to me involved in the story, and I would draw it out as long as I could.

" 'What do we care about two strikes, Campy,' this fan screamed. 'We know you're gonna show these white folks what a great player you are, bear down and make us proud of you.'

"With Campy looking for another curveball, Pierce threw a fastball right down the middle of the plate. Campanella didn't swing and the umpire called, 'Strike three!'

"And as Campy was walking back to the bench, this leather-lunged fan stood up and yollered, 'Yeah! You'd better go back to the bench, you dumb dago!' "

Tips about prospects came from everywhere. Usually, when I got to a new town, the first person I'd go to see was the local barber, because he cut the hair of every young boy in town and knew who the best players were. The best tip I ever got came from a parking lot attendant at Dodger Stadium. I wanted to park in Lot 5, the area closest to the Dodger offices, and he wanted me to park where I was supposed to, Lot 13. When I told him I was a scout and I was late for a meeting, he said he'd let me park in 5 if I agreed to go see a player at South Pasadena High. I wanted that parking spot bad, so I decided to humor the kid. Not only did I end up with a fine parking spot in Lot 5, I signed the player from South Pasadena High, Tommy Hutton, and he has since spent a dozen years in the big leagues.

The best leads come from high school baseball coaches. By the time a player reaches college, every area scout will know about him, but it is still possible to uncover a gem in high school. When I was in school most of the baseball coaches were science teachers trying to pick up a few extra bucks. The only thing they knew about baseball was that it is the sport in which you *don't* wear shoulder pads. But when I started scouting I found that that had changed; baseball coaches knew the game. It's a very difficult job. In most high school athletic programs, baseball is under-financed. Football and basketball are the glamour sports, so those coaches have reasonable budgets and assistant coaches, and are paid a fair stipend; baseball coaches are lucky if they have enough baseballs. But I found that these people are just as dedicated to their players as any football or basketball coach. Much like scouts, they work long hours for little money and almost no recognition, but they do it because they love the sport. I gained a tremendous amount of admiration for high school baseball coaches while scouting for the Dodgers.

The dream of every scout is that he is driving down a country road, all alone, bored, maybe even lost, when he passes a baseball field cut out of the woods. And a game is in progress on that field. And suddenly a young lad comes to bat and hits the ball 450 feet, and the scout signs him and this boy becomes another Mickey Mantle or Willie Mays. That was the dream that kept me going, that kept me on the road, checking out every lead, believing, hoping, that in the next town, over the next hill, I'd find that player.

There is, of course, the famous story of the scout who was driving down that lonely road and found a field cut out of the woods and saw a game in progress and, to his astonishment, a horse came to bat, and that horse hit the first pitch 450 feet. The scout leaped out of his car and went up to the owner of that horse and said, "That was incredible. Let's see him run to first base."

And the owner said, "Run? If he could run he'd be in the Kentucky Derby."

Once, the scout's dream almost came true for me. I was in Greenbelt, Maryland, watching a ball game on a hot Sunday afternoon. I was sitting in the bleachers with my book open, grading players, when a man came over to me and asked, "You a scout?"

That's one way the dream begins. I said I was.

"Well," he told me, "I got a player over yonder who's a fine shortstop and nobody knows about him."

Those are the magic words. "Nobody knows about him?"

"Nobody. Who you scouting for?"

"The Dodgers."

"Oh, I'd love to see him go with the Dodgers."

My ears were beginning to quiver. "How far away is he?"

" 'Bout eight miles."

Eight miles from destiny, I thought. "Let's go." I followed him in my car. He drove down the highway a piece, then cut off the road into the woods. We followed a dirt road for a while, then stopped in front of a dilapidated farmhouse. Bob Feller grew up in a house just like this one, I remembered. The man knocked on the door and a black man answered.

His son wasn't home, he said, he was playing baseball at a picnic. Playing baseball at a picnic! This wasn't just destiny, this was legendary.

I kept thinking the whole thing was going to fall apart, that it couldn't possibly be happening, but each step took me a little closer. We drove another mile deeper into the woods, to a field that had been laid out in a clearing. Stan Musial played on a field like this, I thought. We got there just as two black teams were finishing their game.

The man I'd met in Greenbelt introduced me to the shortstop's coach. As soon as the players heard him say Tom Lasorda, Los Angeles Dodgers' scout, they gathered around. The coach agreed to hit some groundballs to the shortstop.

That young man turned out to be a fine fielder. He had a good throwing arm, he moved well, and he appeared to have good instincts. I was so excited I could barely breathe. "I'd like to see him hit," I said to the coach. "You got somebody who could catch me?" I took off my shirt and, still wearing my Sunday pants and Italian leather loafers, got my glove out of my trunk and started throwing to him. And he hit the ball pretty well.

It was very hot and I was really sweating, but I kept pitching and he kept hitting. He hit my fastball and he hit my curve. I liked him more and more. After about fifteen minutes, one of the other players said, "Boy, I'd sure like to hit off that drop."

"Go ahead," I told him, "step in there." Here were two teams of prospects nobody had scouted. I was willing to pitch to every player on that field, which I did. By the time I was finished my pants were drenched with sweat and the front of my Italian leather loafer was ripped up, but I felt it was worth it. The shortstop was the best player on the field and I wanted to sign him. As soon as I got to a phone I called John Carey and I told him about Greenbelt, Maryland, and the dirt road and the farmhouse and the field in the clearing, and that I wanted to sign the player.

"Nah," he said.

"I want to sign him, John," I repeated.

"Has he got a chance to be another Willie Mays?" John asked.

"Not exactly," I admitted.

"Has he got a chance to be another Roberto Clemente?"

"No, not really."

"Then don't sign him." End of dream. End of legend. End of Italian leather loafers. This player eventually signed with the Washington Senators and played a few years of minor league ball before being released. The worst part of the whole thing was that when I put in for a new pair of loafers on my expense account, Al Campanis rejected it.

Al Campanis and I fought a continuing battle over my expense account. In truth, every scout and every scouting supervisor fight a continuing battle over expense accounts. Once, for example, I had to buy a piece of vital equipment, a new car radio. Without a working radio in his car a scout might just as well drive directly to the funny farm. So I bought the radio and put in for $65. Al rejected it. I submitted it again; Al rejected it again. That was the last time it appeared on my expense account. That bothered Al, because he had never seen me give up after only two attempts. "I'm curious," he said when he called me, "you put in for the radio twice and I rejected it twice. Then you never put in for it again. How come?"

I laughed. "That's what you think," I said. "It was there, you just didn't find it."

Scouts trade expense account stories the way battle veterans trade war stories. I used to tell them that I would put in for 10¢ PTA, 10¢ PTA, 10¢ PTA on every sheet. And each month it added up to a few dollars. Finally, Al couldn't stand it anymore. "I've been in this business a long time," he said, "I thought I knew all the tricks. What the heck is 10¢ PTA?"

"Ten cents, pay toilet—airport," I told him. Obviously, I'd made up this story. I had to stop telling it, however, after I moved out to California and was told by an Angels scout that the Dodgers had someone of their staff who was so cheap he actually put in for "ten cents, PTA."

When I accepted Al's offer to become a scout, I vowed to become the best scout the Dodgers had. Al convinced me that scouting was just as important as any job in the organization, but it was still difficult for me to give up my aspirations to become a manager.

I got my first opportunity to manage a ball club when I was Clay Bryant's player-coach in Montreal in 1958. We were playing Columbus, Ohio, on a Saturday night and the famed minor league umpire Augie Guglielmo ejected Bryant and I had to take over. Jim Koranda, our first baseman, had hit home runs in his first two at bats. In the seventh inning he hit what should have been his third home run, but Gugie called it foul. I thought it was a fair ball and we argued. I mean, we screamed and yelled and hollered. I was furious, but his call stood, foul ball.

As I walked into church the next morning, I saw the back of this bald head. I knew it was Gugie. I very quietly slid into the pew behind him, and whispered in a heavenly sing-song, "Gu-gie, the ball was fa-air."

He looked straight up as if he had seen the light. "Oh, no," he said, "not in church."

After that I had had a few other opportunities to manage and enjoyed it tremendously. But it was like going to a grand buffet and being asked to leave after tasting the salad. I couldn't really savor it. And after the Dodgers decided I was a scout, I accepted the fact that it just wasn't going to happen for me.

Which is when I next got the opportunity to manage. Each spring, the Dodgers would bring me down to Vero Beach as an instructor. One March, Roy Hartsfield, manager of my old Greenville, South Carolina, team in the A level Sally League, had a family emergency and had to leave camp. I was asked to manage Greenville until he returned.

I had always believed that motivation, desire, self-confidence, and hard work, the willingness to pay the price to taste the fruits of victory, were the foundations of success, and this gave me an opportunity to test this theory. Our first game was against the Triple-A Spokane Indians managed by my friend Preston Gomez. A few minutes before I had to go over to Holman Stadium, the Vero Beach ball park, I told camp supervisor John Carey, "You'd better come over to the game, 'cause we're going to beat the Spokane club."

By that time John knew me very well, and knew how much confidence I had in myself, but he still laughed. "There is no way you can beat that ball club," he said flatly.

"Well, you'd better come over there and listen to me talk to my team before the game then." My club was sitting on the bench and I walked up and down in front of them. I was shaking my head in disbelief, they could see I was upset. "Look at that guy over there," I said, pointing to Preston Gomez. "Look at that manager over there. This is really ridiculous, this is really sickening what I just overheard in the lobby. I heard that man, Preston Gomez, go up to Fresco Thompson and say to him, 'Hey, Fresco, how could you have scheduled us against Greenville? That's a disgrace. We're an outstanding Triple-A ball club. We should be playing against the Dodgers, not some mediocre team like Greenville.' "

I paused and sighed and shook my head again. "Can you imagine that," I continued, "can you imagine that man telling his ball club they shouldn't be playing against Humpty-Dumpties like you? Unbelievable. I'll tell you what, if I was a player and I was sitting on this bench and I heard that, I'll guarantee you one thing, I'd really be upset about it. I would not let that man get away with it.

"You guys can do whatever you want, but I know what I would do. If I was pitching, I'd be knocking them on their backsides. If I was a baserunner and I was going into second to break up a double play, I'd knock that shortstop into left field. They'd sure know they were in a ball game if I were playing."

I paused again, then continued, "You know, I was just thinking . . . the worst thing you could possibly do to that man is to beat his team today. I mean, it's probably impossible, those guys are just one step from the major leagues, but . . . do you have any idea what a feather in your caps it would be if you went out there and beat them?"

With that, the big first baseman, Kopatz, jumped up and screamed, "Let's kill 'em!" Everybody else got up and started yelling and hollering and, naturally, I was right in the middle of them yelling and hollering. I knew I had those boys primed.

My Greenville Spinners attacked those Spokane Indians. They played with all the pride and determination a manager tries to instill in his ball club. In the fourth or fifth inning Preston Gomez came up to me and asked, "What is the matter with your guys?"

"What do you mean?"

"They are crazy. They call me dirty names, they curse at me, everything."

"Gee, Preston," I said, "I don't know what to tell you. I just took over Roy's club, I don't even know these guys." We beat Spokane. We won eleven straight games in camp. We beat Double-A teams, the other A teams, everybody we played. We shook that camp up.

I had a new message for them every day. "Psychologically," I told them one morning, "if you show the other team you are in dire need of victory, it could very well affect their play. So I got an idea. This afternoon, during lunch, maybe fifteen minutes before you're supposed to report to the field, I'll shout as loud as I can, 'Greenville ball club!' And no matter what you guys are doing, drop everything and scream, 'Yes, sir!' and then we'll run out of the lobby together."

I ate lunch that day with Fresco Thompson and Al Campanis. As we finished, I said, "You know, these guys playing for Greenville are amazing, they don't even want to stop for lunch."

"Come on, Tommy," Fresco said in a dubious tone.

"It's absolutely true, so help me. Here, watch." Then I stood up and hollered, "Greenville ball club!"

Answering screams came from all over the cafeteria. "Yes, sir!"

"Let's go get 'em!" I yelled, and we charged out of the room, screaming. Everywhere we went in that camp we'd trot in columns of twos, hollering at other teams. We certainly weren't the best team in camp, but we were the team that wanted to win most, the team that enjoyed winning most. By the time spring training ended those players believed in themselves, and I believed I had proven my theory. I knew if I ever had the opportunity to manage again, my teams would play with determination, desire and dedication. I just didn't think I was going to get that chance to manage again.

One cold November night in 1962 Jo and I were sitting around the fire in Norristown when Al called from California. "I need a scout out here," he said, "and I think it would be good for you. I'd like you to move to Los Angeles and work with me."

I didn't know what to say. Although I'd traveled extensively, I'd always come home to Norristown. My family was there, and in Greenville. The home that Jo and I and my brothers had built was there, and we owned it. Laura was ten, Spunky was six; they were in school and they had their friends there. It was a difficult decision.

Jo and I stayed up most of the night discussing it. Both of us realized it was a turning point, we just weren't sure which way to turn. Finally, I asked her, "What do you really want to do?"

I will never forget her answer. "Wherever you go," she said, "if you're happy, we'll all be happy. Whatever you do, if you're miserable, we'll all be miserable. You do what you feel is best for all of us. Wherever you want to go, we'll be right there with you."

I realized I didn't have much choice; if I wanted to progress in baseball, I had to take the job. In California I would be working in the central office and, if I had any ability at all, the proper people would be there to notice it. If I stayed in Pennsylvania, no matter how good a scout I became, I would still be in Pennsylvania, three thousand miles away from the place where all important decisions were made. "Let's try it," I said, "but we won't sell the house. Just in case . . ."

It was rough getting used to California. I'd played there in 1957, but at that time the only directions I had to know were how to get back and forth to the ball park. As a scout, I had to know how to get around most of southern California. I spent approximately half my time being lost on freeways I didn't know existed until I found myself lost on them. It was even more difficult for Jo. We only had one car, so when I was busy being lost, she was stuck in a strange apartment without any close friends nearby.

Professionally, it was the correct decision. Al Campanis began to teach me the game of baseball as I had never seen it before. Al was a disciple of Branch Rickey and taught the Rickey system. We'd be out for dinner with our families and he'd start talking about the importance of running speed: "You can teach a youngster to hit," he would say, "you can teach him to field, but you can't teach him to run . . ."

At two o'clock in the morning, after a ball game, he'd be lecturing on the art of bunting: "Bunting is a fundamental skill that can turn a ball game around . . ." This went on day after day, night after night, when we were alone, when we were with other people, when we were with our families. I used to think, Does he have to do this when we're eating dinner with our families? But I listened, and learned, and learned, and learned.

Besides Al, the other major league scouts in southern California welcomed me and helped me. We were in competition, but we were also all part of professional baseball, and we were all fighting the same battles with our front offices, so a real camaraderie developed. I became very close to people like Ben Wade, Bobby Maddick, Bob Neiman, and Bill Brenzal, who also worked for the Dodgers; Merrill Coombs of the Phillies; the White Sox's Sloppy Thurston; Deacon Jones of the Yankees; the Angels' Rosey Gilhausen; Pittsburgh's Bob Beame, Jerry Gardner, and Howie Haak; the Cubs' Gene Hanley; Boston's Ray Boone and Joe Stephenson, who helped Jo and me settle in Fullerton; and the great Tufie Hashem of the St. Louis Cardinals.

Once, I remember, when Tufie was seriously ill, and depressed, I took him to Adamo's, a tremendous Italian restaurant, to try to cheer him up. After we'd had a few drinks, I started telling him what a wonderful organization the Dodgers were and how proud I was to be working for them. "Look," he said, "I don't want to hear about the Dodgers anymore. I'm tired of hearing how great the Dodgers are, how much you love the Dodgers. Listen, I love the Cardinals as much as you love the Dodgers, but you don't hear me popping off about it all the time."

Now there was a challenge. "You really mean to tell me that you honestly believe you love the Cardinals as much as I love the Dodgers?"

"That's right," he said, "what about it?"

With that, I climbed up onto my chair in the middle of this crowded restaurant and hollered, "I lovve the Dodgers!" Then I looked down at him, and said, "Now I want you to do that about the Cardinals."

He started laughing, shook his head and said, "You really are crazy."

Tufie spent many months in the hospital fighting cancer, and used up most of his savings. The Southern California Scouts drafted a letter asking for contributions to the Tufie Hashem Fund. We sent it to every scout in America. Just scouts—no managers, no players, just the people who were part of that aspect of baseball Tufie loved. The fund eventually grew to $9,000, a tremendous amount of money to come from a generally underpaid group of professional people. It was not only a tribute to Tufie, it was a tribute to every scout in America. We helped take care of the family of one of our own.

Part of my job in California was running Dodger tryout camps. We would invite dozens of players to a park and watch them run, throw, and swing a bat. Any real prospects were given a second tryout, and from that group we selected players for the Dodger Rookies, an amateur team that played a forty-game schedule. The first Dodger tryout session I worked took place in Long Beach. Kenny Meyers, Ben Wade, and I were supervising it. Most of my equipment hadn't arrived from Pennsylvania, so I had to borrow a stopwatch from Al Campanis to time players in the fifty-yard dash.

One of the players at this tryout was a pitcher-outfielder named MacKenzie. I will never forget his name. After watching him pitch and hit we knew he wasn't a prospect and told him so at the end of the session. "Don't let this dampen your spirit," I said. "Just because we don't pick you that doesn't mean you aren't capable of playing professional baseball. Just keep working at it . . ."

He took it well. "Lousy scouts," he said.

Later, as we were packing up, Mackenzie came over to me and said, "Hey, where's the ten bucks I asked you to hold for me before the workout?"

"Look, MacKenzie," I said, "what are you trying to pull? You never gave me any money to hold for you."

MacKenzie then slugged me right on the jaw. I never saw it coming.

I did not go down. And, just as I heard Ben Wade say, "Tommy, don't . . ." I blasted this guy with a left. Then I ripped into him. He was much bigger than I was, but inexperienced. During the fight we fell onto the ground and, fortunately, the impact was softened by Campanis's stopwatch, which was smashed into many pieces.

The fight amazed me. I had gotten into fights as a player and as a coach, I'd seen managers get into fights, but a scout? I'd never heard of anything like that. "Gee, Ben," I said, "is this what the job requires?"

Al Campanis's first question when I told him about the fight was, "Where's my stopwatch?"

"I didn't hurt the kid," I said.

"Where's my stopwatch?"

"He didn't hurt me either."

"Where's my stopwatch?"

"Don't worry," I finally assured him, "I'll let you see it one day." Never did, though, never did.

The most important part of my job in California, as it had been in Pennsylvania, was evaluating and signing prospects, and no young player I ever saw was more of a prospect than Willie Crawford. Even as a high school senior, at Fremont High in Los Angeles, California, it was obvious he was a future major leaguer. This was still before the draft system went into effect, so Willie Crawford was free to sign with any club upon his graduation from high school. Buzzy Bavasi and Al assigned me to convince him to sign with the Dodgers. It was a tremendous challenge. Me, against every other organization in baseball. I wanted to sign him as much as I had wanted to win 20 games in the big leagues.

I spent more time with him than I did with my own family. I'd pick him up after school, I'd visit him at home, I'd eat dinner with his family. I didn't even go to spring traning that year, the first spring I'd missed since 1947, because I wanted to stay close to him. And I got to be very, very close to Willie and his outstanding mother, Clara Crawford. Clara would often invite me for dinner, and on many occasions we shared meals that other scouts had sent as gifts.

The Dodgers' strongest competition for Willie was the Kansas City Athletics. Charlie Finley, the A's owner, wanted Willie as much as we did. Every morning Charlie would call at 7 o'clock, before Willie left for school, just to ask, "And how's my favorite center fielder today?" The A's sent the Crawford family all kinds of wonderful gifts, among them a large autographed photograph of Charlie Finley.

We knew the A's were willing to offer Willie as large a bonus as we were, so his decision would not be based solely on money. This was a young man I was genuinely pleased to see get a large bonus, because Clara had struggled all her life to raise her children and they were very poor. We used to joke that the house was so dilapidated that it would have to be painted before it could be condemned.

Finley did everything he could to convince Willie to sign with the A's. When he found out that his father and Willie's grandfather had once worked in the same steel mill in Bessemer, Alabama, he brought his father to California to talk to Willie's grandfather.

The day before Willie graduated from high school, his grandfather died. Willie graduated on Friday, his grandfather's funeral was on Saturday, and on Sunday each team would meet with Willie and Clara and make their offer. I had dinner with the Crawfords Friday night and made plans to see them on Sunday. I believed the Dodgers had the inside track because the Crawfords were going to give us the twentieth and last visit. That was the spot every scout wanted to be in, because it gave you the opportunity to top everybody else's offer. That was the only time in baseball you wanted to be last.

Finley was nineteenth.

I was supposed to have dinner with Al and Bess Campanis Saturday night, but instead I decided to attend the memorial service for Willie's grandfather. Although I'd only met him once, I believed that this was a way of showing my respect for the family.

As usual, I got lost trying to find the church and got there late. Willie's grandfather, Mr. Keanerd, had been a deacon in the church, so it was packed. By the time I arrived there were no vacant seats, so the ushers led me in the back way. I found myself sitting behind the preacher, in a section with deacons from all over southern California, staring out at the congregation. A moment after I sat down the preacher leaned over and said to me, "I'm sorry, I don't think I know you."

"Reverend," I said, shaking hands, "my name is Tom Lasorda, and I'm a scout for the Los Angeles Dodgers. I came to pay my respects to Deacon Keanerd."

With that, the preacher turned and addressed the congregation. "Ladies and gentlemen, we have with us today a very distinguished man. A man who is very close to the Crawford family." I began looking around, wondering who he was talking about. He continued, "So I think it is only fitting that we should get him up here to say a few words. I would like to introduce to you, Tom . . ." He turned to me. "What did you say your last name was?"

"Lasorda," I said.

"Lasorda," he said.

I got up very slowly, trying to figure out what I could possibly say to eulogize a man I'd met only once. I coughed a lot, trying to gather my thoughts. This was definitely not a place to tell my Campanella story. "Ladies and gentlemen," I began, "we are all here to mourn the passing of Deacon Keanerd . . ." I paused, then began picking up speed. ". . . when actually we should be rejoicing because now the deacon is finally going to face his Lord, his master, and his judge . . ."

A few people in the congregation said "Amen."

". . . in fact, we should be honored because here's a man who is going to face his Lord knowing that the children he raised were wonderful people, that his family loved and cared for him . . ."

More people echoed "Amen, brother."

I was really rolling. ". . . and to see the great number of people who have gathered here today to pay their respects to this man is indicative of the kind of man we all know he was . . ."

The entire church rocked. "Amen, brother!"

I spoke about fifteen minutes, then sat down, sweating but satisfied. It was one thing talking to the Greenville baseball team, it was something else entirely to give a eulogy in church.

I spent most of the following day pacing up and down, waiting to get into the Crawford house to make an offer. Al was with me. Charlie Finley had flown into Los Angeles to present the A's offer himself. When he found out that Al and I were waiting outside to make the final presentation, he told Clara, "I'll make you an offer you will not be able to refuse, but I'll only make that offer if you'll agree to sign it before I walk out of this room." Charlie was trying to shut us out. I've always thought that was an unethical tactic, unless I was doing it.

Clara Crawford explained that she had given her word to Tom Lasorda that she would listen to the Dodger offer and intended to honor her word.

"Wait a minute," Charlie said, "I'm telling you that I'm willing to make an offer that will be impossible to turn down."

Clara insisted she was going to speak to me before signing with anyone.

Charlie couldn't figure it out. "I don't understand," he said. "What do you owe Tom Lasorda?"

"Mr. Finley," she said, "if you had been in church yesterday and heard the speech he gave about my father, you wouldn't be asking that question."

Church? Yesterday? "Are you telling me that Lasorda gave a eulogy at the church?" Charlie asked.

"A nice long one too," Clara replied.

Charlie turned to his scout. "Did you go to the church yesterday?"

The scout shook his head. "No, Charlie, I didn't."

Charlie fired him right there in the living room. Then he tried again, and again, to convince Clara to let him make an irresistible offer. Finally, when he was convinced Willie was not going to sign with anyone before speaking to the Dodgers, Charlie left.

As soon as he was out of the house, we were invited in. But just as we started to make our offer, Charlie was back in the house. "Just hold it now, Charlie," I said, starting to get a bit irritable, "you've had your chance, you're done. It's our turn now, we're in the living room."

He said he just wanted to know where the nearest pay telephone was located.

"It's on the corner," I told him, pointing to the corner. "Now goodbye."

Then we made our offer. "Willie," Al began, "Tommy has told you how much we want you to play for the Los Angeles Dodgers. We're sure you can imagine how exciting it would be for you to play right here, where you grew up, in front of your relatives and friends . . ." As I sat there listening, I realized that this was the World Series of scouting. Here was a potentially great player that every team wanted to sign. The winner might well be getting the ballplayer who would make them a contender, or a champion, for a decade. These battles in the living room helped determine who would be playing the real World Series a few years later. Al Campanis had been absolutely right, it was a job I thoroughly enjoyed.

Willie Crawford accepted the Dodgers' $100,000 offer. As Al started filling out the contracts, he said, "Willie, if that telephone rings before we've finished filling these out, you know that you've agreed to terms." No sooner had he finished speaking than the phone rang.

Charlie Finley was calling from the corner.

The first thing Willie did was buy his mother a new home. Although he never became a superstar, he played fourteen years in the big leagues, twelve of them with the Dodgers. He was a fine player and, even more important, an outstanding young man.

Naturally, I didn't sign every player I went after in California. One that I remember was a seventeen-year-old who played for me on the Dodger Rookie team. I wanted him bad; I believed he was going to play in the big leagues someday. I spent so much time at his house that he began to think I was a boarder. And finally, I had him. I sat down at dinner with him and his mother and we started negotiating. And negotiating. And negotiating. I offered $10,000. His mother said that sounded fine, and I found myself offering $12,000. That sounded fine, too, and then I heard myself offering $15,000. And that sounded fine too. So I went up to $20,000. I couldn't understand how she kept agreeing to the price, and the price kept going up.

Eventually, I had the contract on the table, filled out, and the pen in her hand. The pen was actually in her hand. And she put down the pen. I picked it up. She put it down. "Tommy," she finally explained, "I love the Dodgers and I would love for my son to play for the Los Angeles Dodgers, but I just don't think he's mature enough. I think he should go to college for two years and then we'll sign with you. I give you my word, two years."

Two years later, 1965, the major league draft was instituted and Rick Monday was the number one selection in the first draft. By the Kansas City Athletics. Charlie Finley's Kansas City Athletics. Who signed him to a contract. One for me, one for Charlie Finley.

Two for me. In 1977, my first year as Dodger manager, we obtained Rick Monday in a trade with the Cubs. It had taken me thirteen years, but I had finally gotten my man.

I also strongly recommended the Dodgers draft Tom Seaver, who was pitching for my friend Rod Dedeaux, the outstanding baseball coach at the University of Southern California. We did draft him, but we didn't sign him. Seaver contends the Dodgers didn't offer him a contract as a favor to Dedeaux, forcing him to pitch in college another year. I don't know why the Dodgers didn't sign Seaver, but I certainly don't believe it was because he was playing at USC.

Rod Dedeaux is one of my closest friends. While scouting and coaching, I often worked with his pitching staff, I was USC's unofficial pitching coach, but that never stopped me from recommending or signing a USC player if I believed he could help the Dodgers.

Once, for example, when I was managing Ogden, Utah, in the rookie Pioneer League, Rod threw a party for a group of high school athletes visiting the campus. Casey Stengel was there, Bobby Grich, Tim Foli, some major league players, and some USC players, among them Billy Buckner. At this party I met a high school All-American baseball and football player named Bobby Valentine, who was trying to decide whether to play football at USC or sign a professional baseball contract. Even then Bobby was a shy, retiring young man. When I told him that I had heard what a fine baseball player he was, he said, "I'll tell you something. You see those lights out on the lawn? You turn those lights on, I'll hit off any pitcher here tonight."

Bobby finally decided to sign with the Dodgers and was sent to Ogden to play for me. When he arrived, I had him call Dedeaux to thank him for his interest and his hospitality. After Bobby finished speaking, I got on the phone. Rod was very pleasant. "Okay," he said, "you got Valentine, but I still got Buckner."

And he did, too. For six more days. And when Buckner arrived in Ogden, I made him call Rod too.

I signed a number of USC players. I signed Ray Lamb, who pitched in the big leagues for five years. All he wanted was a chance, but naturally I insisted on giving him money. He was a great bargain at $2,500. And I signed Gary Holman, who played two years of major league baseball. He wanted more than a chance, he wanted money.

Gary was a big first baseman-outfielder from Brea, California. During negotiations, I was the last scout the family spoke to, but they refused to tell me what the top offer was. "Tommy," Mrs. Holman said, "Gary promised Mr. Stephenson that he wouldn't tell anyone what the Red Sox were offering."

"Whoa," I said, "wait a second, I don't understand that. To whose advantage is it for you not to reveal that figure? Not to Gary, not to you. Suppose I want to top it, how can I do that? I mean, I wish everybody I spoke to wouldn't reveal the offer I made, but it's not to their advantage to do that."

"Gary promised," Mrs. Holman repeated, although I could see she was uncomfortable about it, "and I think he should fulfill that promise."

"Absolutely," I agreed. "If Gary promised then he should keep his promise." I looked at Gary and asked, "Did you promise Joe Stephenson you would not tell anyone how much he was offering you?"

"Yeah," he answered.

"Then I won't ask you to break that promise." I looked at Gary's father. "Elmer," I said, "did *you* promise Joe Stephenson you wouldn't reveal that figure?"

"Nope," he said, "I did not." Then he told me what Boston had offered. Gary Holman signed with the Dodgers.

My career as a full-time scout ended in 1965. Once I had believed that no feeling in the world could match the satisfaction that came with pitching my team to a victory. But I had been wrong. It was equally satisfying to watch a young player I had signed to a professional contract progress through the ranks of baseball to the major leagues. They were *my* players, and I enjoyed an overwhelming feeling of pride as I watched them play big league ball. It was a feeling I had never even suspected I could get out of scouting.

Not all of the players I signed made it to the big leagues. A lot of people don't know it, but I was the scout who signed Lou Panella. Unfortunately, I signed the wrong Lou Panella. My Lou Panella was from Roxborough, Pennsylvania, and never made it to the majors. And there was one player I didn't sign, who would have turned out to be the biggest player in baseball history.

That was in spring training, 1970. John Carey and I came back to Dodgertown after dinner one night and began telling everyone about this prospect we'd found. "This guy has more power than anyone I've ever seen," I said. "John and I were on our way to dinner and we saw this game going on, and we stopped. We saw this first baseman hit two of the most tremendous home runs I have ever seen."

Some of the people who knew I occasionally exaggerated were dubious, but nobody, nobody, doubted John Carey. "He's potentially the best player I've ever seen," John said. "We've got him in a motel room right now, he's waiting for his agent to call. We're gonna go get him in the morning, bring him into camp and sign him."

Naturally, everyone got very excited. They wanted to know his name.

"Pee Wee Mullins," I told them. "He's even got the perfect name for a Dodger."

Early the next morning John and I got into my little car to go pick up Pee Wee. We decided to allow my roommate in camp, Dave Hull, an outstanding radio broadcaster, to drive us. As we got ready to go, Wally

Wilson, a reporter for a Santa Monica newspaper, got into the car. "You gotta let me come with you," he said, "I really want this story."

John and I conferred. "All right," we decided, "but you've got to lie down on floor in the back so nobody'll see you when we drive out of camp."

So with Dave Hull driving and Wally Wilson lying on the back floor, we set out to get Pee Wee Mullins. When we reached his motel we gave him a Dodgers' uniform we'd brought for him. It was a little snug, as it only came from our largest player. When we walked out of that motel room Wally was so stunned he didn't even speak.

There was a large crowd waiting for us when we got back to Dodgertown. All the reporters were there, all workouts had stopped and the players were there, even Kay O'Malley, Walter O'Malley's wife, had come over to meet Pee Wee. Of course, I couldn't blame them, I had told everyone that Pee Wee could be the Dodgers' first baseman for the next decade.

So we pulled up outside the press room and opened the car door. John Carey got out. I got out. Dave Hull got out. Wally Wilson got out. And then Pee Wee Mullins, all eight feet of Pee Wee Mullins, the tallest man in the world, wearing a Dodger uniform and carrying a baseball bat, got out of the car.

Mullins, whose real name was Harry Hite, worked for a local meat company. He was so big that the bat he was holding looked like a pencil. John and I had met him the night before, and immediately named him Pee Wee. What else do you call a man who is eight feet tall?

He agreed to go along with our plan as soon as we thought of it. And he was wonderful. When he started getting out of the backseat of our car, then continued getting out of the backseat of our car, and still continued getting out of the backseat of our car, nobody could stop laughing. I glanced at Mrs. O'Malley, and she was laughing so hard tears were running down her cheeks.

Although we didn't sign "Pee Wee Mullins," it was still the finest moment of my scouting career.

SIX

•

I Manage to
Prosper in Utah

I was working in the Dodger Stadium scouting office one afternoon in May 1965 when general manager Buzzy Bavasi asked me to join him, Al Campanis, and Fresco Thompson in his office. I assumed they wanted updated reports on prospects we were looking at. That wasn't what they wanted at all. "Tommy," Buzzy began, "we've been sitting here talking about this for a while, and we'd like you to manage our Pocatello team in the rookie league."

That was totally unexpected, but I was very pleased. Managing was what I had thought I wanted to do before Al Campanis had convinced me that what I really wanted to do was become a scout. And since the Pioneer League, the rookie league, did not begin play until the colleges and high schools finished in June, I could continue to scout as well as manage. Besides, I'd never been to the great city of Pocatello, Idaho. "Buzzy," I told him, "you know I'd be delighted to do anything the Dodgers want me to do."

"Your job," he explained, "will be to develop players for the Dodgers. We think you'll be excellent at that. Winning is secondary, you don't have to win. We just want to make sure our young players get off to a good start."

Telling me I didn't have to win was like telling the Wright Brothers to take a train. I'd spent my entire life striving to win, fighting to win, I didn't know any other way. I understood that my primary job was to introduce young players to professional baseball in the most positive way, but I believed that creating a winning atmosphere was the most positive way. I intended to teach, just as Buzzy wanted me to do, and what I intended to teach was how to win.

The Pioneer League season is sixty games long. The league was created so that players entering baseball after finishing their college or high school seasons would not be thrown into a minor league pennant race without preparation. The rookie league allowed them to compete against players of their own caliber and experience. Clubs were permitted to carry thirty or more people on their roster, and players could be added or cut throughout the season, so that fifty or more different prospects might play for a club in one season.

As a former player, and as a scout, I knew how important the job of manager at Pocatello was. I was the first contact the future Dodgers of America had with the organization. It was my responsibility to instill confidence in them and teach them the fundamentals of the game so they could progress to the major leagues as rapidly as possible. In baseball, the moment a player signs a minor league contract, he becomes a liability. The organization has to give him a bonus, pay his salary and all the expenses associated with instruction, including a minor league coaching staff, travel, meal money, equipment and incidentals, without getting any return. Only when a player reaches the major leagues does he become an asset. My job was to help balance the books.

I had played for a lot of different managers. The little I knew about strategy came from observing these men running their ball clubs. But I did know for certain that the one thing it took to be a winning manager was the ability to squeeze every bit of talent and dedication out of every ballplayer on the team. Throughout my playing career I'd seen that there was only a small difference between the mediocre ballplayer and the very good ballplayer, and that distance could be narrowed through hard work and self-confidence. I believed the mind controlled the mechanisms of the body, and if I could make a player believe in himself, if I could make him really believe he could play in the big leagues, that player would someday play in the big leagues. Hey, I'd seen myself pitch. My career was proof that with determination, someone with limited talent could succeed.

When I accepted the job in the Pioneer League I didn't claim to know more about managing than anyone else, but I did know that I was willing to work harder and longer than anyone in baseball, and I believed that assured success.

"One more thing," Buzzy cautioned me as the meeting in his office broke up, "we don't want you fighting anymore. You've got to promise me that's going to stop."

"Don't worry about it," I said, "those days are over." I was determined not to get into any more fights. I was going to prove to the Dodgers that they had picked the right man for the job. I was going to set a positive example for my players. I really was. Really. "I promise you, Buzzy," I even said, "no more fights."

And then the season started.

We opened in Idaho Falls against the Angels' rookie club. Idaho Fall's manager was a big guy, about 6'4", maybe 220 pounds. We met at home plate and discussed the ground rules, then I trotted down to the third base coaching box to begin my career as a manager. My leadoff hitter got on base. My second hitter got on base. My third hitter got on base. So far I was doing a great job of managing—bases loaded, no outs, and no fights.

Then my fourth hitter checked his swing and bounced a foul groundball down the third-base line. I picked up the ball and looked at it. It was dirty, so I flipped it out of play. As I did, the Angels' manager hollered at me, "Hey, what are you throwing the ball out of play for?"

I thought it was a decent question. "It was dirty," I explained.

"You can't do that," he yelled.

I turned to face him. "What do you mean, I can't do that? They do it every day in baseball. The   ball was dirty so I threw it out of   play."

There was a momentary pause, then the manager shouted, "Hey, Lasorda, just who do you think you are?"

I winced. I had been down this road before. "Yeah," I said, "and who the   do you think you are?"

"You   !" he said.

"   ,   a   ,   and   , and another   come from?" I said.

And that's when he came running out of his dugout. He was huge! He came right at me and gave me absolutely no choice. When he got close enough I threw an outstanding left and dropped him on the spot. All of a sudden, a wave of white uniforms washed out of the Idaho Falls dugout toward me. I started hollering for my guys and a wave of gray uniforms came out of our dugout.

As I watched these two teams rushing into battle, I thought, There goes the job. Two weeks earlier I'd given my word to Buzzy Bavasi that I wouldn't get into any fights, and in the top half of the first inning of the first game I was in the middle of a brawl.

The teams crashed in the middle of the field. There was a big pileup and, eventually, players on the bottom started crawling out from underneath. One of my players, a black pitcher named Leon Everitt, started screaming, "One of my own kind hit me, one of my own kind hit me . . ."

"What do you mean?" I screamed at him.

"A brother," he said, "one of the black players hit me."

"Leon!" I screamed. "Your own kind are the guys in the gray uniforms. The guys in the white uniforms are not your own kind. Now get back in there and hit the people in the white uniforms . . ."

The police finally broke it up. At 9 o'clock the next morning Buzzy was on the telephone. He was not happy. "What's going on up there?" he shouted. "Fred Haney of the Angels just told me you started a free-for-all last night. With the police? I told you when we gave you the job that I didn't want—"

"What did you want me to do?" I interrupted. "The guy was coming after me. He was gonna kill me. Believe me, if I hadn't hit him, you'd be attending my funeral right now."

It was not a tremendous beginning. Things did improve, however, and my teams often went entire ball games without a fight. I managed four years in the Pioneer League—one at Pocatello, and three in Ogden, Utah. After finishing second in 1965, my rookie league teams won the pennant in 1966, 1967, and 1968. I didn't make much money managing there and I worked long, hard hours, but I loved that job. What an incredibly good feeling I got from taking young, inexperienced prospects and molding them, building them, into good players and winners. I can honestly say I was the happiest man in the world.

In fact, I only had one problem managing in the rookie leagues: the players I managed were rookies. I mean, when they came to me at Pocatello or Ogden they were greener than Astroturf. Billy Russell, for example, was a seventeen-year-old from Pittsburg, Kansas, who had played very little baseball. The first time I saw him swing a bat I closed my eyes and shook my head. He thought a curve was something you drive around. He and the curveball were complete strangers. But my experience as a scout taught me to look beyond the obvious and see the potential. Billy had tremendous speed and good hands, he was very agile, and he was willing to work as long as I would work with him. He was willing to pay the price for success.

When Charlie Hough, from Hialeah, Florida, reported to Ogden, he was listed as a first baseman, third baseman, and pitcher. I had to decide where he had the greatest chance to succeed. He swung the bat very well, he looked like he might be a hitter. I looked at him as a third baseman. Good hands, good arm, below average lateral movement. First base requires less lateral movement, so I felt he could field that position. But when I saw him run, I knew he had been born to be a pitcher. The man could not run. I told him that he was the first baseball player I'd ever seen who would finish third in a two-person race against a pregnant woman. I timed everybody else with a stopwatch; he was so slow you could time him with a stopped watch.

Some of the players who started with me had had more experience. Steve Garvey was twenty years old and had played three years of college baseball at Michigan State when he joined me at Ogden. After watching him play I had no doubt that he was a future major leaguer. He was an outstanding player and an outstanding person. He looked like an All-American, wearing his college sweater, every hair in place; he acted like an All-American, respectful and polite; and he played like an All-American.

And then there was Bobby Valentine, one of the most heavily recruited high school football players in the county. He was also a fine baseball player, and as confident as he was good. At our first meeting in Ogden, he told me, "You know, if you see anything that you think I should work on, or if there's something I have to do, just tell me and I'll do it."

"Son," I told him, "there is one thing. I guess nobody told you this, but there is a great tradition in baseball that when a young man reports to his first professional team, he is supposed to take his manager out to dinner. This is very important."

He understood. "And I guess," he said, "that since I'm the Dodgers' number-one draft choice, I should be the first one to take you out, right?"

"That's absolutely correct."

We went to the best steak house in Ogden, and spent the evening talking about professional baseball. I always tried to learn as much as I possibly could about the people who played for me. As we finished dinner, I asked him if he had any questions or problems. "There is one thing," he said.

"What's that?"

"I know this sounds sort of silly," he said, not looking at me, "but see, at my age, I think I should start having some hair on my chest. I don't have any hair on my chest and if I did, you know, it would make me look older."

"Sure," I agreed, "it would." I took a deep breath. "I'll tell you the truth, I've helped a lot of young men grow hair on their chest, but it's like anything else, you've really got to work at it. See that fat on your plate?"

He had cut the fat off his steak and pushed it to the side. "Yeah?"

"The secret is eating a lot of fat. Fat is what does it. You eat all the fat you can, and you won't believe how quickly it'll grow hair on your chest." I looked at his plate. "Here, give me that meat, you don't want it. What you want is that fat."

About three weeks later he came over to me in the clubhouse, and he had a broad smile on his face. "Hey, skip," he said, "you were right. Look at this, there's hair growing on my chest."

Sure enough, some weak-looking hairs were barely growing on his chest. I knew that day that Bobby Valentine was eventually going to play in the major leagues. Any man with the willpower to grow hair on his chest when he wanted to just couldn't miss.

Many of my players were away from home and their families for the first time in their lives, and they were scared, so the first thing I did when a young man reported to me was try to instill confidence in him and make him feel he had become part of a new family, the Dodgers. I would meet with each new player and explain, "Son, there are some things that are very important on this team. The most important is believing that you have the ability to play baseball for the greatest team in the world, the Los Angeles Dodgers. Do you believe that?"

Invariably, they would solemnly nod their heads and say, "I do."

"Good. I do too, otherwise you wouldn't be here. Now, we have a little tradition on this ball club, that no matter where you are, no matter who you're with, no matter what you're doing, when you hear me yell 'Tell me something!' I want you to respond as loudly as you can, 'I believe.'

"And when I shout 'Who do you love?' I want you to respond 'I love the Dodgers!'

"And when I shout 'Where are you going to get your mail?' you respond 'Dodger Stadium.'

"And then when I shout 'Who's gonna sign your paycheck?' I want to hear you screaming 'Mr. O'Malley.' "

Most of the kids couldn't believe I was serious. They had anticipated meeting a calm, professional manager, perhaps someone like their school-teachers, and the first person they met was me, and I was practically ordering them to scream and shout. What I was trying to do was help build their confidence and their team spirit, while teaching them that they could progress in baseball and still have fun.

Eventually, this "tradition" I established received a lot of publicity, and baseball people would come to Pocatello or Ogden, or Spokane or Albuquerque when I was with those clubs, to see my players respond to these questions. My teams were among the few teams in sports history that people came to see perform *off* the field. And my players never let me or themselves down. We'd be working out or in a restaurant or in the clubhouse and all of a sudden I'd shout, "Hey, Valentine, tell me something!"

And no matter where he was, no matter who he was with, no matter what he was doing, Bobby would respond, *"I believe!"*

"Hey, Hough, who do you love?"

"I LOVVVVVVVE the Dodgers!"

"Russell, where you gonna get your mail?"

"I'm gonna get my mail at Dodger Stadium!"

"Garvey, who's gonna sign your paycheck?"

"Mr. O'Malley!"

Only once did someone give me an unexpected answer. "Willie Crawford," I shouted, "Who's gonna sign your checks?"

Willie knew he was still a few years away from the major leagues, and Walter O'Malley was getting older, so Willie responded "Peter O'Malley!"

I had my players shouting and screaming and falling down on their knees and showing outstanding team spirit and enthusiasm. The feeling that they gained from this, particularly when people came to watch them, was that they were part of something unique, something special, which reinforced their self-confidence. I never let up on them. From the first time I saw them in the morning till they went home after night games, I was constantly telling them how good they were, how hard they had to work to play in the big leagues, and how fortunate they were to be members of the Dodger organization. I was always trying to think of new ways of saying the same thing, and one day I told them that they would wear Dodger Blue if the Big Dodger in the Sky wanted it that way. The Big Dodger in the Sky. I liked the way it sounded, I liked the thought. And that was the day the Big Dodger in the Sky was born. Sometimes I'd even get them down on their knees bowing to the Big Dodger while they answered the four questions of Dodgerdom.

During some of my clubhouse speeches I would fall to my own knees and tell them, with absolute sincerity, "I love the Dodgers and I am at peace, because I know the Dodgers love me. They've proven it to me by giving me the privilege of allowing me to wear Dodger Blue. And I am loyal to the Dodgers. How loyal? I am so loyal that I have 'Dodgers' tattooed on my heart. I don't even have red blood flowing in my veins. Cut me open and I will bleed Dodger Blue. That's how loyal I am."

I carried my enthusiasm onto the field. When one of my players hit a home run, made a fine play, or pitched a good ball game, I didn't shake his hand or pat his rump, I hugged him. Why not? I knew how fortunate I was to be able to spend my life in professional baseball, working for the

Dodger organization and outstanding people like the O'Malley family, Buzzy Bavasi, Al Campanis, and Fresco Thompson. I felt like I was the happiest man in the world and I wasn't afraid to show my feelings. None of my actions was planned, my only motive was to help my players progress to the major leagues. I said what I said and I did what I did because I believed.

It was in the minor leagues that my hands-on philosophy was first criticized. Some sportswriters referred to me as a con man. A con man is an individual who tries to sell something for far more value than it has. I was no con man. I was selling a product of tremendous value, major league baseball and the Los Angeles Dodgers.

I cared about my players, off the field as well as on the field. I knew that only a very few of them would ever make the big leagues, but I wanted every one of them to gain something for having played on my team. I spent as much time as possible with my players, certainly more than any manager had ever spent with me. Jo and I had these young men for breakfast, lunch, and dinner; they slept on our couch and borrowed our car. We became very close friends with so many of them, and we were there when they were married, and when their children were born. I got to know my players as people, and friends. I learned about their families, their hobbies, their fears. I tried to learn how they thought. I made them call their parents. I made them write to the coaches who taught them and the scouts who signed them. I wanted their parents, sitting home in Kansas or Florida or Connecticut, to feel confident that their sons were playing for a man who was not only concerned with their progress in baseball, but who also cared about the development of their character.

Of course, I also believed this would help me to win. My job was to teach players the fundamentals of the sport of baseball and then motivate them to want to play it better. If I could teach them well enough, and motivate them sufficiently, I knew we would win. If winning had been my primary objective, I would have simply played my more experienced ball-players—the older players, the players with collegiate experience. Instead, I played those young people who I believed would eventually become the better players, people like Russell and Hough, Valentine, Paciorek, and Buckner.

Teaching took time. If Ogden had a downtown I never got to see it. For three years I was either in my hotel room, at the restaurant, or at the ball park. Usually I'd get to the field at 11 o'clock, work with my players all afternoon, return to the hotel to work on my reports for the Dodgers, and then go back to the ball park for the game.

I tried to make the long workouts fun. We'd split up the squad and play games. I'd pitch for both sides. I'd make bets, offering incredible prizes for anyone able to perform some feat—Charlie Hough still claims I owe him a Cadillac Coupe de Ville for a batting practice home run he hit off my curveball—I'd issue challenges, and I'd keep up a steady stream of conversation. Sometimes this stream would run for hours and I'd have my players laughing, but determined.

It was obvious after watching Bobby Valentine swing a bat, for example, that he was going to have to learn how to hit the high pitch if he was going to play in the big leagues. I pitched hours and hours of batting practice to him, high pitch after high pitch, as we worked on it. "You gotta believe when you step into that batter's box that there is nobody who can get you out," I would scream at him. "Do you believe that?"

"I believe that there's nobody who can get me out!"

"That's right and there isn't. I'm gonna tell you now . . ." and meanwhile, I would be pitching to him, correcting him on each swing. "I'm gonna tell you about this man I knew who had this dog, and every day the dog would do something on the floor. And every day the guy would take the dog, stick the dog's nose in it . . . good swing . . . and then throw that dog out the window. He did this for thirty straight days. And on the thirty-first day, that dog did something on the floor, *but then,* then he stuck his *own* nose in it and jumped out the window! After thirty days of practice, he had learned! And that's what you have to do. Practice, practice, practice. Pay the price. Just follow the pitch all the way in. Do you believe you can hit the high pitch?"

"I *know* I can hit the high pitch . . ."

I did everything I could to teach my players how powerful positive thinking could be for them. "My idol," I would tell them, "is the outstanding boxer Jake LaMotta. Jake LaMotta used to introduce himself as the man who fought Sugar Ray Robinson six times and won all but five of them."

And I practiced what I preached. The very first thing I did when I arrived in Ogden was have stadium club cards printed. I sent them to all the people at Dodger Stadium, telling them that if they visited Ogden, we'd have dinner at the stadium club and I'd have their names posted on the message board at the park. Fortunately, few people took me up on it. We really didn't have a message board at the stadium. In fact, we didn't even have a stadium club.

I was at my best in our clubhouse meeting speeches. "Proper motivation can make you succeed," I would begin. "I knew a man once who was in South America, and he fell into the Amazon River. That man could not swim and he started shouting for help. 'I can't swim,' he screamed,

'I can't swim.' And just then a native came along and saw the man and shouted to him, 'There are piranha in the river.' And let me tell you something, that man learned to swim."

The more I worked with young players, the more I was convinced that many of them did not perform at their ultimate level of ability because they lacked sufficient self-confidence, so I used every motivational technique I could think of to reinforce their confidence. I had a pitcher at Ogden, for example, named Freddie Katawich. The Dodgers did not think he was a major league prospect, so I was told to release him as soon as all the high school and college players arrived.

Katawich was a tall left-handed pitcher from Pennsylvania who had been signed for a very small bonus by John Carey and Ed Liberatore. After watching him pitch, I believed he had more ability than he was showing. With hard work, proper coaching, and motivation, I thought he would be a useful player. At that time the Dodgers' ace relief pitcher was Phil Regan, who was known as the Vulture because every time he saw an opportunity for a save he'd swoop in and scoop it up. So one day I called Katawack into my office and told him that from that moment on, he would officially be known as the Vulture of the Ogden Dodgers. Everytime I brought him in to pitch I'd announce to my infielders, "The Vulture is coming in now and he smells a save and he's going to get it." I told the local sportswriters and they began writing about the Vulture, and Katawich even began referring to himself as the Vulture.

All of a sudden, he started throwing the ball a little bit better. He was coming into ball games and saving them for the team. The better he performed, the more confident he became, the better he performed. It was like watching a man climbing the ladder to success.

I told the front office I couldn't release him because he had improved and had become an effective relief pitcher. They allowed me to keep him. At the end of the season he was drafted by Indianapolis, Cincinnati's Triple-A team, for approximately $12,000.

So the Dodgers had at least made a small profit. But one year later, the San Diego Padres drafted him from Indianapolis for $125,000! This was a player who was signed for almost nothing and was supposed to have been released.

Every player was different and every player required a different approach. That was why it was so important for me to get to know each of them as an individual. Some of them had to be yelled at, others couldn't be yelled at; some needed quiet words of encouragement, others needed a stiff kick. I remember another pitcher I had at Ogden who always seemed to have a sore arm. Our trainer couldn't find anything wrong with his arm, but this pitcher claimed it was sore and he couldn't pitch. I tried hollering at him, that didn't work. I tried to be sympathetic, that didn't work. I just couldn't seem to motivate him. And I knew if I didn't get him pitching soon, I was going to have to cut him. Then I found out he had attended a Bible college and remained very religious.

So one night, as we were getting onto the team bus after a night game, I said loudly enough for everyone on the bus to hear, "Billy, you're pitching tomorrow night."

"I can't," he said, "my arm still hurts."

I held my arm straight out. "Billy, does your arm hurt when you hold it out like this?"

"No, sir."

I held my arm over my head. "Does it hurt when you hold it up here?"

"No, sir."

"Well then, when does it hurt?"

"When I throw the ball."

It was useless to repeat that the trainer and doctor had found nothing wrong with his arm. "Son," I continued, "do you know how long it takes to throw a pitch?" He said he did not, so I told him. "It takes one second. One second to throw a baseball. That means if you make 100 pitches tomorrow night, you will have to endure one minute and forty seconds of pain." I paused, to let that sink in, then I continued, "Billy, do you know how much pain Christ endured when he was crucified?"

His eyes just opened wide. He couldn't believe I was saying this to him. You could've heard a feather crash on that bus at that moment.

"Now, do you mean to tell me," I said, "that you cannot endure one minute and forty seconds of pain for this team? I can't believe that's true." The next night he pitched a three-hit shutout, then proceeded to win his next seven starts.

Sometimes, motivating a player was painful to me. I had an outfielder with a bad foot who wanted to take a few days off. I reminded him that Wally Pipp had taken one afternoon off and was replaced by Lou Gehrig, who then set baseball's consecutive games played record, but that didn't affect him. He knew Lou Gehrig was not playing with the Ogden Dodgers. As I walked into the clubhouse one night I saw he was gently dipping his bad toe into a bucket of scalding hot water. "Why aren't you putting your whole foot in?" I asked.

"It's too hot," he told me.

"Too hot? Too hot?" That was all I needed to hear. "I can't believe you don't have the courage to stick your foot in that water, when you know that's what you need to do to heal your foot. When I was playing, if I had a bad arm I would've gone swimming in water hotter than this if they would let . . ." Eventually, we worked out a deal. If I put my entire foot in the bucket, and kept it in the bucket for one minute, this outfielder would play that night. Steve Garvey was appointed official timekeeper, I wanted to make sure I got an honest count.

I took off my shoes and socks and stuck my foot in that bucket. And it was hot. It was outstandingly hot. I was not going to scream, so I started singing. Loudly. My face began turning pink, then red, then bright red, then lobster red, but I continued to sing. There was simply no way I was going to take my foot out of that bucket before the minute had passed. At the end of one minute I took my foot out of the bucket and sent that outfielder out to play. And then I hobbled into my dressing room, and screamed.

The culmination of my four years in the Pioneer League came on the last day of the 1968 season. We were tied for first with the team we were playing. If we won the game, we won our third consecutive pennant; if we lost, we finished second. About 11 o'clock on the morning of the game, I was in my hotel room working on final reports when one of my infielders knocked on the door. "Skip," he said, "I'm really sorry to have to do this, but my mother just called. My uncle died yesterday and I've got to go home right now."

"Wait," I said, "just wait a second." I knew this player pretty well, and I'd never heard him speak about his uncle. "Just wait a second. Let me ask you, when was the last time you saw your uncle?"

"Boy, I don't know," he said, "probably three or four years ago."

"Four years ago! Four years ago! You gotta be kidding me. If your uncle didn't see you when he was alive, then he sure isn't gonna miss seeing you when he's dead." While I had him thinking about that, I added, "You've gotta play tonight, you can help us win, there's nothing you can do to help your uncle. Play tonight, go home tomorrow."

That settled, I returned to my reports. Minutes later my trainer, Zack Manasian, called. "Skip," he said, "we got a problem. Pat Burke [our catcher] is sick. He's been throwing up all night. The doctor says it's some kind of virus. No way he can play."

Burke was our first-string catcher. We needed him, too. But he's sick, I thought. There's nothing we can do. He'll get over it, I thought. I knew he would play that night, it was just a question of motivating him. "Where is he now?" I asked.

"Up in his room."

"Okay, good." I waited until that afternoon, when my players were getting ready to go out to the ball park. Then I called his room. "How you feeling?" I asked.

"Terrible," he said weakly, "awful."

"Yeah, I know, that stuff is rough when it hits you. Hey, listen, I just had an idea. Instead of lying there by yourself, why don't you come with us out to the park? We'll push a few benches together and you can lie down, at least you won't be alone."

When he stepped off the elevator he looked like the infielder's uncle. His eyes were teary, he was having trouble walking, he was complaining his stomach was killing him. For a moment I almost considered allowing him to be sick, but I got over it. I'd played when I was sicker than he was. When we got to the ball park we pushed two benches together and I got him a blanket and a pillow. "Lie down here," I said sympathetically. Then, just as he started to lie down, I stopped him. "Wait, just hold it, I just had an idea. Rather than getting your clothes all wrinkled up, why don't you put on your baseball uniform?"

So, while the rest of the team was taking batting practice, he put on his uniform, lay down on the benches, and covered himself with the blanket. Fifteen minutes before game time, I went inside to get him. "Okay, Pat," I said, "that's it, let's go."

"Where?"

"You're playing tonight. We need you, you're the only catcher we've got who can do anything and we've got to win this game tonight."

"I can't play," he said, "I'm sick."

"You have to play," I explained, "I've already put your name in the starting line-up."

Somehow, I convinced him to play, and he struggled onto the field. Sandy Vance was pitching for us. We were leading 2–1 in the seventh, but they scored twice on an error to go ahead, 3–2.

Oh, what a sight to behold. The bottom of the ninth inning of the final game of the season, the league pennant at stake, and our first two batters make out. Who comes to bat? The player who wanted to go home to see his dead uncle. I was whooping and hollering in the dugout, but things looked mighty dim. The count went to three balls and two strikes and the batter took a pitch that I thought was strike three, but the umpire called ball four. We were still alive. And now who was coming to bat? Who was our last hope? Pat Burke, our sick catcher.

Unbelievable! What a dramatic situation! Pat had struck out four times, he hadn't even come close to hitting the ball. The fans were screaming at me to pinch-hit. But there was no way, no way. The first

pitch was a strike. Then a ball. The third pitch was a curveball. Pat swung
. . . and missed by eighteen inches. Two strikes, two outs. The next pitch
was a low fastball.

There are some perfect moments in every person's life. This was one
of them. Burke hit a cannon shot over the left-field wall, a tremendous
home run to win the game and the pennant. His manager and his teammates mobbed him at home plate and carried him off the field on their
shoulders. "It was World War III in the Ogden clubhouse," the local
newspaper reported, "seconds after the Dodgers had run up their third
straight Pioneer League pennant flag. Buckets of water, shaving cream
flew in every direction. . . . Some players sat with a blank stare with tears
running unashamedly down their faces. . . . As Ogden's first baseman, Bill
'Mad Dog' Buckner put it, 'You ain't seen nothing yet. Wait'll we get
'em in the World Series in Los Angeles . . . ' "

Amazing. The man who scored the tying run was the player who
wanted to go home, the man who hit the winning home run was too sick
to play. Amazing.

We used to say in Ogden that we led the league in wins, clubhouse
speeches, and police escorts out of town. That was true. From time to
time, I would attempt to motivate my team with a speech before the
game, or after the game. One speech, which is representative of all of
them, took place before an important series with Magic Valley. "We have
four games with this club, we're two and a half games behind them. I
know we can win all four," I began, walking up and down the rows of
lockers, my voice calm, determined, and occasionally rising to provide the
necessary emphasis. "If anybody asked me right now, would you trade
your club even up for the Magic Valley club, I would say definitely not.
Because we have better prospects, we have better ballplayers than that
club will ever think of having. All we've got to do is pull together, have
the same enthusiasm and the same drive that we had when we went into
Caldwell trailing by three games and beat them four out of five to come
out of Caldwell leading the league . . .

"But in order for us to win you must give all of yourself, all your skill,
determination, and desire. Many players say they want to be big leaguers
and many of them try to dress like big leaguers, but if you want to put
forth the effort and hard work that it takes to be a big leaguer it starts
right here. Today. You must put baseball number one in your life. Remember, talent which is used develops, talent which is not used wastes
away . . .

"Do you think they care at Dodger Stadium whether you're a nice guy
or not? No! All they are concerned about is can you play the game. You

have to produce in baseball. As I've told you fellas many times, you must hate the man in the other uniform. There's 365 days in a year, and there won't be one day, Billy Buckner, that one of those guys on the other team will knock on your door and leave you a bushel of groceries. Those guys don't care about you, why should you care about them? When that man is pitching against you, Steve Garvey, he's trying to get you out. Instead, you can nail him, all you have to do is have the desire and the belief in yourself . . .

"Do you think outstanding players in the big leagues were born with successful qualities? No! They developed those qualities through endless hours of practice and hard work. Take Sandy Koufax, for example, here's a man who struggled through his first five years in baseball. Through hard work and personal pride he overcame his weaknesses and went on to become the greatest left-handed pitcher in baseball . . .

"I want you guys to say this over and over. I *believe* I will play in the major leagues because I know it is the only place to play. I *will* play in the major leagues because I believe in myself. I *know* I have the ability to become a major leaguer, all I have to do is put all of my abilities together. I *will* advance in the Dodger organization because I have the positive attitude and dynamic power within myself. I will always maintain this condition and I will learn all I can because I am *determined* to make the major leagues. I have faith in myself and that, along with the abilities I possess, will propel me toward my ultimate goal . . .

"Begin now, start your day, every day, with a positive mental picture. I want you to see yourself, picture yourself, in your mind, wearing a Dodger uniform, playing in beautiful Dodger Stadium. Picture yourself, you are completely poised and perfectly self-controlled. This image that you see in your mind of yourself, the way you will be, will give you the self-confidence and power to achieve your goal . . .

"Say to yourself, I *believe* in myself. I *believe* I have the confidence to play to the best of my ability. Just remember that, because if you go out and hustle against these guys, we *can* beat them four straight. *I know* you can beat this ball club, and *you know* it. All you have to do is play as a team. Remember, self-confidence, self-control, concentration, controlled relaxation, and determination, those are the keys . . .

"The Dodgers afford everyone of you an opportunity for unlimited fame and fortune. But that can only be gotten through hard work, self-discipline, and desire. You *can* do it, you *must* do it, you *will* do it. All you have to do is believe in yourselves. Just remember this, fellas, just remember, when things get a little tough, when Paciorek gets himself into a slump, remember—because God delays does not mean God denies.

Okay, Buckner, are you gonna play in the big leagues?"

"You better believe I'm gonna play in the big leagues."

"Why?"

"'Cause I believe!"

"Vance, are you gonna pitch in the big leagues?"

"You bet I'm gonna pitch in the big leagues . . ."

"Why?"

"Because I'm mean and I believe!"

"Valentine . . ."

That's the way my clubhouse meetings were supposed to go. Unfortunately, not all of them did go as smoothly as that one. Once, I remember, after we'd lost a game I felt we should have won, I closed the clubhouse door and really let loose. I started going right down the line of lockers, stopping in front of each player and telling him, in my own colorful language, exactly what I thought of the way he had been playing. "Buckner," I screamed, "I'm getting tired of you arguing and getting thrown out of so many games all the time. Valentine, when I tell you to steal a base, you gotta steal the base. Garvey, what's the matter with you? I don't know what the you're swinging at half the time. Vance . . ." I just moved right down the entire roster.

Playing for me was an infielder named Gary Pullins, a recent graduate of Brigham Young University. Gary Pullins was one of the finest young men I'd ever met. He didn't drink, he didn't smoke, he didn't curse. He played with great desire and enthusiasm, he hustled, and he was hitting. In fact, there was nothing about him I could criticize. And, as I moved down the line, scolding player after player, and got closer to him, I got a little concerned. I had to say something to him, but what could I say? Everyone on the team knew what a good job he was doing; they were all waiting to see what I would find to criticize about his performance. ". . . Paciorek, don't you know there's no law against hitting the ball to the opposite field? Why do you insist on trying to pull every pitch? Pullins . . . Pullins . . ." I had finally reached Pullins. I looked at him, I sighed, I shook my head disdainfully, "I was just like you when I started out in this game. . . . Now look what these people have done to me!"

On that same team we had an outfielder who did not seem to share my enthusiasm for these team meetings. One night I was in the middle of an all-time sensational inspirational speech. I looked at the faces of my players, they were in awe. Again, I was addressing each player in turn, firing them up, motivating them, bringing them to a peak before sending them onto the field, and then I reached this player—who was sitting in front of his locker reading a newspaper. Without a word, I fell to my knees, looked into the heavens, and started hollering, "Why? Why? You sent him here to drive me crazy, didn't you?"

My clubhouse speeches often led to police escorts out of town. By the time my Ogden Dodgers took the field they were ready to play, and to fight. As the *Los Angeles Times* quoted me in 1968, "[A]n Idaho Falls player was getting on Bobby Valentine, my center fielder. After the game was over he came across the field and challenged Valentine to a fight. He was a karate man and outweighed Valentine by thirty pounds. He got into a karate position, standing like an old-time fighter with one leg stretched out and his hand in an open position. Valentine dropped him. Then both clubs stormed onto the field and we had to pull them apart. They had a police escort to get us out of the city. Actually, fighting has been a little slow this season. We've had about four good ones so far, that's about three behind our usual pace."

My objective at all times was to prepare my players to play for the Los Angeles Dodgers, and part of that preparation was learning to hate the Giants. I knew that some of my players were eventually going to play in the major leagues and I wanted to give them an early start and a good base for hating the Giants. The first thing they saw when they walked into our locker room was a sign reading "Love the Dodgers, But Hate the Giants." "We're gonna kill the Giants," I would scream at them every time we played the Twin Falls Giants, "because they're the Giants and we hate the Giants." I screamed, I yelled, I pleaded with them. Charlie Hough remembers, "The first time we played the Giants I thought we were going to war. I thought they were just high school and college kids like us, but they weren't, they were the Giants and we had to beat them. I don't think we played them once the entire season that we didn't have a fight."

The worst possible thing happened one night against the Twin Falls Giants, we were losing. It was a typical Pioneer League nail-biter, the score was 10–9. Twin Falls' catcher had gotten three hits against us, so when he came to bat in a later inning I went to the mound and told my pitcher to knock him down. I thought if I could get the fight going before the game was over I could motivate my team. The catcher hit the first pitch off the fence for a triple. I was furious. I practically threw my pitcher off the mound and brought in Charlie Hough to pitch. He hadn't had time to warm up properly, but with his stuff warmups wouldn't have helped.

The first batter Charlie faced hit a fly ball to centerfield. The Giants' runner on third tagged up and scored easily after the catch, but as he ran by our catcher, Mike Criscione, he smacked him with his elbow. That was all we needed; once again the wave swept out of our dugout. This was one of the outstanding fights of my minor league career. It lasted a least a half hour. We had three security people in the ball park and they were right in the middle of it, fighting Giants. It got so confusing that people didn't care who they were hitting. I remember Charlie Hough sitting in front of his locker after the game complaining, "My hand is killing me. I had some guy in a headlock and I was hitting him on the head with my right hand . . ."

While a few lockers away, our shortstop was moaning, "I was trapped on the bottom of the pile and somebody had me in a headlock and just kept pounding me on top of the head . . ."

At one point Dodger president Peter O'Malley decided to visit Ogden. I picked him up in Salt Lake City and, as we were driving back to Ogden, he said, "Tommy, I've been reading your game reports and you guys have been getting in a lot of fights. How come?"

I couldn't deny it. "Well," I explained, "my guys are out there trying to win, and they just refuse to let anyone push them around."

"It's not good," he said. "Let me ask you, when these fights take place, what do you do?"

I answered honestly. "Peter, as soon as a fight starts, I run out of our dugout and I start screaming, 'Break it up, break it up . . .' "

"I'm glad to hear that," he said.

When we reached the ball park I began introducing Peter to our ballplayers. It was a great thrill for these youngsters, playing in the rookie league, wearing the Dodger uniform for the first time, and getting to meet the president of the organization. One of the players I wanted Peter to meet was a fine young catcher from Greenville named Randy Kahn.

After they had been introduced, Peter said to Randy, "I see that your team gets into a lot of fights . . ."

"Yes, sir," Randy said proudly.

"Let me ask you a question," Peter continued. "When the team is in these fights, what is your manager doing?"

"Oh, soon as the fight starts, he comes running out of the dugout shouting, 'Break it up, break it up . . .' "

"That's right," I said, "that's exactly what I do."

Unfortunately, Peter continued. "When he does that, do you stop fighting?"

"Oh no," Randy replied. "Tommy told us that when he comes out hollering for us to break it up, that's just to show people he's trying to stop the fight. 'Break it up' really means we're supposed to keep on fighting."

Peter just shook his head in disbelief. Actually, it could've been much worse, he could have asked to see the stadium club.

Once, when Al Campanis came to look at our young players, he asked me who I intended to play that day. "I've divided the squad into three teams," I explained. "I've got my hitting squad, I've got my running squad, and I've got the Green Berets." The Green Berets were my players who would fight at any time for any reason. "Which team do you want to see?"

"All of them," he said.

I hesitated. I knew exactly what was going to happen. "Sure you don't just want to see the hitting team?" Sure enough, my hitters hit, my runners ran, and my fighters got into a brawl in the late innings. After the game all I could do was say to Al, "Well, at least they're good at what they do."

The Pioneer League was as much a place for me to learn as it was for my players. It gave me the opportunity to run a ball club on the field for the first time, to put into use the concepts I'd developed during my fifteen years as a player and five years as a scout. I began to see what would work, and why, and when, and, just as importantly, what wouldn't work. It became obvious to me that the more you forced the other team to throw the ball around, by running, by bunting, by hitting and running, the more opportunities for mistakes you created. And on that level those teams took advantage of those opportunities. They made mistakes. The Pioneer League also gave me the chance to develop and refine my technique for arguing with umpires.

I got plenty of practice. When I was playing, umpires had often frustrated me, disappointed me, or angered me, but, except for that occasion in Cuba when the plate umpire pulled his gun on me, I generally got along pretty well with umpires. But when I was playing I only had myself to argue for, and as a manager I had my entire team to protect, plus myself. And since I had been used to the high caliber of umpiring I had seen in Triple A and the majors, it was difficult for me to accept the mistakes made by the rookie umpires in the rookie league. I had to learn that they were starting out just like players and they were going to make mistakes. Then I had to learn to control my temper. Once, for example, I was screaming at an umpire and he pulled a stopwatch out of his pocket and told me if I didn't leave the field in one minute he would forfeit the game. I responded by grabbing the stopwatch and firing it into the stands.

On another occasion Magic Valley's second baseman dropped the ball on a tag play at second base. The umpire in the field didn't see him drop it and called my runner out. I ranted, I screamed, I cried and I begged him to ask for assistance from the home plate umpire. "He'll tell you the guy dropped the ball."

The field umpire refused to ask the home plate umpire for help. "You kidding me? I haven't spoken to that   for two weeks," he said, "I wouldn't ask that   for anything." How do you argue with that?

Badly, as it turned out. I was ejected from the game and I was outraged. After the game I told local sportswriters, "We simply can't have this kind of umpiring and I will go all the way to the United States Supreme Court if the Dodger organization thinks it's essential that we get adequate umpiring rather than bush league calls." I told them I was going to base my case on unfair practices. I didn't even know what unfair practices were, but I knew that that's what the umpires were practicing against my team. And if it took going all the way to the Supreme Court to get a ruling that Magic Valley's second baseman dropped the ball, I intended to do that. Naturally, I was kidding. I don't think I would have gone much farther than the Court of Appeals.

Gradually, however, as I had more opportunities to argue with umpires, I got much better at it. I didn't argue any less, and I didn't win any more, but I did get better at it.

The most difficult thing for me to get used to as a manager was releasing players. The people who signed professional contracts had been stars in their high school, college, or amateur leagues. They were used to succeeding. And it became my job to tell them that their lifelong dream was not going to come true; that, in my opinion and in the opinion of the Dodgers, they did not have the ability to progress in professional baseball.

Sometimes the players realized it themselves before I told them, and that made it easier. I remember I had a pitcher from Brooklyn, New York, and he was really getting hit hard in one of the first games he pitched. I when out to the mound to take him out of the game and he said, "You know, Skip, I can't understand it. Back in high school in Brooklyn, before I came here, I was striking out sixteen, seventeen guys every game."

I looked at him and explained, "You know those guys you didn't strike out?"

"Yeah?"

"Those are the guys who are here now. The sixteen guys you struck out are still back in Brooklyn."

Few players ever argued with me. "This is very tough for me to do," I'd say, and I wasn't kidding, it was rough, "but it is the opinion of this organization that you don't have the ability to play in the major leagues. You're a fine young man, you've given it all you have and I've appreciated it, but we're going to have to release you. I hope those things you've learned in baseball will help you in whatever you choose to do, and I hope you'll be as tough a competitor off the field as you've been here for me."

I don't remember anyone getting angry, although some players would tell me I was wrong and everyone in the Dodger organization was wrong, and they were going to prove it. "Good," I'd tell them, "I hope you do."

And baseball people do make mistakes. There were people in the front office who thought Billy Russell did not have major league ability, for example, and wanted me to release him. I disagreed. I felt that with a lot of coaching, a lot of patience, and a lot of time working on the ball field, he would play in the big leagues.

Billy felt the pressure. One day he asked to talk to me, and we sat on the bench in the right-field bullpen. "I know there's a big cut coming up," he said, "and I'm worried about it. I want to know how you feel."

"If it'll make you feel any better," I replied, "I'll tell you this much. The only way you'll get released is if I get released as the manager. As long as I'm the manager here, you'll be here, because I believe you have major league ability." You talk about seeing the sun come out on someone's face, he looked as if I had just lifted a building off his shoulders and, relieved of that weight, he began playing the kind of baseball that would eventually make him the shortstop of a world championship ball club.

There is no question about it, sometimes I did get attached to these kids. Seeing them come along, young, talented, sometimes shy like Russell, sometimes confident like Valentine, watching them grow and learn and progress, it was impossible not to root for them. Jo and I became very close to a lot of them in the minor leagues, Billy Russell, Steve Garvey, Valentine, Wimpy Paciorek, Mad Dog Buckner, Tommy Hutton, Ron Cey, Doug Rau, Davey Lopes, Rick Rhoden, Steve Yeager, Joe Ferguson, Jerry Stephenson, Geoff Zahn, and Eddie Solomon. And, of course, Charlie Hough.

Charlie was with me on every team I managed. We were together in Ogden, Spokane, Albuquerque, and the Arizona Instructional League; he was with me in the Dominican and Venezuela and, finally, we made the Dodgers. And at each stop I'd tell him, "Charlie, when I get a job managing in the major leagues, you'll be right there with me."

And at each stop he would respond, "I wish you'd hurry. I'm getting a little old waiting around."

Charlie has always been one of the truly outstanding people in the world. When he reported to me, I made him a pitcher because he had a good fastball, a great curveball, and absolutely no running speed. A year later he had a mediocre fastball, a fair curve, and absolutely no running speed. When he injured his arm and lost some velocity on his fastball, it looked like I was going to have to give him his unconditional release. It was a very painful thought, and I put it off as long as possible.

We were in the Instructional League in the winter of 1969. This is a post-season league for clubs that want to give special attention to young players or allow veteran players to work their way back into shape after an injury. "Charlie," I told him in my office one day, "I'm gonna give it to you straight. You're on the verge of getting released and it is very sad, because I have never met a finer competitor than you are. There isn't a man who has ever put on a baseball uniform who works harder than you do, but what are we gonna do? You're short on your fastball and your curveball isn't what it used to be. So I have to say, if you want to stay in baseball, you're gonna have to come up with another pitch."

He asked if I had any particular pitch in mind.

"Anything," I told him, "anything you think you can master. Screwball, knuckleball, football, anything you can get over the plate."

Charlie went right outside and asked our pitching coach, Goldie Holt, how to grip a knuckleball. A few days later he was actually getting some movement on a knuckleball. I used him as a relief pitcher almost every day and ordered him to throw nothing but knuckleballs. We'd be leading by seven runs and he'd come in and we'd end up losing by five. But you could see he had something going. He'd walk two, strike out two, give up a home run, and then strike out the third batter. When he got it near the plate, no one could hit him, he just had difficulty getting it near the plate.

We didn't even bother getting an oversized catcher's glove for knuckleballs when he joined me in Spokane in 1970, but by July he really had control of that thing. In less than a year he'd progressed from a man taking his last breath in baseball to being a small step out of the big leagues. And I remember the day I knew he was ready to take that small step.

We were playing Hawaii and I had told our catcher, Bob "Scrap Iron" Stinson, not to call for the knuckleball when Charlie had three balls on the batter. We were leading by a run with two out in the ninth inning, but the Islanders had loaded the bases. The count went to three balls, two strikes on the batter, Winston Llenas. Scrap Iron signaled for a fastball, but Charlie shook him off. He signaled for a curve, Charlie shook him off. I went trotting out to the mound to mediate the issue. "What's going on?" I asked Stinson.

"I want the fastball," Scrap Iron told me. "He wants to throw that knuckleball."

I looked at Charlie, and smiled. "You really want to throw it in this situation?"

"Yeah," he said.

"Then throw it." I turned around and went back to the dugout.

Llenas struck out on the next pitch, a tremendous knuckleball. That night I sat down and wrote my report to the Dodgers: "Hough has confidence in his ability to throw the knuckleball for strikes. He has arrived!"

Two weeks later the Dodgers called him up to the major leagues.

Of course, it wasn't easy for Charlie. In his first major league game Walter Alston brought him in against the Pittsburgh Pirates with two outs, two on, and he walked the first hitter he faced to load the bases for Willie Stargell. One thing Charlie always was, was brave. He threw five straight knuckleballs to Stargell, running the count to three balls, two strikes. Then Dodger catcher Jeff Torborg signaled for a fastball.

"What a great idea," Charlie thought, "he's set up for the knuckler, so we'll fool him with a fastball." Only when he was halfway through his windup did he remember that he didn't have a fastball. That's why we taught him the knuckleball in the first place. He threw his fastball down the heart of the plate. Stargell was so surprised he swung right through it. Out, inning and game. Charlie Hough was a major leaguer.

Unfortunately, that started him thinking, and he began mixing up fastballs with his knuckleball. The first three hits he gave up in the major leagues were home runs to Billy Williams, Johnny Callison, and Randy Hundley, all on fastballs.

Which is why he was back with me at Albuquerque in the Pacific Coast League.

By 1969 I was spending the summer managing in Ogden, the fall working in the Arizona Instructional League, the winter managing or coaching in the Caribbean, the spring in Vero Beach as a special instructor, and the time until the Pioneer League season started as a scout. I had always wanted to spend my lifetime in baseball, I just didn't expect it to be compacted into one year.

My experience at Ogden made me believe I might have a career as a manager. I had proven I could win on the lowest level and I had proven I could teach and motivate young players. Doing it in the minors was one thing, but Ogden, Utah, and the rookie league were a long way from Los Angeles and the National League. And I wasn't sure if the Dodgers thought of me as a scout who could manage, a manager who could scout, an instructor who could scout and coach, or a coach who could scout and instruct.

I was sure of one thing, however. In 1968, Buzzy Bavasi left the Dodgers to join the new franchise in San Diego and Fresco Thompson replaced him. Within the year, Fresco Thompson, my friend, died, and Al Campanis became the general manager. It was almost twenty years since he'd told me I would work for him one day, and I was still working for him. Whatever Al Campanis said I was, that's what I was.

When I gave this jacket to President Reagan, I told him I had once been offered a free gall bladder operation in exchange for a Dodger hat, so he could "just imagine what this jacket might be worth someday."

I signed a baseball contract and saw America. During my fifteen-year career I played on the East Coast, in the Midwest, and on the West Coast. I played in North America, Central America, and South America. Imagine where I might have played if I ever had a good fastball. *Top left.* Concord in the North Carolina League, 1945. *Above.* The United States Army with Al Lamont *(left)* and Sgt. Brown, 1947. *Top right.* Mayaguez, Cuba, 1951. *Opposite page, top left.* Montreal Royals, 1953. *Opposite page, top right.* Brooklyn Dodgers, 1955. *Opposite page, bottom.* Kansas City Athletics, 1956.

Top. My mother and father, Carmella and Sabatino Lasorda. *Bottom.* This is where the Lasordas can usually be found—around the dinner table. I'm sitting with my mother; my brothers *(left to right)* Eddy, Harry, Morris, and Smokey Joe are standing behind us. *Opposite page, top.* Tom and Joanne Miller Lasorda, 1950. *Opposite page, bottom.* Tom and Jo Lasorda, 1983.

Top. Laura, our daughter. *Bottom.* Our son, Spunky.

Top. When fans honor a player with a "Day," they usually give him something they would like to see him use. On August 23, 1958, "Tom Lasorda Day" in Montreal, the fans gave Jo, Laura, and me this car. The plan didn't work, however: I still came back the next year. *Bottom.* Proving that I will do anything to keep my players happy, here I am serenading Fernando Valenzuela. When his contract expired reporters asked me what he wanted as inducement to sign a new one. "To start with," I told them, "he wants Texas back."

Top. This picture, taken when I was Walt Alston's third base coach, proves that I worked my way from the ground up to the job of Dodger manager. *Bottom.* A manager must do whatever is necessary to gain the respect of his players. And then he has to try to keep it, as I am doing during this 1977 exhibition game in Santo Domingo.

Top. The family portrait, 1977. *Bottom.* I get along so well with umpires that I often ask them to check my tonsils. Sometimes, we compare tonsils.

Opposite page, top. Sometimes, in the off season, Jo and I like to have a few friends over for a quiet evening. *Opposite page, bottom.* Only in this great country of ours, this land of opportunity, could the sons of Italian immigrants . . . During the 1977 World Series, my friend Frank Sinatra wanted to take me and Yankee manager Billy Martin to dinner. I refused, telling him, "How can you talk about another manager when I'm around? Do I ever mention Julio Iglesias when I'm with you?" *Top.* The work done in spring training may well determine the success of the regular season. For that reason, I run a very strict program, in which each exercise has been scientifically designed to hone the specific skills that will be utilized during the season. *Bottom.* Portrait of three sluggers: me, Reggie, and Billy Martin. When I was hired to manage in Triple A, Billy said I would someday manage in the big leagues if I learned to control my temper. Billy said that.

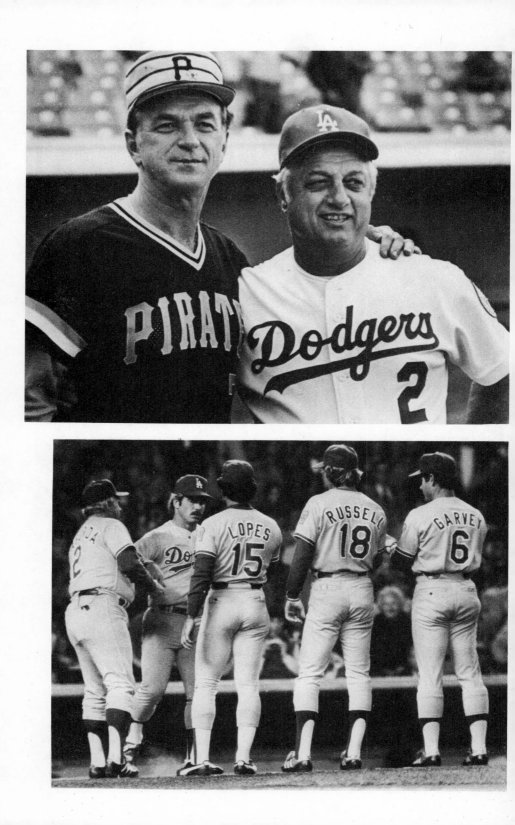

Opposite page, top. By 1979, two years after Pittsburgh Pirate manager Chuck Tanner and I had been hired, we had become the deans of National League managers. *Opposite page, bottom.* Ron Cey, Davey Lopes, Bill Russell, Steve Garvey, and I started together in the minor leagues. They played together longer than any infield in history, culminating with the 1981 World Championship. *Above & left.* In an effort to help me lose weight, clubhouse man Nobe Kawano first tried changing my name on my uniform jersey and then gave me T-shirts reading "Do not feed the manager" in five languages.

Top. Peter O'Malley *(left),* Al Campanis, and I with the 1981 World Championship trophy. *Bottom & opposite page.* An important part of the job of Dodger manager is learning how to celebrate properly. I've always favored the two-hands-in-the-air method, as seen here: as I welcome Rick Monday on his 1981 pennant-winning home run, and as I am drenched in champagne celebrating the 1983 National League pennant victory.

Many teams give managers and coaches raises to show their appreciation. Peter O'Malley surprised me with this fifty-pound granite tombstone after I'd told reporters I wanted my epitaph to read: "Dodger Stadium was his address but every ball park was his home."

SEVEN

•

I Do Pennants

Al Campanis said I was the manager of the Spokane Indians, the Dodgers' club in the Triple-A Pacific Coast League. A manager, he pointed out, had to be a coach, an instructor, and a scout, as well as a psychologist, disciplinarian, and, in my case, a friend.

"Hey, Al," I said, "you're the guy who convinced me I should be a scout, remember? How come now that you're in charge of the operation you want me to manage?"

"Forget scouting," he told me, "managing is what you should be doing."

"What about that thing, that the last one hired is the first one fired?"

"Don't worry about that, that was when I wanted you to scout for me. Now I want you to take over at Spokane."

It was very unusual for a manager to leap from a rookie league to Triple A, and there were a lot of people who didn't believe I could make that jump successfully. My rah-rah let's-be-pals method had worked in the Pioneer League, they argued, where I was working with impressionable kids just out of high school and college, but they doubted experienced professional ballplayers would respond to those techniques.

I didn't care what anyone except Peter O'Malley and Al Campanis thought, and they were confident I could do the job.

"It isn't going to be an easy job," Spokane general manager Elten Schiller warned me. "You're replacing a very popular man, Roy Hartsfield, who's won three divisional titles in a row."

"Fine," I said, "but did he ever win the league championship?"

"No," Elten admitted.

"Well, that's what we're gonna do this season," I said. Naturally, I was elated. I was back in Triple A, where I'd spent most of my playing career, once again knocking on the door to the major leagues. I hadn't really made it as a player, but now I was getting a second chance. The best advice I got came from Minnesota Twins' manager Billy Martin. "You're gonna be a big league manager one day," Billy told me. "All you've got to do is learn how to control your temper." The voice of experience.

As we prepared for spring training in 1969, Al Campanis and I wanted to promote the nucleus of my Ogden club to Spokane. We believed that Valentine, Buckner, Paciorek, Sandy Vance, Joe Ferguson, pitcher Bruce Ellingsen and a few others were capable of competing successfully at that level. We wanted to release the players on the Spokane roster who had no chance to reach the big leagues and force-feed the young players.

Bill Schweppe, our outstanding director of Minor League Operations, disagreed. He didn't want to expose young players to competition they might not be prepared for, and maybe damage their self-confidence. His decision was to let those players get some Double-A experience before testing them against top-caliber minor league competition. So my 1969 Spokane team consisted primarily of players I didn't know very well.

Naturally, this being my first season in Spokane, I wanted to get the people of that city excited about their team. I started in spring training. It was my responsibility to call the Spokane newspapers from Vero Beach after every exhibition game to report the line score and highlights. And every day, I would call them and tell them that we'd won. It didn't matter what had really happened on the field in Dodgertown, in the Spokane newspapers we were undefeated: Spokane wins 5–1 as Tommy Hutton drives in two runs. Billy Russell gets four hits in leading Spokane to an 8–2 victory. Spokane wins 1–0, a great pitchers' battle. Unfortunately, Elten Schiller was an honest man. He happened to be in Albuquerque, New Mexico, the day after I reported us crushing the Dukes, a Dodger Double-A club. Their newspapers reported that they had beaten us. This can't be, Elten realized. When he discovered what I was doing, he told me that I had to start reporting the correct scores.

So I never did it again, or at least until 1972 when the ball club moved to Albuquerque and I had to send our scores back to New Mexico.

My first season as a Triple-A manager began smoothly. Roy Hartsfield, who had gone up to the Dodgers to coach, was a more traditional type manager than I was, so it took the players some time to get used to me. Trust and friendship, I knew, could not be forced, they have to grow, and that took time. Then, eighteen games into our season, a Dodger infielder was injured and Campanis told me he needed a replacement.

"You got no problem," I told him, "the guy I got playing shortstop for me, Billy Grabarkewitz, is pound for pound as good a hitter as anybody in baseball. Take him, he can help you."

Campanis agreed, then asked me if I wanted the shortstop on our Double-A club, Jimmy Johnson, promoted to Spokane to replace Grabarkewitz. "No," I told him. I knew exactly who I wanted. "Let me have Bobby Valentine."

There was a long pause on the other end of the phone. I knew what Al was thinking. Bobby Valentine was an outfielder. Finally, he asked, as if he hadn't heard correctly, "To play shortstop?"

"That's right." During the winter we had decided to convert outfielders Valentine and Bill Russell to shortstop, because Dodgers shortstop Maury Wills was starting to wear down. Russell had made the big club as a backup outfielder. That left Valentine.

"You're crazy, you know that," he said. The only experience Valentine had had at shortstop was three weeks during spring training. "There's no way you can play him at shortstop in Triple A. They'll run both of you out of town."

"Let 'em try," I said, "but he's the guy I want. Let me tell you that kid is a winner. He loves to play and he can play." Campanis agreed, reluctantly. When Valentine reported I stuck him in the lineup. And from that very first day, he was terrible. He made a lot of errors, he ended up leading the league in errors, in fact. But it was just so obvious that he was going to be an outstanding major league player that I decided to suffer through this learning period with him. My job was, first, to mold major league players and, second, to win, and that's what I was doing.

It caused dissension on the team, however. Some of my players started complaining that this nineteen-year-old kid was costing them ball games. Finally, in late June, it came to a climax. As I was putting on my uniform one afternoon, Dick McLaughlin, my coach, told me the players had asked him to speak to me about Valentine. They wanted me to take him out of the lineup. This was the first real challenge I had faced as a manager and I had to meet it. It was exactly the kind of situation that people critical of my philosophy of managing had said I would not be able to handle. I realized that my future as a manager might well depend on how I reacted. "All right," I said to Dick, "let's air it out. Get 'em all up here right now." So Dick brought the team off the field for a meeting.

This was not an inspirational meeting. I wasn't trying to motivate anyone. What I intended to do was let my players know who was running the ball club. After everyone had settled down I started walking back and forth, back and forth, not saying a word, just watching them. Finally, after about five minutes of silence, I began. "Evidently," I said, "there are some people here who seem to think I'm not running this club right, they seem to think I shouldn't be playing this young man at shortstop."

I paused, and took a deep breath. "Now, before I get into that, I'm gonna stop for a few minutes so that all of you can go over to Valentine and ask him for his autograph, because when he's playing in the big leagues and you guys are working in a factory somewhere, you're gonna be telling everybody how you had the opportunity and the honor to play on the same ball club as him. So do it now, you won't have the chance to do it later because you won't be in baseball."

There was total silence in that clubhouse. I started walking a little faster. I was starting to get really angry. Suddenly, I stopped in front of the pitcher who had stirred up this problem and glared at him. "If you don't like the way I'm running this ball club, get up, get up right now, and I'll drop you like a bad habit. 'Cause as long as I'm the manager of this club, Bobby Valentine is gonna be my shortstop because he's gonna play in the big leagues someday. Now if you don't like that, if any of you don't like that, see me when this meeting's over and I'll be glad to make arrangements to send you somewhere else."

No one came up to me after the meeting, no one ever again complained about Valentine's play at shortstop, and I never had another serious problem at Spokane. I'd proven I could be tough when I had to be tough.

Bobby Valentine and I worked incredibly hard to turn him into a shortstop. After each game I'd remind him, "Be here at 11 o'clock tomorrow morning," and he'd be there and I'd hit hundreds of groundballs to him. Finally, he got so tired of these daily workouts that he began sneaking out of the locker room after games and I'd have to phone him to remind him, "Be here at 11 o'clock tomorrow morning," and he'd be there. Then it got to the point where he wouldn't answer his telephone and I'd have to drive over to his apartment to pick him up so he could be there at 11 o'clock.

One day my wife, Jo, said to me, "You know, he's going to hate you for pushing him like this. You're working him too hard."

Jo and I had a long-standing agreement, she didn't tell me how to manage and I didn't tell her how to do the dishes, but I knew she cared about Bobby. "He may dislike me now," I explained, "but he's gonna love me later because he's gonna be an outstanding player." The following season, 1970, he was the Most Valuable Player in the Pacific Coast League, hitting .340 and leading the PCL in seven offensive categories.

He eventually played portions of ten seasons in the big leagues and, had he not been severely injured a number of times, he would have been an outstanding major league player.

The Spokane Indians finished second in 1969, a very disappointing second, although we set a league record by stealing 207 bases. But we couldn't run if we didn't get on base. My education as a manager was continuing. I had a different experience each day and I tried to learn something from each one. It became obvious to me that the most important part of a manager's job is getting his team mentally and physically prepared to play, because once the game started there were a limited number of moves I could make. Any manager or coach naive enough to believe he's responsible for winning a game is in serious trouble. I knew that if I didn't show up one night my team still had an excellent chance of winning; but if I showed up the next night and the team didn't, I had no chance of winning.

Naturally, because we didn't win, I was criticized. Once again I was told that a manager could not be close to his players and command their respect. In order to win, I was going to have to change. I realized there was only one way to end that criticism—win the 1970 Pacific Coast League championship.

The first day my squad got together in Vero Beach I told them that we were going to win, and the way we were going to win was to pay the price. "We're gonna work like my wife shops," I warned them, "all day long." And we did. We were on the field from early in the morning till late in the afternoon. My pitchers ran laps until they were sick. Finally, they threatened to revolt, they threatened to mutiny. So I called a meeting. "I understand you people think you're doing too much running," I said.

"*Yeah!*" Well, at least I had brought them together. Pitcher Jerry Stephenson spoke for the whole staff when he complained, "The only time we get a break is when George Lott [my coach] is counting laps," he said, "'cause he can't count that high."

"Okay," I told them after listening to their complaints, "this is a democracy and I'm gonna run things in a democratic fashion. I'll give you a choice, you can either run sixty laps at 11 o'clock in the morning and then you're finished for the day, or you can work out all day and run twenty laps at 5 o'clock."

My years in Latin America had taught me how to run a democracy, my way.

I've never had a team better prepared for a season than on opening day, 1970. I had no doubt we were going to win the championship. In fact, we opened in Salt Lake City on April 14, 1970, Jo and my twentieth wedding anniversary, and I was handed a microphone and asked to introduce my starting players. "Ladies and gentlemen," I began, "I would like to introduce to you the 1970 Pacific Coast League champions, the Spokane Indians . . ."

That's confidence.

We won our divisional pennant by an incredible 26 games, then beat the Hawaii Islanders in 4 straight games for the league championship. We led the standings every day of the season. We had a *team* batting average of .299. What a team we had; more than half of them eventually played in the major leagues, including Bob Stinson, Tommy Hutton, Bobby Valentine, Steve Garvey, Tom Paciorek, Bill Russell, Davey Lopes, Bill Buckner, Sandy Vance, Doyle Alexander, Charlie Hough, Bobby O'Brien, Jerry Stephenson, Jose Pena, Von Joshua, and Mike Strahler.

The only problem we had was complacency. It's difficult to keep a team motivated when they're leading the league by 15 games. You really have to go some to keep them from getting overconfident. We had our only real losing streak in June, when we lost six in a row, and I called a team meeting. "I told you guys in spring training," I began, "that if you work together, if you pull together, if you play like one ball club, you'll be number one in this league. That's exactly where you are right now. But just let me tell you a little story about a guy I once knew who was out in a boat, because you guys think you have this thing locked up. This man was one thousand yards offshore, he could see the beach, and his boat capsized. And that man swam and swam and swam with all his heart and all his energy and all the drive that he had. And, when he got four yards offshore, he drowned. You guys are still four yards offshore, and you will be until you clinch the pennant.

"Some of you get a base hit and you get to first base and stop. You got as far as a one-legged man could get. When you leave the batter's box, you gotta want two. On a double you gotta want a triple. So let's get out there today, gang, and let's get them!"

At the end of the season I was selected the Minor League Manager of the Year by *The Sporting News,* a tremendous honor. Suddenly, I was being praised for the same things I had been criticized for before the season started. "I think the biggest asset Tom has in comparing him with other managers," said general manager Elten Schiller, "is that he is able to get close to his players and still maintain discipline. It's a rare quality. He gets right next to his players, gets to know them inside and out, jokes with them, eats with them, has a good time with them, but still has their respect. And that's what counts."

Actually, Elten was wrong about one thing. I didn't exactly eat *with* my players, more often I ate *for* them. My players proudly claimed that I didn't buy one meal that season. Actually, the only reason I did what I did was to help break down the barriers that traditionally existed between players and their manager. What I did was, I would go into a restaurant and find some of my players. Then I would come up behind them and ask, "What's that you're eating?"

Steak, or something else, they'd answer.

So I'd reach over their shoulder, cut off a hunk, and eat it. "That's right," I'd reply, "that is steak." One day in Phoenix I walked into the restaurant and saw a man with his back to me wearing a black banlon shirt, the same black banlon shirt that Jerry Stephenson wore every day. So I snuck up behind him, reached over his shoulder, and grabbed a hunk off his plate. "What's this you're eating?" I asked.

"Fish," he said angrily, as he turned around. It was not Jerry Stephenson. It wasn't even a ballplayer. It was someone I had never seen before in my life. My players in the restaurant were rolling on the floor laughing; I figured I was going to have to fight this guy.

Somehow, I talked my way out of it. But as this man reached the cash register, he hollered at me across the entire place, "Hey, buddy, if you really want to know, it was halibut!"

On another occasion I went to pick up my coach, George Lott, because we were going to speak at a luncheon. He was getting ready as I walked into his hotel room, and I spotted a full bottle of soda on the table between the twin beds. "Hey, George," I shouted, picking up the bottle and taking a sip, "What's th—"

I found out even before George answered. It was chewing tobacco juice he'd spit into the empty bottle. Fortunately, that experience did not stop me from sharing other people's meals.

That was some team, some season. We had the stars of tomorrow, we had grizzled veterans, we had people who overcame adversity, we had coach George Lott (whose wife wanted to buy their son an encyclopedia, but George wanted him to walk to school like every other kid), and we had the Comeback Player, Jerry Stephenson. On the 1969 club we had had a pitcher I just didn't feel was Dodger-minded—he would actually applaud when the big team lost—and I told Bill Schweppe to get rid of him. Bill worked out a deal with another club, which gave us a list of five players to choose from. One name on the list was pitcher Jerry Stephenson. Jerry had won a total of 10 games in his three previous minor league seasons, but I'd seen him pitch and knew he could throw hard. His problem was he just didn't have good control. But I remembered how

Jerry's father, Red Sox scout Joe Stephenson, had taken such good care of me and Jo when we moved to Los Angeles, and I felt that here was an opportunity to repay his kindness. "Take Stephenson," I told Bill Schweppe, proving the value of consideration for others, and a good fastball.

In February 1970, I was working at Dodger Stadium when Jerry came in to sign his contract. It was the first time we'd met. I took him over to a large window overlooking the magnificent ball park and said, "You see that field down there? Well, before this season's over, you'll be pitching down there."

Jerry looked at me and laughed. "They told me you were crazy," he said, "and I didn't believe them. Now I know it's true. I've won 10 games in the minor leagues in three seasons, and you're telling me I'm gonna pitch for the Dodgers?"

"Absolutely," I continued, "you'll be pitching there in 1970. You have all the ability, the only reason you haven't won many games is that you haven't believed in yourself. But let me tell you, son, by the time this year's over, you *will* believe in yourself!" I started that day and never let up on him. I made him run till his legs were wobbly, I talked to him till his ears hurt, I screamed at him until he had a headache, but I forced him to believe in himself. And, pitching for the Spokane Indians that season, Jerry Stephenson won 20 games and led the league in strikeouts. That September, just as I had predicted, he was on the hill of thrills in Dodger Stadium, pitching for the Los Angeles Dodgers.

The only thing that marred an otherwise perfect season took place in the fourth game of the playoffs. We'd beaten the Hawaii Islanders three straight, and Bobby Valentine, our leadoff hitter, had gotten eight or nine hits. On the very first pitch of that fourth game, Hawaii pitcher Greg Washburn hit Bobby in the head. I was coaching third base and I immediately knew it was bad. I heard a *thud,* and the ball dropped straight down, and Bobby collapsed. Oh, my God, I thought, and ran toward the plate. I didn't even think of Bobby's career, I was afraid he had been killed.

He was conscious when I got to him, and there wasn't very much blood, but part of his left temple had caved in. One very lucky thing was that an outstanding surgeon happened to be at the game and he came running right down to help. I just stood there, feeling helpless, tears in my eyes. All the Hawaii players kept saying, Washburn didn't do it on purpose, he didn't do it on purpose. If I thought he had, I would've gone after him right there.

Bobby was in tremendous pain, but he said, "Skip, do me one favor . . ."

"Anything, son," I told him.

"Don't let them carry me off the field on a stretcher. I want to walk off. I don't want to be carried off."

"You got my word on it," I promised. So a group of us walked with him, supporting him, to the clubhouse in center field. I was on the verge of tears. It broke my heart to see this young athlete with such tremendous talent unable to even stand up without help. Incredibly, and happily, Bobby came back and was playing in the big leagues in 1971.

The big problem for me in 1971 was trying to do better than in 1970. How do you improve on a season like that? Winning a pennant is difficult enough, winning the pennant two years in a row is twice as tough. This is particularly true in the minor leagues, because if your players are good enough to win the pennant, at least some of them are going to be promoted, so every year you're losing your best people. We did not get off to an outstanding start in 1971. Some of our players from the 1970 team were playing in the big leagues, among them Valentine, Russell, Garvey, and Buckner, we had some people learning how to play new positions, and our pitching was not as strong as it had been the previous year. In May, we lost seven games in a row. It was time for a clubhouse meeting.

A team, just like an individual player, sometimes needs words of encouragement and other times needs a good bawling out. The key is to know when to be supportive and when to be outrageous. I never really planned what I would say in these meetings, or how I would say it, I just let it happen. As any man who ever played for me will confirm, I never ran out of words.

"I'm really proud of you guys," I began that meeting, which I was, "and I don't want to see any of you hanging your heads. You guys have gone out there and you've done everything you possibly could to win. You're just not getting the breaks. You've been hustling, you've been giving it all you have, and I'm proud of you."

And then a thought came into my mind, and I shared it with my team. "About three weeks ago," I said, "the sportswriters of America took a poll on the greatest team in major league baseball history. The team they selected was the 1927 Yankees, a team with Babe Ruth, Lou Gehrig, Tony Lazzeri, Earle Combs, and Waite Hoyt . . . And I'll tell you something, the 1927 Yankees, with that team, once lost nine straight games. If a great ball club like that one could lose nine in a row, you guys shouldn't feel too bad about losing seven in a row." I looked around that clubhouse, at Hough and Paciorek, Joe Ferguson, Davey Lopes, Ron Cey, and I saw that they had really been listening to me. "Come on," I finished, "let's just go have a cold one. We'll get 'em tomorrow." And we did get 'em tomorrow, starting a six-game winning streak that got us right back into pennant contention.

I'd told Jo all about the meeting and, during the winning streak that followed, she said, "Gee, that was a really great thing you told those players about the 1927 Yankees. That really seems to have made a difference." And, after twenty-one years of marriage, she knew me very well. "But did the '27 Yankees really lose nine games in a row?"

I shrugged. "How do I know? That was the year I was born. But let me tell you, it sure sounded good to those kids."

In mid-season that year I met Clete Boyer in a hotel lobby in Spokane. Clete had been released by the Atlanta Braves and had signed with Hawaii. He told me that the Braves had also released Hoyt Wilhelm, the knuckleballer who was one of the greatest relief pitchers of all time and who recently became the first relief pitcher elected to the Hall of Fame. Hoyt had pitched in the big leagues for twenty years. As soon as I heard he was a free agent, I got an idea.

I wanted to sign Hoyt Wilhelm to pitch for the Spokane Indians. So what if he was forty-eight years old? I had many reasons: I believed he could still pitch. I knew he would be a tremendous gate attraction. I thought he would really be able to help Charlie Hough, who was continuing to have problems controlling his own knuckleball. And finally, I liked the idea of managing a player who was older than I was.

I immediately called Bill Schweppe. "What would you think if we could sign Hoyt Wilhelm?"

"You're kidding, right?" he said. I thought he knew me better than that. "We can't sign him," he continued. "You think after twenty years in the majors he's gonna come and pitch in the minors?"

"I can get him," I said.

Bill paused. He did know I could be pretty persuasive. "Well," he said, "if you think you're gonna pay him a lot of money, no way."

"I don't believe we have to pay him a lot of money. Well?"

He paused again. And sighed. "If we don't have to pay him a lot of money, I guess . . ." Spoken like a true Farm Director.

Jo and I had become friends with Hoyt and his charming wife, Peg, in Cuba in 1950. I called their home in Columbus, Georgia, and eventually got in touch with him. After we exchanged pleasantries, I went to work. "You know, Hoyt, baseball's been very good to you."

"Yes," he agreed, "it certainly has."

"So don't you think it might be time for you to do something for baseball?"

"Tommy, I'd do almost anything for baseball," he answered. "What'd you have in mind?"

"Well, Hoyt, I don't have to tell you that the minor leagues are in trouble, what with the big leagues expanding and all the televised games, and we really need a shot in the arm. And I was thinking, what a tremendous thrill it would be for everyone if Hoyt Wilhelm came to Spokane and pitched Triple-A baseball. Now, you know we don't have a lot of money in Triple A, so I can't offer you very much, but if you would come here and pitch you would give baseball fans a tremendous thrill.

"And, you know, if you come here and pitch for me, you got a chance of going back to the big leagues. There's a lot of scouts who follow our team."

I heard him chuckling on the other end of the phone. I knew he liked the idea. "Now what are you talking about?" he asked.

"I think . . . I can probably get you $2,000 a month." I was positive we'd make back whatever we had to pay him the first night he pitched in Spokane.

One of the many wonderful things about baseball are the outstanding people you meet during a career in the game. Like Hoyt Wilhelm. "Money's not a problem, Tommy," he said. "I agree with you, it could be a lot of fun. The only problem is, do you have anybody there who can catch my knuckleball?"

I'd get out there and catch it myself, barehanded, if I had to in order to get him to Spokane. "I'm gonna tell you something about my catcher," I began, trying to figure out what I was going to tell him. "You wanna know if my catcher, Sergio Robles, can catch a knuckleball? Lemme tell you a little story. He lives in a rooming house with one of our pitchers, Mike Strahler. A few weeks ago the man who owned the house had a heart attack, and the lady of the house, Katy, asked Sergio and Mike to help her clean out the garage and they agreed to help her. Now, when they went into the garage they found there was a bird in the rafters. So Strahler told Robles, 'Open the garage door and I'll flush him out.' Sergio opened the door and Mike got up there with a broom handle and that bird took off and, this was the incredible part, Hoyt, as this frightened bird was flying out the door . . . my catcher caught him.

"Hoyt, if he can catch a bird in flight, he can catch your knuckleball."

"Where do you want me to meet the team?" Hoyt asked.

Naturally, no one believed me when I told them Hoyt Wilhelm, the greatest relief pitcher in baseball history, was going to join the team. Campanis said there was no way Wilhelm would play minor league baseball for $2,000 a month. Charlie Hough knew this was another one of my jokes. Hoyt Wilhelm joined the team in Salt Lake City.

I used him immediately and he pitched six good innings. Six excellent innings. I called Campanis after the game. "You'd better get here right away," I told him. "This guy can still pitch. He can really help your ball club."

Wilhelm next pitched in Hawaii and, with Campanis watching, pitched another outstanding ball game. Finally, we returned to Spokane. We announced Hoyt Wilhelm Day the first time he was scheduled to pitch, and filled the ball park. He had another good game. And then Campanis called up Wilhelm to the Dodgers.

It worked out perfectly. He helped our attendance, he worked with Charlie Hough, he pitched well for us and we didn't have to pay him the whole $2000.

I hadn't been kidding when I told Wilhelm the minor leagues were in trouble. With the competition from televised major league games, as well as all the other recreational activities, it was getting tougher and tougher to get people out to the minor league ball parks. It wasn't at all like it had been when I pitched in Montreal and baseball was the only game in town. To compete successfully, baseball had to learn to market its product, to advertise, and I did everything I could to help. I spoke anywhere they would have me. I spoke at thirty-two different schools in four months. If more than three people were waiting on a corner for a traffic light to change, I was there urging them to come out to the ball park for a wonderful and inexpensive evening of entertainment. I spoke at a group luncheon practically every day. It was a difficult job, but somebody had to do it. Naturally, I suffered. I sacrificed my waistline for baseball. The only thing I minded about that was when Ron "The Penguin" Cey started telling people the team was afraid they were going to have to start running laps around Lasorda.

I wasn't the only one working to increase minor league attendance. I remember once we were playing in Eugene, Oregon. Frank Lucchesi, a good friend, was managing the Eugene Phillies, and we had planned to have dinner after the ball game. When I went into his clubhouse to meet him, he was just finishing his local radio show. "And another thing," I heard him say, "I've just about had it with the antics of Spokane's manager, Lasorda. I really don't like that guy, so all you fans should come out to the ball park tomorrow because I'm gonna get him once and for all." Then he smiled at me.

During dinner, we decided to really put on a show for the fans, maybe even get a good rivalry going, which would help both clubs' attendance. In the sixth inning I was going to come out and start arguing with the umpire. We were confident I could find something to argue about. He was going to shout something at me from his bench, I was going to respond, he was going to come at me, and we were going to really start fighting, we were going to wrestle each other to the ground.

In the fifth inning the next day my hitter took a half swing and the umpire called it a strike. I walked halfway down the foul line from the third base coach's box and started arguing with him. "How the   can you make a   call like that? How the   can you miss that so badly?"

Bill Hatch, the umpire, took off his mask and came halfway up the foul line to meet me. He hollered. I shouted. He yelled. I screamed. He roared. And *only* then did I kick a tiny little bit of dirt on him. So he ejected me, and that's when I really got upset. I was all over him. "Why you   ," I said. "How the   make a call like that? That's the worst   . . ." We were nose-to-nose when I suddenly felt someone tugging at my shoulder. I yanked myself free and continued telling Hatch what I thought of his attitude. Then I felt that tugging at my shoulder again. I turned around, it was Lucchesi. "Tommy," he said, "this is only the *fifth* inning."

"Leave me alone, Frank," I said, pulling free.

Naturally, he thought it was part of the show, and grabbed me by the back of my shirt. "You got the wrong inning, Tommy, you weren't supposed to do nothing till the sixth inning."

He was trying to get his arms around me to drag me down, I was trying to pull free so I could continue arguing with Hatch. "Get your hands off me, Frank, this   just threw me out of the ball game!"

Lucchesi immediately let me go. "What? This guy? He can't do that to you!" And with that Lucchesi climbed all over Hatch. The two of us really went at him. I'm sure the fans had absolutely no idea what was going on, but they got an outstanding show. This is probably the only time in organized baseball history that a manager argued with an umpire for ejecting the opposing manager.

Spokane finished third in 1971, and the Dodger organization was finished in Spokane. At the end of that season the Dodgers had to choose between Spokane and Albuquerque, New Mexico, as the home of their Triple-A club. It was a tremendously difficult decision, but Albuquerque was selected, primarily because it had a new ball park. Believe me, I was sorry to leave Spokane. It was a wonderful city and we left many good friends there, people like Elten Schiller; Frank Rotunda, who owned the Town and Country Restaurant; the outstanding Felice family, in whose home my family ate many times; Kenny Merkle; Chuck Stewart; Dick Wright; Denny Spellacy; Herb Hunter; Joel and Rose O'Leary; Father Welsh, a professor of law at Gonzaga University; and Father Tom Mulcahy, the hair-cutting right-handed priest who pitched batting practice.

I met Father Mulcahy just after I arrived in Spokane. He had been signed as a player by Bing Crosby and had pitched in the Pirates' organization, getting as high as Triple A. After leaving baseball he'd become a Jesuit priest, assigned to Gonzaga. He asked me if he might pitch batting practice for us. I've never turned down a priest who wanted to pitch batting practice in my life, so I agreed. Father Mulcahy turned out to be an outstanding member of the Spokane baseball organization and a very close friend of the Lasorda family. Everybody loved him. And, in addition to pitching batting practice, he cut hair, free. What more could any baseball player ask of a priest?

Religious things, actually. He also said Mass for us every Sunday morning. One day Lucchesi's Eugene club was in town and, after Father Mulcahy had finished tossing batting practice, he was standing by the batting cage. He was still in uniform, chewing tobacco, and looked about as much like a priest as . . . as I did. Eugene's Joe Lis, who had played for me in Venezuela, came over and asked, "Is that guy really a priest?"

I told him that he definitely was.

"A Catholic priest?"

"Yeah, a Catholic priest."

Joe was a little dubious, but he asked Father Mulcahy if he would hear his confession before the game. The two of them walked, alone, into the outfield. That night Joe Lis had three home runs and a double, forcing me to post a rule covering Father Mulcahy: no taking confession from a visiting player *before* a game.

I knew I would miss Spokane, but I was looking forward to being in Albuquerque. Wherever I am, I figure, that's a good place to be. I prepared for my first season as manager of the Albuquerque Dukes just as I had for my first year at Spokane—according to my daily reports, the Dukes didn't lose a game in spring training that year. It was actually almost true, we had a fine club, put together by general manager Charlie Blaney, who is now the director of Dodgertown. We celebrated the Dukes' first year in Triple A by winning our division pennant, then beating Eugene in the PCL championship series.

Even before I'd settled in Albuquerque I had started hearing rumors that I was being considered for various major league managing jobs. I wasn't really surprised; in seven minor league seasons my teams finished first four times, second twice, and third once. In the Caribbean, my teams had won four pennants in six seasons. Naturally, I was flattered to be mentioned for big league jobs, but I was also a bit troubled. There was only one job I really wanted, manager of the Los Angeles Dodgers, and it was taken. It was taken by Walter Alston, a man I'd played for, a man I considered an excellent manager, a man I respected. I knew, however, that he wasn't going to manage the Dodgers forever. And when he was ready to step down, I knew that Peter O'Malley and Al Campanis were going to hire the man they considered best for the job, no matter what their personal feelings. I decided to keep working as hard as I could and when the time came to make a change at the helm of the big club, I planned to be the best man for the job. I was gambling that my dedication, my loyalty, and my ability would warrant me the job. Besides, it was easy for me to stay in Albuquerque—although I had received a few feelers, no major league team had actually offered me a job.

Managing in Triple A was a tremendous experience. These were players who were either on their way to the major leagues or who had played there and were on their way down the baseball ladder. The toughest part of managing in the Pioneer League had been cutting players, having to tell them they weren't good enough to make it in baseball. At Spokane, and then Albuquerque, it was just the opposite; I got to tell these young people they were going up to the big leagues. It was always a thrill for me. I can remember the look on each of their faces when I told them. I thought Billy Russell was going to burst with happiness. Charlie Hough thought I was kidding. When catcher Joe Ferguson was called up, I took him out to breakfast with me and my son, Spunky, at Uncle John's Pancake House in Tucson, Arizona.

"Joe," I began, speaking softly, "I got some bad news for you. Bill Schweppe called me last night, he wants you to go down to Double A for a little while . . ."

"I'm not going," Joe said firmly, "no way. I don't care what I have to do . . ."

"Listen, Fergy," I told him, "don't think this isn't hurting me. You know how much I love you. This is killing me to do this, but they make the moves. What do you want me to do?"

"There is absolutely no way I'm going down to Double A," he repeated. "Call Campanis and Schweppe and tell them that I said—"

"Okay, okay," I interrupted, "but lemme ask you, how would you feel if I told you you were going up to the big leagues?"

"Oh, that'd be different, that'd be great."

"All right then, give me back your meal money." Those were the worst words a manager could ever say to a ballplayer. That meant they were not staying with the club for the road trip.

"I'm not giving you back any money," he said firmly, "because I'm not going to Double A."

I frowned. "All right, okay, you win. You can go to the big leagues."

"What?" The man did not trust me.

"You heard me. All joking aside, Fergy, Al called me. He wants you in L.A." Fergy took the news calmly. He started jumping up and down, screaming for joy, and hugging me and Spunky.

I was proud to be able to send my players to the big leagues, because I knew they were taking a part of me with them. I knew I had done my job, I had helped them accomplish their dream. I wish I had a penny for every pitch I threw to Valentine and Garvey, Buckner, Paciorek, Ferguson, Steve Yeager, Russell, Lopes, Cey . . . At the beginning of each minor league season I had a little speech I would make to my ball clubs. I told them a story, a story about a young man who was performing in New York City's famed Carnegie Hall, the greatest auditorium in the world. And this young man gives the finest performance of his entire life, and at the end, the audience is standing up and cheering him. While up in the balcony there's a man with a tear in his eye, and it's this young man's father, the man who sacrificed so that his son could make it, the man who motivated him, who directed him, the man who generated his interest. "So," I would tell my players, "when you're in Dodger Stadium, and you get a hit to win a ball game, and all your teammates are extending their hands, look, look over your shoulder, because there's Old Tom, rooting for you, with a tear in his eye."

That was really the way I felt about my job. I was a teacher, and the way I could judge my success was by the success of my students.

Part of my job as a Triple-A manager was converting players to different positions. In Triple A it was possible to determine which players would be able to hit big league pitching, then we had to start moving them around to fill projected holes on the big club. "Coconut snatching" was what Mr. Rickey had called it. On the islands, he used to say, it would take two fellows to gather coconuts from a palm tree. There was the coconut catcher, who stood safely on the ground, and the coconut snatcher, who climbed the tree and threw the coconuts down to the coconut catcher. Eventually, if the coconut snatcher was smart enough, he would be able to talk the coconut catcher into trading positions. So, in the Dodger organization, moving from one position to another became known as coconut snatching.

Bobby Valentine was not the only player we snatched. Outfielder Davey Lopes became a second baseman. Outfielder Bill Russell became a shortstop. Outfielders Joe Ferguson and Bob Stinson became catchers. Catcher Ted Sizemore moved to second base. Pitcher Bobby Darwin moved to the outfield. Steve Garvey switched from third base to first base. Bill Buckner moved from first base to the outfield. Third baseman Bill Sudakis became a catcher.

Lopes and Ferguson, in particular, did not want to make the transition to other positions. I first met David Lopes in Vero Beach in spring training, in 1970. I actually heard him before I saw him. John Carey and I were walking toward Diamond Number 1 when I heard the sweet sound of a bat hammering a ball. The corner of the clubhouse blocked my view, so I couldn't see who hit it, but suddenly I saw this player round first and head for second, he didn't slow down at all going around second, and he made a head-first slide safely into third base. "Who is that guy, John?" I asked.

"His name's David Lopes."

He had literally run into my life. "I want him on the Spokane club tomorrow," I said. As camp director, John Carey could arrange that.

"Come on, Tommy," John said, "He's just played a little at Daytona Beach, not even a full season. Give him a chance to get some experience."

"I want him, John," I said firmly, "I want him in Spokane." And after Lopes had spent a few days with my ball club, I knew I had been right. He was a bona fide, blue-chip, big league prospect. His only problem was that he was an outfielder, and the organization had an abundance of talented outfielders. We needed shortstops and second basemen. Since Russell and Valentine were already working out at shortstop, I told Davey I wanted to make him a second baseman. He resisted the idea at first, but once I'd convinced him he would get to the big leagues a lot faster as an infielder, he accepted it. The day he agreed to make the switch I put him in a Triple A game at second base. He had been born to play that position. The last player I'd seen make the difficult throw across his body with power and accuracy like Lopes could do it was the Pirates' great Bill Mazeroski. By 1973, two years after we snatched him, Davey Lopes was playing second base for the Dodgers, and played a vital role on four pennant-winning clubs.

When Al Campanis decided we needed catchers in the system, I suggested we move 6'2", 200-pound Joe Ferguson behind the plate. Al thought it was a good idea. Joe Ferguson did not. "Tommy," he said, "I love you like I do my own father, but there is no way in the world you're gonna get me behind that plate. I just don't wanna do it."

I tried the obvious arguments; he would make it to the big leagues sooner, we had an excess of speedy outfielders, he was the perfect size to be a catcher, but still he resisted. Finally, I just had to shake my head and tell him, "You know, I don't understand you. Here's this tremendous opportunity we're giving you . . . hey, listen, didn't you ever hear of a guy by the name of Gabby Hartnett?"

He said, "Yes, sir, I have."

"Well, Gabby Hartnett started as an outfielder, he became a catcher, and he went into the Hall of Fame. And did you ever hear of a guy named Mickey Cochrane?"

"Sure, I read about him."

"Him too. Mickey Cochrane started as an outfielder, became a catcher, and went into the Hall of Fame. You ever heard about Ernie Lombardi?"

"Yeah, he lives up near where I do in San Francisco."

"Hey, Ernie Lombardi started out as an outfielder too, and he became an outstanding catcher."

Fergy thought about that for a moment. "Okay," he said, "I'll try it. But no promises." Then he went into the dugout, put on the catcher's equipment, and started catching batting practice. He never went back to the outfield.

That night I called Campanis to tell him Fergy had agreed to make the transition. "Great," Al said, "how'd you talk him into it?"

"Wasn't too difficult," I said. "I just told him that Gabby Hartnett, Mickey Cochrane, and Ernie Lombardi had all started their careers as outfielders and changed to catching."

After a pause, Al said softly, "Tom, those guys were never outfielders."

"Hey, Al," I answered, "you know that and I know that, but Ferguson doesn't know it. And he's catching."

Bobby Darwin, on the other hand, was eager to move from the pitcher's mound to the outfield. He'd been pitching in the minor leagues nine years and hadn't impressed anyone in two major league trials. But he could hit. I'd watched him in batting practice, and the ball just shot off his bat. So, when he was struggling through another mediocre year as a pitcher in 1971, I told him I didn't think he was going to make it back to the bigs that way, but that he might have a major league future as an outfielder.

Bobby later told a reporter, "The way he talked to me, if he had told me the moon was made of green cheese after all, I would've believed him. He knew the answers to questions I hadn't even asked him yet."

We were playing the hated Phoenix Giants the night Campanis gave me permission to make the switch, and I started Bobby in the outfield. He came to bat for the first time as an everyday player in the second inning with two men on base. As he stepped into the batter's box, a fan sitting behind me at third base started screaming, "What are you trying to do, Lasorda? This isn't the rookie league. We're fighting for a pennant and you're playing a pitcher in the outfield? We oughta run you right outta town, you no good . . ." As well as other things.

I looked up into the sky and said to the Big Dodger, "Lord, if you ever let a guy get ahold of one, let him do it right now."

Giants pitcher Rich Robertson threw, Darwin swung, Darwin connected, that baseball shot over the left-field wall like it had come out of a cannon. I started whooping and hollering, and as Bobby rounded third base, I gave him a big pop on the backside and finally, just as I started to turn around to find the fan who'd been screaming at me, I heard his loud voice. "Lasorda," he screeched, "you dumb   . How come you haven't been playing that guy in the outfield all season!"

Outfielder Bobby Darwin eventually played parts of seven seasons in the majors.

The quickest conversion I ever made was turning my third baseman, Cleo James, into a center fielder in one game. Cleo had been kicking around the minor leagues for a long time, and I knew we were probably going to release him at the end of the season. But one night, before a game, I spotted a friend of mine from my scouting days, a scout with the Cubs, sitting in the stands. We started talking and he told me he was desperate for a center fielder. The Cubs were battling for the National League pennant and were short of outfielders.

"Hey," I told him, "you're really in luck. I've got an outstanding center fielder, Cleo James. Believe me, this guy can go get 'em."

The scout's ears perked up. "I thought he was a third baseman."

"He was, yeah," I agreed, "but that was before. Now he's a center fielder. You watch him, you'll like him."

As soon as I finished this conversation I rushed back into my clubhouse. "Change the starting lineup!" I told my coach, Dick McLaughlin. "Move Cleo to center field." Truthfully, it wasn't a completely new position for him, he had played it on occasion.

Unbelieveable! Incredible! The first batter of the ball game hit a line drive into right center. Cleo James outran the baseball, coming out of nowhere, dove, rolled over twice, and came up holding the baseball in the tip of his glove. He looked like he was holding a scoop of ice cream, but he held onto it, a sensational catch.

The Cubs purchased his contract that week for $25,000, and he ended up playing ninety games for them—in the outfield.

During the four years I spent in Triple A I proved I could manage on that level of competition and, just as important, proved I was able to motivate veteran players as well as the kids. Each year in spring training the Dodgers would assign me one player to work closely with, and in 1970 it was first baseman Wes Parker. Parker was an outstanding fielder, but in six major league seasons had never hit better than .278. After watching him in batting practice, I told Campanis I couldn't find any obvious mechanical problems in his swing. He wasn't uppercutting, he didn't overstride, and he waited nicely on the ball. "I think he can hit for average in the big leagues," I said.

"But he doesn't," Al pointed out.

"I think he just doesn't have enough confidence in his ability as a hitter," I said, and then I set out to prove, once again, that a lack of confidence can be just as damaging to a hitter as a flawed swing.

Wes was extremely receptive to the prospect of working with me. We knew each other, but were not close friends. That changed that spring. I was with him every spare minute I had. I'd throw batting practice to him early in the morning and I'd throw more batting practice to him after the exhibition games. As we walked toward the cage, I'd start shouting to gather an audience, "Come on," I'd scream at visitors to Dodgertown, "may I have your attention please. Step right down this way and watch the 1970 National League batting champion, Mr. Wes Parker, working out for your delight. Watch this young man who loves the great game of baseball. Do you love this great game, Wes?"

"I love the game, Tommy."

A few people would stop by the cage to see what this madman was screaming about, and they would attract other people, and suddenly we had a crowd. "Wes Parker," I would demand, "who's the best hitting first baseman in baseball?"

"Wes Parker!" he'd answer.

"Folks," I said, addressing the spectators, "you can now go back to your homes and tell your friends that you saw Mr. Wes Parker hit them out of sight in Vero Beach, Florida. That you saw the 1970 batting champion, Wes Parker, a man who knows that you can get wholesale prices for a washing machine and you can get wholesale prices for a television set, but that you must pay retail prices for success . . ."

Once, an older woman watching me pitch said to John Carey, "He really doesn't throw very hard, does he?"

John Carey then yelled to me, "Tommy, there's a lady here who says you don't throw very hard."

I stopped, put my hands on my hips and hollered at her, "Let me tell you something, lady. I throw just as hard as the great Sandy Koufax. It's just that my ball doesn't get there as quick."

When Wes Parker and I were in the batting cage I'd keep up an endless stream of chatter. I'd challenge him to try to get a hit off me, I'd bet him he couldn't, I'd be offering advice. "Selective!" I'd scream at him. "You gotta pick out the pitch you want to hit. You got to be as selective at the plate as you are with women. You're careful when you pick a woman to go out with, right? So you got to be just as selective when you're picking out a pitch to swing at!

"I'm telling you, Wes Parker, hitting is the toughest thing in the world to do. Statistics prove it. You take a doctor, he operates on ten people. Seven of them die. Is he a good doctor? You take a cabdriver. He makes ten trips. He gets lost seven out of ten times. Is he a good cabdriver? A basketball player takes ten foul shots and misses seven out of ten. Is he a good foul shooter? If a football quarterback throws ten passes and completes three of them, is he a good quarterback? If an engineer builds ten bridges and seven of them collapse, how good an engineer is he? But in baseball, a man who gets three hits in ten times at bat is an outstanding hitter. Baseball is the only job in the world that if you fail seven out of ten times you're a success. And you can be that outstanding hitter. You just have to work and work at it."

By the time the big club was ready to break camp and head north Wes Parker and I had become close friends. "Tommy," he told me, "I want you to know that when I'm around you, you make me believe in myself. I'm really sorry you're not gonna be with the ball club, because I need you."

"Wes, that isn't true," I said. "More than anything, you need to believe in yourself." I believed that was true for Wes Parker as a hitter, for me as a manager, and for anyone else in any profession. If you believe it, you can achieve it. Success begins with confidence. It comes in cans, not can'ts. Really believing you can do something is the beginning of doing it. Doubts just get in the way. "Look," I continued, "I got an idea. Meet me in the lobby with your tape recorder tonight and we'll talk."

We met after dinner, and sat on a little bench, under a dim light. "You told me I make you believe in yourself, right?" I said, before turning on the recorder.

"That's right," he agreed. "I wish you could be with me during the season."

"I will be," I said. "Turn on that tape recorder." Then I started. "The first thing I want to ask you is that if the Dodgers are beating the Reds 3–2 in the bottom of the ninth inning of the final game of the season, and the winner of this game goes into the playoffs, and Cincinnati has the bases loaded and Pete Rose is the batter, who do you want Pete Rose to hit the ball to?"

"Me," he said without hesitation.

"Right. Why?"

"Because I'm the best fielder in the league."

"Good. Okay, now, this time you're in Dodger Stadium and the Dodgers are losing 3–2 in the bottom of the ninth inning of the final game of the season and the winner of this game goes into the playoffs. The bases are loaded and there are two outs, who would you want to be at bat?"

Parker paused. "Who's pitching?"

"See, there's your problem right there. When I asked you who you wanted the ball hit to, you didn't even hesitate, because you believe that you are the best, you believe there isn't anybody in baseball who can catch the ball better than you can. But when I asked you who you wanted at bat you hesitated, because you don't have confidence in your ability to hit.

"Let me ask you another question. Suppose I told you that I was going to meet you here at 6 o'clock tomorrow morning and I was going to fight you and kill you. What are you gonna do between now and tomorrow morning? Are you gonna be running around having a good time, not worrying about me, or are you gonna try to prepare for the fight by finding out what type of fighter I am? Am I an infighter? Do I like to slug or box? Am I a dirty fighter? What are you gonna do?"

"I'm gonna find out everything I can about you," he said.

"Beautiful. Now, the same thing applies to pitchers. When you're going up against a pitcher the next day, you have to picture yourself mentally and physically ready to hit that pitcher. You've got to step into the batter's box *believing* that there isn't a man alive who can get you out. You have to want to live for the day you can drive in the big run for the Dodgers. You've got to *believe* that you are the best with the bat. The night before you're going to hit against Juan Marichal or Bob Gibson or Bob Veale you have to picture yourself hitting them, you have to *know* you can hit them.

"You must never even think, 'I can't hit this guy.' What you've got to be saying is, 'This guy can't get me out.' You have to really *believe* you are the best hitter in baseball . . ." When we'd finished making the tape, I told him to listen to it every day throughout the summer and to call me whenever he needed a boost. "I know you can hit," I told him, "and I really believe you can be one of the best hitters in the major leagues. I want you to repeat, over and over, every day, 'I believe I am the best hitter in baseball.' "

And that season he almost was. Wes Parker hit .319 and drove in 111 runs. As soon as he started believing he was one of the best hitters in baseball, he became one of the best hitters in baseball. The following winter I received a letter from him. "Dear Tom," he wrote, "I want to tell you how much I appreciate all you've done for me. I had the best year of my career because you made me believe in myself. . . . I can never repay you for what you've done for me . . ." But he tried. Enclosed was a check for $1,000, which we used to air-condition our home.

I believe in the power of positive thought. It is something I have seen work numerous times, and it is something I try to teach my players. In 1983, the Dodgers snatched Pedro Guerrero from right field and moved him to third base. In 1984, he was having some problems playing third, so I decided to talk to him. I brought him into my office and said, "Okay, Pete, I want you to picture this, we're beating Atlanta by one run in the ninth inning of the final game of the season, and the winner of this game goes into the playoffs. There are two outs, they've got the bases loaded and Dale Murphy is the hitter. What are you thinking?"

At least he was honest. "I'm thinking, please Lord, don't let him hit the ball to me."

I sighed. "Is that all?"

"No," he said, "and then I'm thinking, and please Lord, don't let him hit it to Steve Sax either."

Obviously, on occasion my motivational techniques are not as successful as I want them to be. A similiar thing happened to me one night in Spokane. We were beating Tucson by a run in the eighth inning, but they had the bases loaded with two outs. I figured it would be a good time to go out there and pump up my pitcher, a little left-hander named Bobby O'Brien. I walked slowly out to the mound and said, "Bobby, if the heavens opened up right now and you could hear the voice of the Big Dodger in the Sky, and he said to you, 'Bobby, you're gonna die and come up to heaven, and this is the last batter you're ever gonna face,' how would you like to meet the Lord? Getting this man out or letting him get a hit off you?"

"I'd want to face him getting this guy out," Bobby replied.

"That's right, you would. Now, how do you know that after you throw the next pitch you are not going to die? This might really be the last hitter you're ever going to face. And if it is, you'll want to face the Lord getting him out." I felt confident Bobby was going to go after that batter with all the drive and aggressiveness I knew he had inside. Unfortunately, before I could get settled in the dugout, the batter lined a base hit to right field, knocking in both runners and putting us behind. "Bobby," I said with great pain at the end of the inning, "what happened?"

"It's like this, skip," he said, taking a deep breath, "you had me so worried about dying, I couldn't concentrate on the batter."

One of the things I realized early in my career as a manager was that before I could convince anyone that believing in himself could make a difference, I had to convince him that I knew what I was talking about. I had to prove that my belief in my own abilities enabled me to accomplish difficult tasks. Because if a player saw me fail, there would be no reason for him to believe anything I said.

Proving it took many forms. Beating my players in pool. Pitching two hours of batting practice in the Arizona sunshine. Convincing a stranger not to fight me when I ate halibut off his plate. Speaking to large groups with little preparation and no fear. And flying first class in Triple A ball. Whenever we would fly from city to city in the minor leagues, we wouldn't fly first class, we wouldn't fly coach, we wouldn't even fly economy, we would fly last class. They didn't even have a name for it. No food, no movie, one seat and one seatbelt, that was it. So, naturally, I decided I was always going to fly first class. I did not do it for myself, for the comfort of the large seat, for the meal, for the beverages, for the movie; I did it to show my team that with self-confidence and a belief in oneself, anything was possible.

No matter where my teams flew, I ended up flying first class. This greatly impressed my players, who were proud of the Old Skipper, and they wanted to know how I had accomplished this truly incredible feat. I would tell them, and this was in 1969, 1970 . . . "I can't say anything now, you'll have to wait and read it in my book." No matter how hard they tried to discover my secret method, I would tell them, "You'll read how in my book." So, I really hate to let this secret out, but this is my book, and I did promise. I will now reveal my technique, which will enable anyone to be upgraded to first class.

On second thought, this is such a tremendous secret, and so valuable, that I think I should wait until my second book to reveal it. All I will say about it here is that it requires outstanding determination, strong will, and it has something to do with the United States Postal Service. Details other than those, I'm afraid, cannot be revealed at this time.

I was not selfish about sharing the fruits of this skill, however. Every time I got upgraded and there was an empty seat in first class, I'd ask the stewardess if she could go in the back and bring up my team physician, Dr. Herbert Vike. Now, Herbie Vike was our trainer, and he was as much a doctor as I am a submarine commander. But when the stewardess heard that word "physician," she was agreeable.

I never forgot that my team was sitting in the back of the plane, either, and I knew that I wouldn't have been there except for my players. And when I looked back, way back, and saw those big players cramped into those tiny seats, I could hardly stand it, so I'd ask the stewardess if she could close the curtain. And sometime, because I always had a problem deciding what meal to order, I'd send the menu back to my boys to get their assistance in making my selection.

In fact, getting food was almost as much of a challenge as getting a first-class seat. The very first time I faced that problem was on a flight from Phoenix to Hawaii. Just as we were boarding in Phoenix, Herbie Vike told me, "You'd better tell everybody to pick up box lunches when we change planes in L.A."

"You're kidding me, right?" I said.

He was not kidding me. "The class we're flying, we don't get any food. We don't even get drinks, so you'd better tell everybody if they want anything to eat before we get to Hawaii they'd better buy it in L.A."

"Wait a minute," I said, "do they have food on that plane?"

"Sure they have food on that plane, but you ain't gonna get any of it."

"I'm gonna tell you something right now, Herbie, I'm not buying any box lunch in L.A., and I'm gonna eat."

"No way," he said, "no way." Naturally, everyone on the team heard about this, and it became a tremendous challenge.

I was sitting quietly on the plane when the stewardesses began serving dinner. I called one of them over to me and said softly, "Miss, I'll take one of those steaks."

"I'm sorry, sir," she said politely, "I can let you sit here, but the fare you're flying on does not include meals, so we don't have enough."

"Miss," I repeated, "I really think you should bring me one of those steaks."

"I'm very sorry, but I can't."

"Let me explain something to you, miss," I said, always politely, "I've got a bad heart and if I don't get anything to eat and I have another heart attack I'm gonna hold the airline responsible because I cautioned you that I have a bad heart and must have something to eat. That means you will have to be subpoenaed and go to court as a witness, so rather than causing all that difficulty, I'd like a steak medium rare, please."

After I'd finished my steak the stewardess came over and asked me how I felt. "Not bad," I said, "I think one more steak will get me through the trip."

As I was eating that second dinner, I started talking to the stewardess. I discovered that her father worked for a close friend of mine at Sears, someone we both knew. "That's just great," I said to her. "I see him all the time. I'll tell him you said hello. How many steaks do you have left?"

"Ten," she said.

"Herbie!" I screamed. He came up. "Point out the starting lineup to her, they're all getting steak dinners."

"Hey, Skip," he said, "that's not right. You can't give it to just the starters and not the rest."

"You get the tenth one," I said.

"I'll show you who they are," he said to the stewardess.

After that, my team listened when I told them anything was possible.

Of course, some players never learn. Jerry Reuss, for instance, recently bet me $20 that I could not get an Italian meal during a twenty-minute stopover the Dodgers were making in Chicago.

It was just too easy. As our plane taxied up to the terminal at O'Hare, a van pulled up and delivered twenty pizzas. I had simply radioed a friend of mine named Eddy Minasian, who had called Connie's Pizza, who delivered.

Some of the people who have been with me through the years are still amazed by the things that can be accomplished with self-confidence. Happy Hooton was with me one day in Florida when the owner of a clothing store offered Dodger players a sizable discount on sports jackets. Unfortunately, I couldn't find anything that I liked in the proper size. And then I spotted a blue blazer, hanging on a rack by itself. I tried it on and it fit perfectly, although there was a slight bulge in the inside breast pocket. The bulge turned out to be the owner of the store's sunglasses, the blue blazer turned out to be the jacket he'd worn to work that day. Now, what impressed Hooton was not that I talked the man into giving me the jacket—that was a given—it was that I also talked him into taking all of us out to lunch so I could wear my new jacket.

So, was Hooton really going to doubt me when I told them I knew he could throw his knuckle-curve for a strike? Really?

Was I a good minor league manager? If a manager is judged on winning, I would have to say: five firsts, two seconds, and a third-place finish in eight years of managing in the lowest and highest minor leagues. If a manager is judged on helping to mold players and send them to the big leagues, I would have to say: Steve Garvey, Davey Lopes, Ron Cey, Billy Russell, Bill Buckner, Tom Paciorek, Doyle Alexander, Jerry Stephenson, Bobby O'Brien, Mike Strahler, Charlie Hough, Jose Pena, Sandy Vance, Bob Stinson, Tommy Hutton, Bobby Valentine, Jim Schafer, Freddie Norman, Cleo James, Chuck Coggins, Billy Grabarkewitz, Johnny Gamble, Steve Huntz, Jimmy Hibbs, Bobby Darwin, Sergio Robles, Timmy Johnson, Bobby Randall, Joe Ferguson, Steve Yeager, Von Joshua, Bruce Ellingsen, Rick Rhoden, Stan Wall, Eddie Solomon, Bob Gallagher, Lee Lacy, and Geoff Zahn.

And, finally, Tom Lasorda. Peter O'Malley came down to the Dominican during the winter of 1972. "Al and I were discussing your future," he said during dinner his first night there, "and we want you to forget about managing in the minor leagues and . . ."

EIGHT

•

My Blue Heaven

". . . join the Dodgers coaching staff." Danny Ozark was leaving to manage the Philadelphia Phillies and Roy Hartsfield was joining the Atlanta Braves as a coach, and they wanted me to fill one of the vacancies.

After four years of sending people up to the big leagues, my time had come. I just wasn't sure I wanted to go. "I don't know," I said. "Al was absolutely right, I really do enjoy managing. I'm not sure I want to give it up."

"You want to manage in the big leagues someday, don't you?" Peter asked.

"Sure. Course."

"Okay, well then, believe me, the easiest way to get a job is from the coaching ranks . . ."

I wasn't sure that was true. "Who gets to be President first, a senator or a congressman? There's a lot of guys who got major league jobs directly from the minor leagues. You know, you can get forgotten pretty quickly as a coach."

Peter paused. He knew me very well. "Tommy," he pointed out, "I'm confident you won't let anybody forget about you."

I knew I had no real choice. I'd spent too many years being loyal to the Dodger organization to refuse. If they wanted me to coach, I intended to be the best coach in major league baseball. The only thing that concerned me were the feelings of manager Walter Alston. I knew that the moment my promotion was announced people would begin asking if I was after his job. Well, I was after his job—but only when he was ready to give it up. "How does Walter feel about this?" I asked.

"He's all for it. He'll be glad to have you."

So, after a seventeen-year absence, I was back in the big leagues. I really was reluctant to give up the minor league managing job, I loved running my own team my own way and I loved working with the kids, but I'd been selling Los Angeles Dodgers baseball for so long I couldn't help but be tremendously excited.

Walt was extremely supportive. He told me I would be his third-base coach. And I told him how pleased I was to be working for him. "I'll try to be the same kind of coach for you that I would want working for me," I said.

I really was the obvious choice for the job. Seventeen players on the Dodgers' twenty-five-man major league squad had been with me in the minor leagues, and I'd worked with most of the others in spring training. My job was to supervise the pre-game workout, coach third base during games, do whatever additional chores Walt needed done, and help create a positive, winning atmosphere.

Walt Alston was a quiet, private, serious man. I was exactly the opposite. But it was a mix that worked very well. I had played for him at Montreal, I had worked with him while scouting, I had spent many years assisting him in spring training, and I ended up coaching for him in the major leagues for four seasons. Never once did he ask me to change or to tone down my enthusiasm, and never, ever, did he appear threatened by my close relationships to the Dodger players. He knew that I was loyal to him, and the Dodgers, and he pretty much let me do whatever I wanted to do.

One year in spring training, for example, I established the 111 Percent Club for the nonroster players I was supervising. George Allen, then coaching the Los Angeles Rams, was quoted as saying his players gave 110 percent. I told my people I wanted even more than that. So each day John Carey, Del Crandall, Jim Muhe, and I selected a group of players who had hustled most that day, then the players voted for the winner. Naturally, we awarded outstanding prizes. Our first winner received a guided tour of the major league locker room, during which he had his photograph taken, *in color,* sitting in the locker of his favorite major league player while eating a major league ham and cheese sandwich. On another day the winner was allowed to use my personal electric heater. One of our most desirable prizes was the privilege of assisting the chief of clubhouse sanitation in feeding the ducks in the pond adjoining Holman Stadium. Still another winner had the honor of riding in the backseat of the car that drove to Melbourne, Florida, to pick up Don Drysdale. And our grand prize winner was invited to lunch with Walter O'Malley and *twice* during the meal was permitted to say, "Please pass the salt, Walter." You think there wasn't a lot of hustle in that camp? I'll tell you one thing, they never had an incentive program like that when I was playing.

On another spring training occasion, I thought I'd liven things up by putting a ringer into an exhibition game between our Bakersfield and Albuquerque farm clubs. Fred Claire, then a sportswriter for a Long Beach, California, newspaper, but now the Dodgers' executive vice-president, had told me he had played some baseball in school and asked permission to work out with one of our farm clubs. So I put him in uniform and sent him into the game to replace Dukes shortstop Bobby Valentine.

Bobby always disliked being taken out of games, but I told him Claire was a prospect we really wanted to look at.

Fred Claire distinguished himself in the field; he didn't get hurt.

When he came to bat for the first time I was sitting next to National League umpire Billy Williams. "Watch this kid, Billy," I said. "He's just out of college and we gave him a $100,000 bonus. He could be a great one."

Fred struck out on three straight fastballs. He didn't even foul tip a pitch.

Billy didn't know what to say. He hesitated a moment, then said softly, "I think maybe you paid $999,999 too much, Tommy."

As I promised Walter Alston, I did as good a job for him as I would expect my coaches to do for me. Before games I'd pitch batting practice if the team we were playing was starting a left-handed pitcher, and I'd punctuate each pitch with a comment. "Hitting is the toughest thing to do in sports, Garvey," I'd scream. "If I throw ten pitches to the greatest professional golfer in the world, he wouldn't hit one, yet I could hit that golf ball nine out of ten swings!" After batting practice I'd hit hundreds of grounders and fly balls to fielders, using the long, slender fungo bat. I made those players work, warning them, "It's called a fungo bat because when I pick it up the fun goes out of the game," but I also tried to make it enjoyable, challenging them to catch a certain number in a row or trying to bang one off some part of their body.

When the game began I took my position in the third base coach's box. Not exactly *in* the box, but in the general vicinity of the box. I liked to move around, diving on the ground if I wanted my players to slide. I was an aggressive, gambling coach, and, like any gambler, sometimes I'd win and other times . . . Probably my worst moment came during our stretch drive in September 1974. We were tied with the Phillies in the ninth inning, two outs, Manny Mota on first base. Ken McMullen drove a line shot off the left-field wall. Greg Luzinski was playing left for the Phillies and I decided Manny could score easily. I waved him around third just as Luzinski made a perfect throw to shortstop Larry Bowa, who then made a perfect throw to catcher Bob Boone. Manny was out by fifteen feet. I wanted to dig a hole, crawl in, pull the dirt over me, and then plant it with sod so no one would know where I had been. I felt awful, terrible, and helpless, but there was nothing I could do about it. Fortunately, we won the game in the twelfth inning.

Walter never said a word to me about it.

But I continued to believe that aggressive baseball causes the defense to make mistakes. In a similar situation, we were tied with Montreal in the bottom of the ninth, one out, Joe Ferguson our runner on third base. Now once, when I was managing and coaching third base in the Dominican, Ferguson had been my runner on second base when Tom Paciorek bounced a single past the shortstop into left field. Somehow, the outfielder picked up the ball and threw Ferguson out at *second base*. I couldn't believe it. I started screaming and yelling at Ferguson. He screamed and yelled right back, "Hey, Skip," he shouted, "what are you yelling about? That could've happened to anybody!" Happened to anybody? I had been in baseball twenty-five years and I had never seen a runner who started at second base get thrown out at second base on a hit.

So this time Ferguson, the potential winning run, was on third. The batter hit a routine fly ball to the Expos' Kenny Singleton. I knew Singleton had an outstanding throwing arm. I knew Ferguson had no speed. I remembered what had happened in the Dominican. But I decided to take a chance and send Ferguson to the plate. I don't know why.

Singleton's one-bounce throw had Ferguson beaten by twenty feet. But when it bounced, it hit a rock and sailed over catcher Barry Foote's head. Ferguson scored the winning run. Which again demonstrated to me that aggressive baseball—and a well-placed rock—can win ball games.

The thing I did best for Walter was help create a loose, happy ball club. I've always believed one of the most important sounds in any clubhouse is laughter, because a team that is laughing is happy, a happy team is a relaxed team, a relaxed team is a confident team, a confident team is a winning team. Laughter is food for the soul, and I wanted any team I was with to be as well fed as I was. And Walt Alston let me have fun. We'd be on the Dodger plane, the Kay-O II, named after Walter O'Malley's beautiful wife, Kay, and I'd be walking up and down the aisle screaming, "Remember this, gentlemen of the fourth estate. Remember this, Alan

Malamud of the *Herald-Examiner*. Mark my words, Mr. Bud Furillo of
KABC radio. Listen closely, John Hall of the *Register*. I hereby predict
Bill Russell will hit .300 soon. He is capable of hitting .300 because he
has extroadinary talents . . ."

Walter would be sitting in the front seat, listening, smiling, enjoying
my performance.

". . . Bill Russell can run like a deer. He can throw like a rifle shoots
a bullet. He can swing like a major league player. More important, he
wears the Dodger Blue. There is no better trademark. It stands for speed,
strong bodies, .300 hitters . . ."

Russell would be shaking his head, his cheeks turning red, and smiling.

". . . There is no player on this team with blond or black hair. Russell's
isn't red. Everything is blue. They say blue is supposed to mean sadness,
but don't you believe it. I'm here to tell you right now blue is happiness.
That's why blue is for boys. Boys are always happy in blue, especially
Dodger Blue. That's why they called that painting a long time ago *Blue
Boy*. That's why they called that song 'My Blue Heaven.' Look at Russell.
He's an exact replica of that painting *Blue Boy*. Look at that smile. Would
you call that sad . . ."

Writers Mel Durslag of the *Herald-Examiner* and Jim Murray of the
Los Angeles Times would be desperately turning up the volume on their
headsets. But I didn't care, I continued to tell my message to the world.

". . . I'll tell you what, Bill Russell. See this watch? It's expensive. It
has everything on it. Instead of waiting until I die to will it to you, I'm
gonna promise you here and now it's yours when you hit .300. And you're
gonna do it, mark my words.

"You're gonna do it just as surely as the members of the fourth estate
will finish their stories aboard this plane. Look at that Gordy Verrell
type. Look at that Bob Hunter typing away. That's what you call dedication to Dodger Blue. That's why we took over first place in the National League today. We wanted to make their stories better. We did it
for you, Gorden Edes, of the *Los Angeles Times*, and you Ken Gurnick
of the *Examiner*.

"These great journalists deserve it! Look, all but one of them typing on
a blue typewriter. Don't give that guy any answers when he asks you
questions . . .

". . . We are going to fly over blue mountains. We are going to fly over
the blue desert. We are going to fly over the blue chips of Las Vegas. We
are going to fly over the blue pools of Palm Springs. We are going to land
in the blue smog of Los Angeles International Airport. I love the smog
as much as I love rain. Rain isn't really bigger than baseball. I don't see

why we have rainouts. Anyone in Dodger Blue should love to play in any kind of weather.

"Look at you, Ron Cey, the Penguin. I named you the Penguin because you are a cold weather man. But I have supreme confidence that you're a special kind of penguin. You will make an effort to acclimatize yourself to hot weather. You'll open up a whole new world for all those other penguins who are afraid to get out of the cold.

"We'll have penguins at Catalina. We'll have penguins at Dodger Stadium. We'll have blue penguins instead of black and white. I love penguins. That's why you, Penguin, are going to be the best third baseman in the history of the game. You don't want to let me down."

Fortunately, it was not difficult for me to carry on a monologue like this for an entire plane trip, or for four seasons.

I wasn't the only one on the team who told the jokes, or played the jokes. Sometimes, in fact, the jokes were played on me. I became the outlet, the target, the member of management on whom employees, or management, could play jokes that everyone would enjoy.

Once, for example, during my first season with the Dodgers, I found a letter from Peter O'Malley waiting for me when the team arrived in Houston. When I opened the envelope, I discovered that the first page was missing. But the second page read, "and very serious consequences involved, I'm sure you will agree, Tom, that I had no alternative but to give them the information they requested. I certainly hope that this will in no way affect our friendship. Peter."

Serious consequences? No alternative? Them? What "information"? I had no idea what this letter was about, but I was extremely concerned. I immediately called Peter's office. He wasn't there and was not expected. I called his home. He wasn't there either and no one knew when he would be back. I went to the ball park, but I couldn't concentrate. I was really worried. I couldn't even guess what this was about. I must have said a hundred prayers at third base that night, and none of them were for the team.

The one thing that never occurred to me was that this was a practical joke. I was so used to playing jokes on other people, I didn't expect them to play them on me. This, of course, was unlike the Attack of the Green Phantom, which I knew was a joke. Or at least I think I knew it was a joke.

The Green Phantom first appeared in spring training. One of my real peeves was players who spent too much time in the trainer's room. "When I was pitching," I'd complain, "the only thing our trainer had was one bottle of rubbing alcohol, and before the game was over he'd drink it."

Consequently, I rarely used the whirlpool or other devices in the trainer's room. One day, though, my arm stiffened up and I decided to give it a whirlpool treatment. Since I didn't want the players to know about this, I enlisted John Carey as a guard. "I want you to warn me if any players are coming in the locker room while I'm in the whirlpool," I said.

"Here, Tom," he said, handing me a straw, "if anyone comes in, take this straw, duck under the water, and breathe through it."

A few minutes after I got into the whirlpool, John warned me that someone was coming and I ducked under the water, breathing through the straw. Unfortunately, someone twisted the end of the straw protruding out of the water. I almost drowned.

When I went into the clubhouse the next day someone, or something, had painted across the whirlpool "U.S.S. Lasorda" and signed it "The Green Phantom."

A few days later I found a can of ant spray and a can of weed killer in my locker, with labels pasted on them reading "Lasorda's Shaving Lotion" and "Lasorda's Deodorant." Both were signed . . . "The Green Phantom."

Naturally, the entire squad was as concerned as I was about finding out the identity of this perpetrator. "I can now deduce that this Phantom has a college degree," I told the team when I found those labels, "because he spelled the word 'deodorant' correctly. That immediately eliminates half the people in this room."

The next night the Phantom removed all the furniture, including my bed, from my room, leaving a baseball, painted green, and a clue. The clue led to an abandoned storage room in which I found my furniture. The day after that the Phantom painted everything in my locker green—my shoes, gloves, shorts, my uniform, everything was green. "You have to pay the price," I said, "and I'm paying it."

Throughout the entire spring the Green Phantom plagued me. He had me called out of the Dodgertown movie theater to receive a telegram that had no message—but for which I had to tip the delivery boy a dollar. He wrote me threatening poems and he challenged me to uncover his identity. Of course, I knew who it was the entire time. I figured it out right away. But everyone in the camp was enjoying this duel of wits so much I didn't want to spoil their fun. Really, I did know. Honestly. The Green Phantom was . . .

I can't. I would like to reveal his identity, but I believe there are some things better left inside the clubhouse, and this is one of them.

The one thing Al Campanis and Peter O'Malley both requested when I joined the Dodgers was that I please, please do not get into any fights.

They pointed out that my temper might prevent me from getting a big league managing job. I knew they were right, and I told them they would not have to worry about me getting into fights anymore, those days were over, done, finished. It was different when I was an active player, or an active scout, or a minor league manager, then I was practically required to fight. "I've hung up my fists," I said.

And I kept *that* promise too, at least for the next five months.

In August, we were in San Francisco for a weekend series with the hated Giants. The hated Giants were managed by Charlie Fox. I'd managed against him in the minor leagues, so we knew each other. In the seventh inning of the Friday night game, Giants relief pitcher Elias Sosa decked our pitcher, Andy Messersmith. Both benches emptied, but no punches were thrown. I knew Sosa from the Dominican, and we had had problems down there, so I really let him know how I felt about him. I hit him with a barrage of threats, calling him every unpleasant name I could think of, some of them more than twice.

On Saturday morning, I was standing near the batting cage when Charlie Fox came over to me and said, "Don't be getting on my pitchers no more."

"I will if I want to, Charlie," I told him, "because that guy's a no-good   . He was throwing at our players all winter and he's doing it again."

"Yeah? Then why don't you say it to me? You do and I'll kick your   . How come you didn't look for me in that fight last night?"

The players around the cage waiting to hit thought we were kidding. I didn't know about Fox, but I knew I was serious. "'Cause you're too old," I told him, "but if you want me, the only thing between us is daylight." That was it. He came right at me and I took a couple of shots at him. He swung at me, but missed. Then, just as I was getting warmed up, my own catcher, Chris Cannizzaro, and Giants coach John McNamara grabbed Fox, while Giants coach Joey Amalifitano held me.

"That's enough," Chris was screaming, "that's not necessary, 'specially before a game. During the game is different." And when Fox refused to calm down, Chris added, "Come on, Charlie, don't you realize you're being restrained by two guys who were signed by the same scout?"

Other than that, though, my fighting days were about over.

Ironically, Sosa was one of my better relief pitchers when I took over the Dodgers, and Amalifitano became my coach.

As I knew would happen when I accepted the coaching job, sportswriters and fans immediately began speculating that I was in line for Alston's job. Every time a writer needed a story, he wrote some version of "Is Tom

Lasorda the next dodger manager?" I began to think my name was "heir-apparent Tom Lasorda." No matter where I went, no matter what group I spoke to, I would always be asked, "Are you going to be the next Dodger manager?" It was tough. It was hard. The Dodgers already had a manager, and he was my friend. I always responded the same way. "Of course it's everybody's ambition, including mine, to manage the Dodgers, if and when the time comes. I just hope Alston lasts a long time. I played for him six years. He's a great man to play for and work for.

"I've never been told the job will be mine when Walt steps down, but I know that when that happens the O'Malleys and Al Campanis are going to find the best man they can for the job. I just hope and pray that my contributions and dedication will warrant my selection."

I was being truthful, the Dodgers had made no promises to me. When Walter O'Malley was asked if I would succeed Walt, he said, "When Walter Alston leaves, Tommy certainly would be high on our list of candidates. He knows baseball, he knows our organization, he knows our personnel. He was a big winner as a minor league manager and he is great at teaching young men how to play this game. He also gets along well with veteran players and this is important. But he'd have to go through a screening process with a lot of other people. And if we did pick him, it would be for a variety of reasons and not just one."

I was certainly not the only candidate mentioned. For a while, Gene Mauch was supposed to succeed Walt. Then there was speculation that Jim Gilliam, who had played for Walt, managed in the Winter Leagues, and was with me on the coaching staff, might get the job. There was nothing any of us could do but wait, wait until Walt decided to retire.

To make my situation even more difficult, writers began naming me as a candidate for every managerial vacancy. At various times I was supposedly offered jobs in Atlanta, Montreal, Pittsburgh, and Kansas City. I tried to be honest with the writers when they asked me if I'd be interested in these jobs. "I've been in the Dodger organization for twenty-five (or twenty-six or twenty-seven or . . .) years and I don't want to leave. But all of these players I brought up aren't getting any younger and I'd like to manage them in the majors before they get much older. If I was offered another job I'd first have to talk it over with Peter O'Malley. If he told me to stay, I would, because I want to stay with the Dodgers as long as they want me. But I would ask him how long I'll have to wait to manage here. If it was a long time, I would have to consider other offers."

And there were other offers. I met with John McHale, general manager of the Montreal Expos, for three hours in a conference room at Denver airport. If I was not going to manage in Los Angeles, Montreal would be very attractive to me. It's an outstanding city and I have many wonderful friends there. At the conclusion of the meeting John McHale told me I'd be hearing from him in a few days.

I really hoped he would not offer me the job, it was a decision I preferred not to have to make. But a few days later I was at Dodger Stadium, preparing to leave for the Dominican to manage the Licey club, when McHale called. Peter O'Malley knew what the call was about and suggested I take it in his office. "Tommy," John McHale said, "we'd like to offer you a three-year contract to manage the Montreal team. I know you're leaving for Santo Domingo, and there'll be a ticket waiting for you there to fly to Montreal to meet our reporters . . ."

There it was. I finally had to make a choice. Take the offer and become a major league manager at a salary almost twice what the Dodgers were paying me, or wait, with no guarantee I would get the job when Alston stepped down.

I just couldn't see myself telling people about the Big Expo in the Sky. "John," I said, "you're one of the finest people I've ever met in baseball and I truly appreciate your considering me. I'm extremely honored, but I'm afraid I'm going to have to turn down the job."

"You know," he said pleasantly, "I had a feeling you were going to say that."

"Lemme tell you this though. If I ever left the Dodgers, it would have to be for a man like you. But I'm just not ready to go yet." When I walked out of the office, Peter looked at me questioningly. "I turned it down," I said.

"Good," he said, and that was all he said.

Later, when I told Al Campanis I had decided to stay in that third base coach's box, he said, "Tommy, wouldn't it have been terrible if you took another job and then saw another man named manager of the Dodgers?"

He was right, it would have been terrible. And so I waited.

But there were moments during the 1976 season that, as I was standing in the vicinity of the third base coach's box, I thought to myself, Can you believe that you turned down a job that would have doubled your salary? That you could have been managing your own club? And when we played the Expos, I did find myself staring into their dugout and wondering what it would have been like to be sitting there.

I just couldn't do it. Jo and I both agreed, we had too much love for the O'Malleys and the Campanises and all the people with whom we'd spent so much of our lives to leave the Dodgers. Now, with no guarantee, I had proven my loyalty. It was just a matter of time until I found out if the Dodger organization felt that same loyalty toward me. Deep inside, I believed that it did.

I didn't exactly wait quietly, that wouldn't have been me. Los Angeles is the entertainment capital of the world and, because I was not exactly the average seen-but-not-heard third base coach, I began receiving some attention. A lot of attention, actually.

My television career had begun in Kansas City in 1956, when I appeared on the action-packed show "Bowlin' with Dolan," and won a banlon shirt. After that, I often appeared on the local sports shows in Pocatello, Ogden, Spokane, and Albuquerque. I was a household name in Ogden, Utah. In 1972, when I was managing Albuquerque, a local station did a half-hour documentary about me. And my first national appearance came on my friend Joe Garagiola's "World of Baseball."

Joe and I had known each other for years, and once I had taken him to a party at Joe Ferguson's house. As we drove there, I told him, "Joe, I'm gonna show you something today you have never seen in your entire career in baseball."

He laughed. "I've been in baseball a long time, Tommy."

I laughed too. I knew what I was going to show him.

At Ferguson's, after I'd introduced Garagiola to everyone there, I said loudly, "Paciorek, come over here." He did. "Tell me something."

Wimpy dropped to his knees, lifted his head to the heavens, and screamed, "I *LOVVVE* the Dodgers."

"And the Dodgers love you, son," I said. Then I yelled, "Charlie Hough, get over here." Charlie came right over. "Charlie Hough, tell me something."

Charlie dropped to his knees, lifted his head to the heavens, and screamed, "I *LOVVVE* the Dodgers."

Garagiola's mouth was open and no words were coming out. I knew this was something he had never seen before. "And the Dodgers love you, too, son." Lopes. Crawford. Ferguson. Russell and everyone else there followed. And it was not a case of me showing off what these players would do for me, it was all of us showing what we could do together. And having a good time doing it. It was the beginning of an outstanding party.

The following winter Garagiola invited me to lunch. Any time anyone wants to see me they can guarantee I'll show up by inviting me for a meal. "I've been thinking about this for a long time," Joe said. That thing you showed me at Ferguson's party, can you get those guys to do it on television?"

"Joe," I replied, "I can get those guys to do it on Fifth Avenue in New

York City during the Christmas rush hour!" Garagiola showed up in spring training with a camera crew and we taped an entire show.

By 1974, Garagiola was announcing NBC's "Game of the Week," and he was trying to do some things that had never been done before. In order to give the fans a taste of what it was really like to be down on the field, he asked me if I would wear a microphone while coaching third base. Me? Talk? I would've paid for the microphone.

With the permission of baseball commissioner Bowie Kuhn, the Dodgers, and Walt Alston, I was miked during a Dodgers–Chicago Cubs game. My mike would be activated when the Dodgers were batting in the second and fifth innings. While my mike was on, the announcers would not say a word. It was just me and the entire United States of America.

Was I nervous? Did I feel any pressure? Pressure, I believe, is what you put on yourself by worrying about failure. When you know you are going to succeed there is no pressure. I knew I'd be fine, it was the players I was worried about. To make things interesting for the viewers, the players had to provide some action. When nothing's going on, third base can really be a wilderness outpost.

Nothing happened in the second inning. I did my best to fill the silence, talking about getting signs from Alston and relaying to the batter. When Billy Buckner smashed a line shot through the infield I said, "Gee, the way we're hitting the ball, they better get those married people off the infield or somebody's gonna get killed."

If the fifth inning wasn't more exciting, I realized, my show was going to close on opening night. As we came to bat in the fifth inning I could see that Cubs pitcher Ken Frailing was starting to get tired. "Put the camera on Frailing's face," I said. "Get a good look at him. There is a man who did not sleep well last night. He was awake all night, tossing and turning, worrying about facing this great Dodger ball club."

We got a couple of hits and Penguin came to bat. I knew he was going to save me. "Ron Cey, the Penguin, is at bat," I said, "and if Frailing tries to get a low fastball by him, he's going to hit it up in the seats." On the next pitch, the very next pitch, Frailing tried to throw a low fastball past Cey and the Penguin hit it up in the seats. Talk about a star being born on one pitch. Penguin hit the home run, but I got the credit for it. As he was rounding the bases, I was whooping it up for him, and as he ran by me, I said softly, so that only America could hear, "Thanks, Penguin, for making me a hero."

Garagiola's producers like it so much they gave me the greatest possible reward: They turned on my mike for another half-inning.

The success of that appearance led to others. A contestant on "Truth or Consequences," for example, was told he would be dressed in a Dodger uniform and brought to Dodger Stadium, where I would instruct him how to catch flies batted by Tommy John.

That's exactly what happened. Tommy John knocked some insect-type flies out of a glass jar and the contestant tried to catch them with a butterfly net as I shouted, "Keep your eyes on the flies, don't take your eyes off the flies."

That was a considerable advancement from "Bowlin' with Dolan," but nothing like what happened after I'd managed the Dodgers to the 1977 pennant. Then I was invited to appear on some of television's most popular programs, including "Today," "Tonight," and "Tomorrow," as well as "Dance Fever."

Los Angeles is a city of celebrities, and it is impossible to work for the Dodgers without meeting many of them. Movie and television stars are baseball fans just like everyone else. Once, for example, Jo and I were at Robert Wagner's birthday party when we were introduced to Bette Davis. In Ogden, the biggest celebrity we'd met was the owner of the big used car lot, so we were both in awe at meeting Bette Davis. "Miss Davis," I said, "it's a tremendous thrill to meet you. I've always considered you to be the Sandy Koufax of the film industry."

That was my way of saying I thought she was the very best, but I wasn't sure she understood what I was talking about until she responded, "I felt so sorry for the Dodgers last week when Joe Morgan hit that hanging curve for a home run." Bette Davis, I discovered, was almost as big a Dodger fan as I was.

The only celebrity outside of baseball we knew when we moved to California was Chuck Connors—and we knew him from baseball. But gradually we began to meet some of the people who had given us so much pleasure over the years, among them comedian Pat Henry, who was Frank Sinatra's opening act.

In 1976 the Dodgers were in Chicago and I was with Al Campanis and one of my closest friends in the world, Eddie Minasian. When Eddie mentioned that Pat Henry was also in town, we left a message at his hotel telling him where we were. About 10 o'clock that night Pat called and said, "Come over here right away. I told Frank you called and he'd like to meet you."

I didn't have to ask who Frank was anymore than I would've had to ask who Babe was. There was only one Babe, and there is only one Frank. We went right over to the hotel, and Pat brought us in to meet Frank Sinatra.

For me, this was like meeting Babe Ruth, or the President of the

United States. When I was growing up in Norristown I idolized Frank Sinatra. I was so proud of him, an Italian boy like me, the son of immigrants like me, from a poor family like me, growing up to be cheered by millions and millions of people.

Frank Sinatra, I found out, had been an outstanding Dodger fan since Leo Durocher had been one of Walt Alston's coaches. So we talked baseball for a while, and then he said to me, "You should be managing the Dodgers."

That was always a tough spot for me to be in. I didn't want anyone to believe I had anything but the utmost respect for my boss, so I gave him the stock answer, "If the Lord's willing, I will be someday."

"I'll tell you what," he said, "when you become manager of the Dodgers, I'll come out and sing the National Anthem for you."

I knew he was kidding, but I appreciated it. I've done some exaggerating in my time, but even I wouldn't tell too many people about this. They might have believed me when I said Gabby Hartnett had been an outfielder, they might have believed me when I told them about the man who drowned four yards offshore, they even might have believed that the greatest team in sports history had lost nine games in a row. But Frank Sinatra singing the National Anthem at Dodger Stadium for me? There are some things even *I* don't believe.

As it turned out, I didn't have much longer to wait. I was sitting in the locker room after a game on September 28, 1976, when someone came in, I don't remember who it was, and said, "Walt's just announced his retirement."

I took a deep breath. This was it, this was the moment I'd been waiting for. Alston's announcement took me completely by surprise, he hadn't said a thing about his plans to anybody. I just sat there. I don't know what I expected to happen. I didn't know if Peter O'Malley and Al Campanis were going to come into the clubhouse and tap me on the shoulder, or if they were going to announce that someone else had been hired to manage the Dodgers. I was caught halfway between my dream and reality. So, not knowing what else to do, I continued doing what I had been doing after thirty years of baseball games, getting dressed to go home.

Before I left Dodger Stadium that night Peter O'Malley found me and told me point-blank that I was the leading candidate to replace Walter Alston, but that no final decision had been made. He promised he would call me the following morning at 9 o'clock.

Normally, in our home in Fullerton, the telephone rings every minute, twice a minute. I usually let Jo answer it, in case the caller is someone I don't want to talk to, although, as Jo points out, we've been married more than three decades and there still hasn't been anybody who has called that I didn't want to talk to. But that morning I guarded the phone. I didn't let Jo or either of the kids use it. I just sat there, waiting. Fortunately, our phone is in the kitchen, which made the waiting slightly easier. I knew Peter's call was going to change my life. I was either going to be the manager of the Los Angeles Dodgers or a soon-to-be former Dodger coach. If the Dodgers didn't want me, I knew some team would.

I waited. Have you ever seen a telephone grow? This one did. As it got closer to 9 o'clock that telephone got bigger and bigger.

I was confident I was going to get the job.

On the other hand, Jim Gilliam was a tremendous man, no one could criticize his selection. Maybe I was a little too flamboyant. Maybe I yelled a little too much. Why hadn't Peter said something more positive the night before?

At 9 o'clock, exactly, the phone did not ring. A year later, at 9:02, Peter called and asked me to come to his office.

That was the longest twenty-five miles I have ever driven. They've got to offer me the job, I kept thinking, I know they're going to. But maybe they aren't going to offer me the job and Peter wants to explain why not in person. I tried to concentrate on keeping my car on the freeway.

I sat down in Peter's office and crossed my hands in my lap. "Tommy," he said, "we'd like to make you manager of the Dodgers . . ."

I breathed for the first time in hours. I had hoped, I had prayed, many people told me I was going to get the job, but until Peter said those words, there were always doubts in my mind. "Peter," I said, making one of the great understatements of my life, "I accept. This is the greatest thing that has ever happened to me . . ." I felt so good, so proud; my love for the Dodgers, my loyalty, had been repaid. Only in America could the son of an Italian immigrant, a runny-nosed little left-handed pitcher with a decent curveball, a player good enough only to be the third-string pitcher on his high school baseball team . . . grow up to become the manager of the greatest team in baseball.

I immediately called Jo. "I got the job," I said.

"I knew you would. I'm so proud . . ."

"I got the job."

"You deserve it, too. You worked so hard . . ."

"I got the job."

Sports reporters were waiting in the stadium club for the announcement of the new Dodger manager. Most of them believed the official announcement was only a formality, assuming I had the job locked up.

But as they waited, and waited, one writer said loudly, "Anybody see [Dodger coach] Jeff Torborg here yet?"

Finally, I walked in with Peter, Al, and Walt Alston to meet the reporters for the first time as Dodger manager. "To be named manager of the Dodgers," I began, "to replace the greatest manager in baseball . . . well, it's like inheriting the Hope Diamond.

"I believe managing is like holding a dove in your hand," I continued, "if you hold it too tightly, you kill it, but if you hold it too loosely, you lose it."

A reporter asked the question I would be asked all winter, would I continue to socialize with my players. "That depends," I admitted, "on who's paying the check. Look, I happen to believe I can be close to my players and still command their respect. I love my son, Spunky, but I discipline him when he needs it. I'll do the same thing with my players."

Another reporter asked if I hoped to match Walt Alston's twenty-three seasons as manager of the Dodgers. "All I want to do is live twenty-three more years," I answered. "I'm forty-nine now and that would put me at seventy-two and that ain't bad!"

After the press conference, I did my first interview as manager of the Los Angeles Dodgers. My friend, baseball's greatest announcer, Vin Scully, asked, "You're replacing a legend, don't you feel that puts a lot of pressure on you?"

Walter Alston had managed the Dodgers in Brooklyn and Los Angeles for twenty-three years. The only two men in baseball history to manage one team longer than that were Connie Mack, who owned his team, and the New York Giants' John McGraw. Walter won more than 2,000 ball games, he won seven pennants and four World Series. He was a certain Hall-of-Famer. Did I feel any pressure in replacing him?

"Vin," I answered honestly, "I'm worried about the guy who's gonna replace me. That's the guy who's gonna have it tough."

Walter Alston and I both had bittersweet feelings. I knew he was happy for me, but sad to be leaving the field. I was thrilled for me, but also sad to see my friend taking off the uniform for the last time. He asked me to take over the team for the final four games of the season. "But bear down," he warned me, "because these four games count on my record."

In a vaguely similar situation when I was an active player, Walt selected Karl Spooner to pitch instead of me. This time, he gave me the decision. The Dodgers won my first game as manager, beating the Houston Astros 1–0.

The telephone rang continuously for months as reporters called from all over the country. "I have a wait problem," I told them, "I can't wait for next season to get started because the Dodgers will be champions in 1977." They asked about the length of my contract. Alston had signed twenty-three one-year pacts. "I signed a multimonth contract," I said. How much? "I told Peter O'Malley he wasn't a very good businessman. If he had waited a little longer I would've agreed to pay him more." Seriously, how much? "I never looked at the figure. Let other people hold out, I'm just thrilled to be holding on."

But the one question I was asked repeatedly, on the day I was named manager, throughout the winter, and every day in spring training, was: How could I expect to remain close to my players and still command their respect? No manager in baseball history had socialized with his players the way I did, and certainly no manager had ever gone around hugging them. A number of sportswriters predicted the "Dodger Love Boat" would spring a leak the first time we lost four or five games in a row. Other people said knowingly that I had been able to get away with that kind of behavior as a coach because I didn't have to discipline the players, but I would not be able to act the same way as a manager. It was as if I were introducing something dangerous to baseball, rather than mutual respect between me and my players. It was the same criticism I had heard in Pocatello and Ogden and Spokane and Albuquerque, and I had my answer down pretty good.

"When I was growing up," I explained, "my father would put on his blue sports jacket with a pair of green pants. 'Pop,' my brothers and I would tell him, 'you can't wear that coat with those pants. They don't match.' And he would say, 'Yeah? Who wrote that rule? You show me a law in the United States of America that says I can't wear this coat with these pants!'

"I don't believe there's a law that says a manager can't be friendly with his players and still command their respect. There's no rule prohibiting me from telling my players that I think they're great, because I do think they're great. Let me ask you, if I'm invited with four of my players to speak at the Lions Club, where do I sit? Am I going to sit with my players? Of course. So what's the difference if we don't get invited to the Lions Club and just go out to eat together?"

Among the first calls I received after being named manager was from Frank Sinatra's secretary, Dorothy, asking me when I'd like Frank Sinatra to sing the National Anthem at Dodger Stadium. He had remembered, he had been serious. "Well, I think it would be great for him to sing it on opening day next season," I said, "because that's when I officially start. We can start out together."

I hadn't been kidding reporters when I told them about my "wait" problem, I really couldn't wait for the 1977 season to begin. I wasn't just taking over a team, I was taking over the team of players I'd grown up with in the minor leagues. Steve Garvey, seven years in the big leagues and still looking as if he'd just stepped off the Michigan State campus, was my first baseman. Davey Lopes, who I'd heard before I'd seen one day in Vero Beach, was my second baseman. Billy Russell, the red-headed kid who had worried about being cut from my Pioneer League team, was my shortstop. And the great Penguin, a man who failed to beat me in pool for an entire season in Albuquerque, was my third baseman. Rick Rhoden and Doug Rau, who I'd had in Triple A, and Happy Hooton, who I yelled into losing weight in the Caribbean, were three of my five starting pitchers. Charlie Hough, the former infielder who I stuck on the pitcher's mound and convinced to learn the knuckleball, was my leading reliever. And my pitchers were going to be caught by Steve Yeager and Joe Ferguson, who caught them in Albuquerque. In all, eighteen players on the roster had been with me in the minor leagues or Winter Leagues. So I wasn't just taking over a team, this was my family.

A few people were missing. Valentine had broken his leg crashing into a wall for the Angels and his career was in jeopardy. Wimpy Paciorek had been traded to the Braves in 1976. And, just after I had been named manager, Mad Dog Buckner was traded to the Cubs. Trades are made by general managers, not managers, and we needed a center fielder who could run. I came home one afternoon and found Jo sitting there crying. "What's the matter?" I said, fearful that something had happened to one of our kids.

In a sense, I was right. She had just heard on the radio that Billy Buckner had been traded. These kids were hers as much as mine, and it just broke her heart every time one of them left. My explanation that we needed a centerfielder really did not make her feel better. The centerfielder we got, ironically, was Rick Monday, who had played for me on the Dodger Rookie team I'd managed during my scouting career, and who almost signed with me. Well, I had finally gotten him.

The Dodgers had finished 10 games behind Cincinnati in 1976, the second consecutive year we'd trailed the Reds. In both seasons we'd been out in front and in both seasons we let the Reds catch us. My job in 1977 was to find eleven games.

I had no doubts we would do it, and told anyone who asked every time they asked. I knew my players were better than the Reds' players, I just had to get a little more out of them. My philosophy of managing had always been basic: If I put on a hit-and-run play, or Sparky Anderson puts on a hit-and-run play, or Chuck Tanner puts on a hit-and-run play, the success of that play does not depend on me, Anderson, or Tanner. The best we could do is get the right player up to bat at the right time. So I concentrated on getting the maximum ability out of each player.

I started by writing a letter to every player on the team. "Dear Steve," I'd write, "it is a privilege and honor to have been selected your manager. We have the nucleus of a very fine ball club. Each player is gifted with talent and will play a major role in the success of the Dodgers, but there is only one way we can win a pennant and that is for twenty-five players, the coaches, and manager to pull and work together. We have to be totally involved and totally prepared . . ."

Then I visited or spoke to every player. I told them exactly what their role on the team would be and what I expected from them. I called Billy Russell in Oklahoma, for example, and asked, "Is there a wall by the phone?" There was. "Well, write on that wall 35–45. Got that? Write 35–45."

"I got it," he said, "but what does it mean?"

"That's how many bases you're going to steal this year," I told him.

I told Garvey we needed home run power from him. "You had 200 hits in '75 and '76," I pointed out, "and look where we finished. You hit 13 home runs last year and I know you're capable of doing better than that. When you come to bat in the late innings with men on base, I don't want you thinking base hit, I want you trying to jack that ball out of the park."

"Every time you open a game by getting on base," I told our leadoff hitter, Davey Lopes, "you're going to be stealing. I want you running with reckless abandon, but I want to see more discipline from you at the plate. If you can get 100 walks, combined with your 150 hits, you can be the best base-stealer in baseball."

We'd gotten Dusty Baker from the Braves in 1976 to provide the power we'd desperately needed, and he'd hit a very disappointing four home runs for us. A lot of people were saying the trade had been a mistake, and that we needed an outfielder to take his place. "You haven't heard that from me, though," I told him, "and you won't, because you're gonna be my left fielder from the first day of spring training to the final game of the World Series. I've seen the way you run, throw, hit for power, and hit for average when you're healthy, and I know you can do it again." I told reporters that Dusty had been a great player and "we weren't guessing when we traded for him," and that I was confident he would be a great player for the Dodgers.

Right fielder Reggie Smith had acquired a reputation as a malcontent while playing for Boston and St. Louis. "Reggie," I said, "I've been watching you play for three years. I know how good you are, and I'm relying on you to demonstrate your superstar talent. I need you. I really and truly need you, and I want you to help me."

Reggie looked at me and said, "You know, nobody's ever told me that before." I knew at that moment that Reggie Smith was going to have some kind of season in 1977.

I spoke to everybody, not just the starters. I didn't want any player on the club trying to guess what his role would be. I told my reserves they were like understudies in a Broadway show. They had to understand how important their jobs were and they had to be ready to play if anything happened to one of our starters. Baseball is a team game played over a long season, I reminded them, and the best *team*, not just the best collection of players, wins.

Once everyone knew what I expected of them, I made some changes in our batting order. I moved Russell from eighth to second to take advantage of his speed and his ability to make contact and hit behind the runners. I dropped Garvey from third to fifth, moved up Reggie Smith to third, and Cey to the cleanup spot, so pitchers, knowing Garvey was following them, couldn't afford to walk them and would have to give them good pitches to hit.

On the first day of spring training or "refinement of capabilities camp," as I prefer to call it, I said, "I'm tired of watching someone else in the World Series. What we're striving for is to win the World Series. That is our supreme objective. If you players believe as much as I believe, then I have the utmost confidence we'll do it.

"Unity, hard work, confidence, and ability to execute, coupled with the fact you guys are outstanding players, will enable us to reach our goal if we're willing to pay the price. It's not always the strongest who wins the fight, nor the swiftest who wins the race, nor the best team who finishes first, but the one who wants victory the most."

From the first workout of spring I kept my eight starters together. Yeager, Garvey, Lopes, Russell, Cey, Smith, Monday, and Baker practiced as a group, played in games as a group, and got taken out of games as a group. Before the exhibition season opened, I kept them together on their own practice field, away from everyone else, like a heavyweight champion preparing for a title bout. During exhibition games, when one played they all played and when one rested they all rested. "They're the Octopus," I told reporters, "because if you're lucky enough to hold down one tentacle, another one will rise up and get you."

This had never been done before and, naturally, a lot of people knew it wouldn't work. I had them running in the outfield as a group before a game with the Reds, and my former teammate, Cincinnati manager

Sparky Anderson predicted, "By September they'll all be running in different directions."

"Sparky's right," I said, "they're going to be running in eight different directions—to get to eight different banks to deposit the money they receive for winning the world's championship."

We had an outstanding spring, winning 17 of 24 exhibition games, the best record in baseball, as well as leading the league in reporters, photographers, and autograph seekers. I tried to answer every question, I know I signed every piece of paper put in front of me, and I tried to heed the sage advice once given to me by Stan Musial. "Always stand in the middle when you're having a group picture taken," Stan the Man had told me, "because that way they can't cut you out of it."

The first thing I did when we got back to Los Angeles to open the season was move the manager's office. Walt had operated out of a tiny space barely large enough for him and one coach leaning in the door. He was happy there. I took a large trainer's room, moved the whirlpools to another empty space, and installed a desk, some chairs, a couch, a television set, a refrigerator, and a beer tap. I made arrangements to have food, I mean real food, delivered to my office after every game. I wanted that office to be a place that my players felt comfortable walking in and out of, where they could sit down and have something to eat, watch television, even use my telephone—for local calls. I wanted to create a relaxed, enjoyable atmosphere.

I hung a lovely photograph of Jo, Laura, and Spunky on the cement wall. Then I was ready to start the season.

How could any baseball season that begins with Frank Sinatra singing the National Anthem turn out to be anything but sensational? There were a lot of people watching the Dodgers carefully to see how the team reacted to me. If we had gotten off to a poor start, the critics would have been all over me. I suspect that more than one person would have said that I had been proven wrong, you just couldn't treat ball players like people.

On the very first pitch of the very first game of my very first season as Dodger manager, the hated Giants' Gary Thomasson hit Don Sutton's fastball for a home run. Some way to start a season, or a career. After that, however, the rest of the game, and the season, was tremendous. We won that first game 5–1. Then we won 21 of our next 25, giving us the third best season-opening record in baseball history. We won 10 of 11 on our first road trip. By May 13, we were 11 games in front of the second place Reds, the largest lead any Los Angeles Dodger team had ever enjoyed. Penguin, getting better pitches to swing at because Garvey was batting behind him, hit .429 with 9 home runs and a record-setting 29 runs batted in for the month of April.

"You're doing pretty good now," read a telegram from comedian Don Rickles, who had become a close friend, "but if you start losing, don't tell anybody you know me. P.S. Do you really know Sinatra?"

Not everybody was impressed, of course. Now that I had proven I could manage a major league ball club while it was winning, people wanted to know how I would react when the team suffered its first, inevitable, losing streak.

"I never even thought about it," I told a Philadelphia reporter who asked.

"You must have," he insisted. "You've sat and watched this team lose for the past two years. You must have thought about how you would handle a losing streak."

"I haven't. I don't know why you even ask that. Why think about losing?"

"Because it's inevitable," he answered.

"Tell me something," I countered, "are you gonna pay your taxes next year?"

"Sure."

"Have you thought about it?"

"No."

I smiled. "See?"

Sparky Anderson wasn't impressed either. "We've given them a good lead," he said. "It doesn't bother us. They always come back to us in July. Don't ask me why, but they always come back to us."

"Sparky's entitled to his opinion," I responded. "Opinions are like rear ends. Everybody's got one."

Sparky responded to that by calling me "Walking Eagle," claiming "He's so full of it he can't fly."

Still, we kept winning. It was a season in which I tasted the fruits of victory, and then tasted some more of the fruits of victory, and then a little more. The fruits of victory, I learned, are not low calorie. Reporters began calling me "a heavyweight among managers" as I gained thirty-five pounds. And Steve Garvey, my friend Steve Garvey, noted, "The only thing Lasorda hasn't handled this season is his weight."

Once, I remember, I was sitting in my office before a game, enjoying a plate of linguini, getting ready to throw some batting practice, when Al Campanis walked in. "Gee," he said, "Earl Weaver looks at computers before a game, my manager eats linguini."

"It's for my health, Al," I explained. "It's like a heart stress test. Let me ask you, where does Sears test its Die-Hard batteries, Malibu, California, or Anchorage, Alaska? They take 'em to Alaska and bury them in ice. Then, if they can start a car, they can start a car anywhere, right? Now if I go out there and throw 300 pitches after eating a big plate of linguini and my heart holds up, it'll hold up under any circumstances. So I'm really eating this for the good of the Dodger organization."

As I had hoped, my office became a gathering place for my players, their friends, friends of their friends, people waiting for a bus, reporters, and, naturally in the entertainment capital of the world, entertainers. On a typical night during the season it was possible there'd be more celebrities in my office than at the Beverly Hills Hotel Polo Lounge. Milton Berle, Jack Carter, Walter Matthau, Robert Wagner, Norm Crosby, Tony Orlando, Ron Masak, Vic Damone, Jerry Vale, Harvey Korman, Ernie Banks, or Gregory Peck might just walk in. It was incredible to me that these people would wander into the office of the son of an Italian immigrant, a runny-nosed little left-handed pitcher with a decent curveball, a player . . . There were nights that we had more people in my office than some clubs had in their ball park. So I began to fix up the place a little. Put some wood paneling on the walls. Threw an outstanding Dodger Blue rug with the Dodger emblem on the floor. And I began hanging up a few photographs of some of my players, some celebrities, then a few more photographs, and just a few more, maybe a couple on the far wall, two over the door, and eventually most of the four walls were covered. I did, however, restrict the wall opposite my desk to photographs of my friend Frank Sinatra.

Sinatra earned that space. Not just by attending Dodger games or singing the National Anthem, but by being there when I needed him. After my mother suffered a stroke, and was in very poor health, Sinatra found time to go to Norristown and spend an afternoon with her. I had done a lot of things in my lifetime to make my mother and father proud of me, I had married an outstanding woman and had two wonderful children, I had become manager of the Los Angeles Dodgers, I had helped people whenever I could, and I had earned a good living. But the day Frank Sinatra showed up at my house in Norristown, I was made.

A few days after his visit, he had a limousine pick up my mother and, accompanied by a doctor and a nurse, she was his guest at a concert. He gave her flowers, he took her around to meet everyone, and gave her one of the last great evenings of her life.

A few months later her health got much worse, and the family gathered in Norristown. I remember sitting alone with her, talking about my father, their life together, my four brothers and the very successful restaurant they had opened in Exton, Pennsylvania (in which they raised the price of a Tommy Lasorda Special from $3.50 to $12.50 the day we won the pennant). I told her I believed I had been the luckiest man in the world that my father had lived long enough to see his sons happy and successful, that I was proud of her and I hoped she was proud of me. Later, when my brother Joe was with her, she asked, "How much does Tommy get for making a speech?"

"Twenty-five hundred dollars," he said, shaking his head. No one in my family could believe people would actually pay to listen to me.

"Give him the whole twenty-five hundred," my mother told Joe, "'cause he just made the best speech I ever heard."

One of the people I became close with that season was Don Rickles. Although he seems hard and tough on the outside, on the inside he really has a heart of lead. Because I didn't want his feelings to be hurt when I gave Sinatra an entire wall, I gave Rickles his own corner. And, after we'd clinched the pennant, I put him in uniform one day and let him work as a ballboy. I told him I could only pay him $15 for the game, but promised him top billing over the other ballboys. That was enough for him. The primary job of a ballboy during the game is to run from the dugout to the home plate umpire to give the umpire new baseballs when he needs them. Rickles did an excellent job throughout the game; he didn't drop one ball and he didn't get lost.

From opening day to the final day of the 1977 season, we were never out of first place although we did falter a bit after the All-Star Game. In late August I felt the team was starting to coast on its 9½-game lead and called a clubhouse meeting. The meeting lasted fourteen minutes and I told them exactly what I thought of the way they had been playing ball. After the meeting Don Sutton handed me a note. "Congratulations," it read, "you have just set the all-time record by using a certain four-letter word 124 times, by precise count, in fourteen minutes." We then went out and beat the Cubs.

To make the season even sweeter, we clinched the Western Division championship against the hated San Francisco Giants. I remember sitting in the dugout, watching the final out of that game, feeling so elated, so proud. These really were the kids I'd grown up with in baseball. I'd taught Russell how to hit a curveball, I'd moved Lopes to second base, and here they were dethroning the world champion Cincinnati Reds. It was a feeling of culmination. We had finished ten games behind the Reds in '76, and beat them by ten in 1977, an incredible twenty-game turnaround. We had proven that ballplayers could be hugged and still play winning baseball.

I'd yelled, I'd screamed, I'd argued with my players. I don't keep anger inside me very well. And when we did fight I reminded them that the reason a jockey in the Kentucky Derby carries a whip is because even the greatest racehorses have to be reminded to do what they know how to do from time to time.

Every player contributed to the victory. Garvey hit 33 home runs and knocked in 115, 35 more than in 1976. Russell hit .278, the best he had ever done. Yeager lifted his average 42 points while hitting a career-high 16 home runs. Reggie Smith had the best year of his career, batting .307 with 32 home runs and 104 RBIs. Dusty Baker had a tremendous season, .291 with 30 home runs. The Penguin had career highs of 30 home runs and 110 RBI's. Davey Lopes hit .283, 42 points higher than '76, and knocked in 33 more runs. For the first time in Tommy John's outstanding career he won 20 games, while losing only 7. Burt Hooton won 12, lost 7, and had the lowest earned run average of his career to that point. Rick Rhoden had a career-high 16 wins against 10 losses. Doug Rau was 14–8, and Charlie Hough led the relief corps with 22 saves.

Not one player set a baseball record, no one led the National League in any significant category, and all we did was win the pennant. The team set two records, however. Never before in major league history had four players on the same team each hit 30 or more home runs in a season. On the last day of the season, Garvey, Cey, and Smith had their 30, Baker had . . . 29. It came down to his last at bat. Houston's J. R. Richard was on the mound. Every player on our bench was on the top step, screaming for Dusty. And when he hit the home run to set the record the dugout exploded. It was as if we had . . . won the pennant.

Our other record was really set by our fans. We shattered a fifteen-year-old attendance mark by drawing 2,955,087 true blue Dodger fans to Dodger Stadium, or what I had started to call "My Blue Heaven On Earth."

The Philadelphia Phillies had won the Eastern Division title, and we met them for the right to represent the National League in the Fall Classic. The Phillies won the opener of the best-of-five series, 7–5. I was disappointed, but encouraged by the fact that we had fought back from a 5–1 deficit to score four times off Steve Carlton. Still, we had a difficult task ahead of us, we had to win three of four games, and three of them were to be played in Philadelphia.

I wanted to give the team a lift the next day, so for one of the few times in my career, I brought a guest motivator into the clubhouse before the game, our former ballboy, Don Rickles. "Look at Lasorda," he began, "look at that stomach. You think he's worried about you? No way. If you guys lose he's gonna tie a cord around his neck and get work as a balloon."

Rickles had kind words for everyone. Tommy John, for example, was sitting in front of his locker wearing long johns. "Look at him," Rickles said, "he makes a million dollars a year and he's wearing trick-or-treat underwear.

"Lee Lacy, what're you laughing at? You're the only one on this team *owing* points on your batting average."

Rickles looked at Dusty Baker and threw both his arms straight into the air. "It's okay, Dusty, I'm clean. I'll give you everything, the house, the wife, just don't get mad . . .

"Oh, Davey Lopes, I want to tell you, it's okay. I spoke to my neighbors. You can move in Friday . . ."

We beat the Phillies three straight games, proving some teams will do anything not to have to listen to another lecture from Don Rickles.

The fourth and final game was played in a rainstorm. The Phillies' Veterans Stadium had an artificial surface, and many people thought I was making a mistake starting sinkerball pitcher Tommy John. John depended on his sinker causing batters to hit groundballs, and groundballs shot through that plastic infield. I didn't even think about not starting Tommy John. I remembered what Walt Alston told me as I led cheers from the Brooklyn Dodger bench in 1954, you go with the people who got you there. Tommy John was an outstanding pitcher who would've started that fourth game for me if we were playing on ice. He pitched a tremendous game, giving up only seven hits in winning, 4–1.

After the game, some Philadelphia reporters complained that the game never should have been played under those terrible conditions. "Conditions?" I screamed. "Are you kidding me? This is the most beautiful night of my life."

We drank champagne that night and the fruits of victory never tasted sweeter. "Tell Peter O'Malley he'd better get a vineyard," I shouted, "because we ain't gonna stop winning. We have tasted the fruits of victory, and we love it."

I had come a long way with these players, from squirting shaving cream at each other to celebrate winning the Pioneer League pennant to champagne as National League champions. "There's nobody in the world who can knock a tear out of me," I admitted, "but tonight there are tears in my eyes."

I spent half the celebration dousing people with champagne and the other half reminding my players, "Four more yards! Four more yards to shore!" We'd won the pennant, but now we had the World Series, the Fall Classic, in front of us.

It was a tremendous matchup. For the first time since 1963, the Dodgers were to meet the New York Yankees for the championship of the world. Me managing against Billy Martin, with every seat in the ball park filled and every television set in the country turned on to watch us. I was returning to Yankee Stadium, the ball park of my dreams, the place where I'd marched out of the bullpen in a meaningless exhibition game to get out Yogi Berra, the place where I'd fought Billy Martin, and Hank Bauer, and I was returning as manager of the National League champions. It was fall, and the thrill was in the air. I was going back in style.

I've been in a lot of ball games in my career. I've seen a lot of batters get a lot of important hits. I've seen almost anything that can happen on a ball field happen. Certain moments are unforgettable, of course. Reggie Jackson's three home runs on three swings in the final game of the '77 Series. Rick Monday's two-out home run in the ninth inning of the '81 playoffs off Steve Rogers to give us a 2–1 victory and the pennant. The historic confrontation between Bob Welch and Reggie Jackson in the ninth inning of the second game of the '78 World Series. The controversial play in the fourth game of the same Series when Reggie deflected Russell's throw to first base with his hip, turning the game, and the Series, around. The determination of young Fernando Valenzuela in the third game of the '81 Series when he gave up nine hits and seven walks, but staggered to a 5–4 victory. I can remember each one of those as if they took place yesterday, but don't ask me if Hooton pitched the second or the third game of the '77 or '78 World Series. After more than three decades of baseball, the details begin to blend together into a lovely Dodger Blue. Did Sutton pitch a particular game in the '77 or '78 World Series? Did that play take place during the '72 season or was it '75? Who made that catch? Monday? Guerrero? Did Fernando pitch the fourth game or the fifth game?

I do remember what Reggie Jackson did to us in 1977, though, I remember it very well. He killed us. In six games he hit 5 home runs, knocked in 8, scored 10, and hit .450. It had started out to be a tremendous Classic. In the first game we scored in the ninth to tie the score 3–3, but lost in twelve innings, 4–3. We had had some opportunities to win, but couldn't pull the trigger. In the second game, Burt Hooton pitched the biggest game of his life, holding the Yankees to five hits and beating them 6–1. So we had split a pair of games in New York, and we were going home to our stadium and our fans for the next three games. I was confident we were going to be the 1977 world champions.

It did not happen precisely as I had planned. Mike Torrez beat us 5–3 in the third game. Doug Rau started the fourth game for us and the Yankees started banging him around in the second inning. I went out to the mound to bring in a relief pitcher—and Dougie didn't want to come out. We had an argument on the pitcher's mound in Dodger Stadium in the fourth game of the World Series. "There's a left-handed hitter coming up," the left-handed throwing Rau said. "I can strike this guy out!"

"Yeah?" I replied, but not precisely in these words, "Then how come the three runners on base are all left-handed hitters?" Rick Rhodern relieved and pitched seven solid innings, but it was too late. We lost the game four, 4–2.

We were down three games to one, and two of the remaining three games were scheduled to be played in New York City. I called a clubhouse meeting before the fifth game. If we lost it, the Series was over. I didn't scream, I didn't blame anybody, I just told my team exactly what I thought of them. "You beat one helluva club this year in Cincinnati," I said. "Then came the playoffs and everybody thought Philadelphia was going to wipe you off the face of the earth. We split two games with them here in Los Angeles and nobody gave us any chance when we had to go back to Philadelphia. But we beat them there.

"Now we're two down with the Yankees and we've got to win the next three. I know you can do it. The odds against winning three games in a row are very high, but if we win today, then we only have to win two in a row, and those odds are much lower. In my heart I honestly feel we have the better ball club. I honestly feel if we win today, we're gonna win all the rest of the games. But whether we do or not, I want you to hold your heads up high. Regardless of what happens out there today, I want you all to know how proud of you I am, and I want to thank you for everything you did this year."

Davey Lopes led off the game with a triple. Russell singled him home, and we beat the Yankees 10–4.

In the sixth game, the last game as it turned out, Reggie Jackson put on one of the greatest displays of power in baseball history, hitting three home runs on the only three swings he took in the ball game, to lead the Yankees to an 8–4 victory. He hit the first one off Hooton, the second off Sosa, and the last shot, a titanic shot, off Charlie Hough's knuckleball. I knew I was watching history being made, but that didn't make me enjoy it. Charlie told me that after Reggie hit the third home run and was trotting around the bases, he was watching him and thinking, What a season that guy has had tonight.

"Don't feel bad, Charlie," I said, "that guy's hit a lot of them before tonight."

But Charlie pointed out that few of them had gone quite as far as that last one.

In the second game of the Series, a foul ball had bounced off the ground and hit my catcher, Steve Yeager, in the groin. He was in tremendous pain, balancing himself on his hands and knees, trying to get his breath back. I put my arm around his shoulder and said softly, "It'll only hurt for a little while."

That's the way I felt about losing the 1977 World Series. As I told my team, next to winning the World Series, the best thing that could happen to a team was losing the World Series, that there were twenty-four other teams who would have loved to have been right where we were. I just didn't want that loss to spoil an otherwise perfect season.

I flew home to Los Angeles, and I was sick to my stomach for a week —and I had a lot of stomach to be sick to. But once the depression had worn off, I was able to appreciate the season. The United Press International voted me Manager of the Year, which I knew really meant team of the year. The "Love Boat" hadn't sunk. We'd shown our detractors that a manager and players who liked each other could win, win often, and win big.

Naturally, a few weeks after the World Series, reporters began writing that my love-'em-and-hug-'em philosophy had worked one season because it was new and because the team had gotten off to such a tremendous start we never faced adversity. That glow would wear off, they predicted. And how would I react when we didn't win the pennant?

"I hope I never find out," I said.

NINE

•

Blue Seasoning

The Big Dodger in the Sky has seen fit to bestow upon me and mine a multitude of great moments during my years as leader of the flock. In the changing seasons we have experienced good and bad, highs and lows, ups and downs, thrills and chills, the many wins and the too many losses. We have breathed the air at the summit, and we have tilled the soil in the valley. We have walked among the stars and supped at the many tables of our brethren, the many tables, and we have withstood the slings and arrows of the vigilant scribes. We have been well rewarded for our faith, and we have had our beliefs severely tested. And yea! though twenty-four of twenty-six managers have fallen around us, mortally wounded, some of them mortally wounded more than once, we alone have survived.

We alone, except for Chuck Tanner in Pittsburgh, but he was hired a few days after we.

In 1978, we repeated as National League champions, finishing 2½ games ahead of Sparky Anderson's Reds, then beat the Phillies in the playoffs again. And again, we met the Yankees in the World Series. I have to believe if the Big Dodger had really wanted us to win that Series he would have given us a sign—and that sign would have been to make Yankee third baseman Graig Nettles sick. We won the first game. In the ninth inning of the second game we held a 4–3 lead, but Bucky Dent was on second and Paul Blair was on first with one out and Thurman Munson and Reggie Jackson due up. I went out to the mound and brought in twenty-one-year-old Bob Welch to pitch. It was only his second year in professional baseball, but we'd brought him up in mid-season and he'd won seven games, including three shutouts, and saved three more. Now I was bringing him in to face two of the greatest clutch hitters in baseball history with the game on the line. What could I say to him? I just handed him the baseball and suggested, "Throw strikes."

Munson lined out to right field. Mr. October, Reggie Jackson, came to bat. He had already driven in the Yankees' first three runs. It was the greatest confrontation I've ever seen, the veteran slugger against the kid pitcher. Fastball hitter against fastball pitcher. The ninth inning of a World Series game with the tying run on second and the winning run on first with two outs. I settled down in the dugout, crossed my arms, and stopped breathing. I was fully aware we were watching a duel that would become a baseball legend. Welch threw a fastball for strike one. Then another fastball outside, ball one. Welch was just rearing back and throwing. He wasn't going to try to fool him with a breaking pitch. This was simply heat against heat, *mano a mano.*

Welch threw another fastball. Reggie fouled it off. And another. Again Reggie fouled it off. Another. Again Reggie fouled it off. Everyone in the dugouts, on the field, in the stands, realized they were witnessing a historic moment. It could only end with a strikeout or a home run.

Jackson looked at another pitch. Ball two. Welch again went into his windup and fired. Jackson shifted his weight and swung . . . Strike three! We roared out of our dugout to congratulate Bobby Welch. Reggie stood at home plate for a moment, looking at Welch, paying tribute. What an outstanding moment.

We had won the first two games. I was confident we were going to win the Series. We would have won the third game, too, which pretty much would have locked it up for us, but Nettles made four incredible plays to take at least six runs away from us. After the game a reporter asked Reggie Jackson, "Are the Yankees better than the Dodgers?"

"If they hit the ball to Nettles, we're better," he replied. Unfortunately, for the rest of the Series, we continued to hit the ball to Nettles.

We should have won the fourth game, too. We were leading 3-0 in the sixth when the Yankees scored one run, and had baserunners on first and second with one out. Chris Chambliss hit a line drive that Russell knocked down, then he picked the ball up, stepped on second to force Jackson, and threw to first to try to complete the inning-ending double play. But Jackson deliberately let Russell's throw hit him in the hip. The ball bounced away, allowing Munson to score from second base. There was no question in my mind that Jackson had interfered with Russell's throw and I wanted to share my knowledge with the umpires. I shared it loudly. I shared it for a long time. I jumped up and down trying to share it. I wanted Chambliss called out for Jackson's interference, eliminating Munson's run, but the umpires refused to do so. Frank Pulli was the umpire at first base and I think he is an outstanding umpire, but I know he was wrong on that play. I have never been as frustrated on a baseball field. Even today, years later, after seeing the replay countless times, I'm *still* frustrated. I told Russell he was too much of a gentleman on his throw. He should have aimed directly at Reggie's forehead. Reggie may have loved the Yankees, but he wouldn't have risked his life for them.

Eventually, the Yankees tied the score. We went into extra innings, which we would not have done if Munson had not scored, and lost in the tenth inning when Lou Piniella singled off Bob Welch.

The next day was even tougher. We lost both the fifth game and the Pope. The Yankees beat us 12–2 and, in Rome, Italy, the College of Cardinals elected a non-Italian Pope for the first time in 450 years.

We lost the sixth game and the World Series the next day as Brian Doyle, a minor leaguer who had been called up late in the season to replace the injured Willie Randolph, and Bucky Dent each had three hits. Doyle, who had hit .192 for the season, the best he did in parts of four big league seasons, hit .438 for the Series. I just have two words to say about that. Brian Doyle?

In 1979 two men met on the street and the first guy asked, "How are things?"

"Not so good," the second man answered. "Business is just terrible. January was bad, February was awful, March was brutal."

"You think you've got problems," the first man said. "My whole family was in a train wreck and they all got killed. What could be worse than that?"

"April."

That about sums up 1979. Throughout the season, every time I thought to myself, things could be worse, sure enough, they got worse. Now, I'm not making excuses, but we did lose free agent Tommy John to the Yankees, and our leading relief pitcher in 1978, Terry Forster, had elbow surgery and finished the season with two saves, and Andy Messersmith did injure the radial nerve running from his shoulder to his elbow and Doug Rau did tear the rotator cuff in his shoulder and was out for most of the season and Bob Welch did have a sore arm and could only pitch once in two months. I'm really not making excuses, but that is 40 percent of our pitching staff.

And I certainly don't want to alibi, but Reggie Smith did injure his leg and neck and couldn't play after the All-Star Game and the Penguin, our leading hitter, did pull a hamstring muscle, and our center fielder, Rick Monday, did tear his Achilles tendon, but I really don't want to alibi.

We were in last place in July. I was scheduled to be interviewed on Larry King's late-night national radio show and when I got to his studio he told me he wouldn't have been surprised if I had canceled my appearance, because the team was doing so badly.

"Hey," I said, "anybody can show up when they're on top, that's easy. But what kind of man would I be if I allowed adversity to change me? This is a test of character, a challenge, a chance to show I am the same person in good times and bad times."

"That's a great attitude," Larry said.

"Yeah," I agreed, "besides, who could sleep when things are going this bad?"

In addition, we had some serious problems in the clubhouse. Before a game in New York one day I was standing outside our locker room talking to former umpire Tommy Gorman when somebody came running up to me and told me Steve Garvey and Don Sutton were fighting inside. By the time I got there, it had been broken up.

I called both players into my office to find out what had happened. Sutton, Garvey said, had claimed in a newspaper interview that Garvey was a fraud, that Reggie Smith, not Garvey, was the team leader. The two players angrily exchanged words and then started throwing punches. It wasn't much of a fight, professionally speaking, but with all the problems the team was already battling, it was the last thing we needed. Both of these men were outstanding baseball players and outstanding people, and both of them really felt bad it had happened.

"I don't care if you like each other or not," I told the entire team, "I played with a lot of people for five or six years and never went to their home or shared a meal with them because we had nothing in common off the field, but on the field we had one thing in common, we wanted to win. I can't make you like each other, but what I am asking you to do is come in here ready to play as a team. We've got twenty-five guys here, and if twelve of them are pulling on one end of the rope and thirteen are pulling on the other end, believe me, we're not going anywhere. But if we all pull together . . ."

I didn't fine either player and I didn't ask either player to apologize. But Sutton, completely on his own, decided to make a public apology.

That was not the only problem we had in the clubhouse. When a team is not winning, players get very unhappy. And just as it is impossible for every player on the team to like every other player, it is impossible to get every player to like the manager. Believe me, I tried. But only nine players can be in the game at one time, and that means sixteen other players have to sit on the bench. A lot of them don't think they should be there. I've had problems with players in my career. Every manager has. The Penguin got mad because I dropped him from fifth to sixth in the batting order without telling him. Ferguson and Monday were upset when I sat them on the bench. Every starting pitcher gets angry at being taken out of a game. Reggie Smith got mad because I had Burt Hooton bunting while we were seven runs ahead. Dusty Baker got upset when I gave *him* the bunt sign. Major league baseball players are highly competitive, often egotistical, proud men. Naturally they're going to get angry when things aren't going their way. I know I certainly was when I was playing. Casey Stengel once said that the key to managing was keeping the players on the team who hate you away from the players on the team who are undecided about you. I always figure twelve players on the team are going to love the manager, twelve players are going to hate the manager, and the twenty-fifth player is going to have a gun loaded with three bullets and three blanks.

When we returned from the All-Star Game break we had a team meeting. It was open and honest and a lot of people got a lot of things that had been bothering them off their chests. From that point on, we played exceptionally well. We had the best record in the National League for the second half of the season, finishing third overall.

In December, a Los Angeles newspaper conducted a poll asking its readers: "Should Lasorda manage the Dodgers next season?" Gee, that's kind of tough. Two Western Division titles and two National League championships in three years and this newspaper was wondering if I should be fired. Fortunately, I had learned early in my career that being criticized is part of a manager's job, and that it is impossible to win an argument with anyone who buys ink by the gallon. So I ignored the poll. Besides, I won 5,822 votes to 2,123.

Some years a team will win the pennant, some years a team will lose the pennant, and, in 1980, we tied for the pennant. The 1980 Dodgers made the most incredible comeback I have ever seen. Trailing the Houston Astros by three games, we played them the last three games of the season. We had to win all three games to tie for the pennant. And we played three of the most exciting baseball games I've ever seen, winning all three as Steve Garvey, Ron Cey, and Joe Ferguson each hit game-winning home runs to force a one-game playoff. After we had come back like that, losing the playoff game to the Astros would be like having Little Red Riding Hood eaten by the Big Bad Wolf. Fairy-tale comebacks just don't end that way.

Pass the ketchup, please. That's one of the serious problems with major league baseball, games don't always end the way I want them to. We lost, 7–1.

At our welcome-home luncheon in 1981, I promised the Los Angeles Chamber of Commerce that the Dodgers would win the world championship that season. And I was right. The fact that I make that same promise every year should in no way diminish the magnitude of that prediction. That was the year that the Baseball Players Association called a strike. This proved something I have said for many years; that without his players a manager is nothing. The managers were ready to manage, but when the players refused to play, the season had to be suspended. I spent my time during the strike going to any baseball game I could find. I saw many minor league games, I saw college games, I saw semi-pro games, I even saw a few Little League games. I was surprised at some of the things parents would yell at their children who had made an error or struck out. I wondered what they would do if they *didn't* love these kids. As I later told a group at a Little League banquet, don't yell at your children when they strike out three times—I've seen Steve Garvey strike out three times in a game, and he's being paid a lot more than most Little Leaguers.

Being without baseball in summer was like being without air, without linguini. Things got so bad I almost did housework. Fortunately, I caught myself in time. "I married you for better or worse," I told Jo, "not for dirty dishes." As I said to her when we were first married, I don't cut the grass, I don't carry out the garbage, I don't do the dishes, and I don't shovel snow. It's really for your own good, I explained, and then told her about the man in Minnesota, who was just settling down to watch a football game one Sunday afternoon when his wife screamed at him, "Get outside and shovel the snow off the driveway." So he put on his heavy coat, went outside, and started shoveling. Unfortunately, he was not used to exercise, and had a heart attack, and died. A year later his widow was in Paris, France, with his insurance money, looking at the Eiffel Tower and thinking, If only my poor husband were here to enjoy this with me.

Well, if she had let him watch that football game, he would have been.

Jo once asked me if I worried about *her* having a heart attack while mowing the lawn. "Of course I do," I replied. "That's why I bought you the power mower for Christmas."

Since the Dodgers had been in first place when the strike had begun, we were awarded the first half championship. At the conclusion of the condensed season, we played the second half winners, the Astros, in a best-of-five divisional playoff. Houston won the first two games. We were in serious trouble, no team in history had ever come back to win a divisional playoff after losing the first two games. Of course, this was the first divisional playoff. Happy Hooton gave up three hits and beat them in the third game. The incredible Fernando Valenzuela gave up four hits and won the fourth game. And Jerry Reuss gave up five hits but shut out Houston to win the fifth and deciding game.

We then met the Montreal Expos in a best-of-five series for the National League championship. The Expos had lost 18 of the last 19 games they'd played at Dodger Stadium. This time they won one of two and we flew to Montreal for the final three games. They won the third game, putting them ahead two games to one. With the remaining two games to be played in Montreal, we were in serious trouble. But before we went out to play the fourth game, Dusty Baker handed me a slip of paper with a verse from the Bible, Romans 5:3–5, written on it.

I read it to the team. " 'Suffering produces endurance, and endurance produces character, and character produces hope, and hope does not disappoint us.' " It made a difference. Not as much difference, however, as Dusty Baker's three hits and three RBIs. Hooton, who had pitched 7 ⅓ innings in winning the first game, pitched 7 ⅓ innings and won the fourth game. The fifth and final game would decide the championship of the National League.

Center field in Montreal is the closest position in baseball to the North Pole. It felt that way that day. It was cold in Canada. Reporters asked me if I thought my California team was going to be at a disadvantage because of the cold. "Only if it snows on our side of the field and not theirs," I said, but, in fact, I was concerned that the cold was going to be a factor. I had pitched in snowstorms up there and I knew how difficult it could be to play in that kind of weather. I just didn't want my players thinking about it.

"Where do you think Montreal's players are from?" I asked my team before the game. "Antartica? They're from Florida, Pennsylvania, California, and Texas, just like we are." It wasn't necessary for me to point out that we had the Penguin on our side.

But as a psychological ploy, I told my team I did not want them wearing their warmup jackets when they were introduced. I remember standing next to Davey Lopes along the third base foul line, as the wind whipped across the field, telling him, "Whatever you do, don't shiver."

Rick Monday's two-out ninth inning home run, and Valenzuela's three-hit pitching, gave us a 2–1 victory and the National League pennant. For the third time in five years, we were going to play the New York Yankees in the World Series. I was thrilled to be in the Series again, but I was elated that we were playing the Yankees. I didn't just want to win the world championship, I wanted to beat the Yankees for it.

Starting pitcher Rick Sutcliffe had been on our disabled list at the end of the season, so we decided to replace him with a relief pitcher on our post-season roster. When the league asked me to name the player I wanted to add, I said, "That's easy, Goose Gossage."

They explained that it had to be one of our players. Gossage was the Yankees star relief pitcher.

Sutcliffe was irate when he found out he was not going to be on the post-season roster. Supposedly, he came into my office, turned over my desk, and threw things around the room, stopping just as he was about to throw something at a photograph of Frank Sinatra, realizing that that was going too far.

That story is absolutely not true. Rick Sutcliffe did not turn over my desk.

Sutcliffe has always been a tremendous competitor and an outstanding pitcher. Every time he walked out on the field, he gave his team everything he had. He never shortchanged anyone. I don't blame him for being upset, I probably would have done exactly the same thing in the same situation. When he found out he was not going to be on our post-season roster he came into my office and knocked some papers off my desk. But he did not turn it over. He barely even tilted it.

I had been waiting three years for another opportunity to beat the Yankees. Brian Doyle was gone and I knew there was absolutely no way Graig Nettles could duplicate his performance in the 1978 World Series. On the fourth pitch of the first game, Davey Lopes hit a shot down the third base line. Nettles dived for it, knocked it down, scrambled around and picked it up, then fired to first to throw out Lopes.

At least I was sure Brian Doyle was gone.

The Yankees won the first two games. After the second game, someone in the crush of reporters filling our clubhouse asked Davey Lopes for about the hundredth time, "Do you think you can come back and win the Series after losing the first two games like the Yankees did in 1978?"

Davey sighed, and started to give his stock answer, "I don't have any doubts that we . . ." and then he looked up and saw that the person asking the question was Dodger outfielder Jay Johnstone.

The Yankees had won the first two games, but we were going home to Dodger Stadium for the next three games. I reminded everybody that we had been down two games to none against Houston in the best-of-five game division series and had come back to win. We had been down two games to one against Montreal in the best-of-five league championship series and had come back to win. And now we were down two games to none against the Yankees in a best-of-seven series. "Seems to me," I said, "we've got them right where we want them."

I did one unusual thing to better our chances, however. Whenever we went into St. Louis during the regular season, Sean Roarty, son of my good friend Mike Roarty, an Anheiser-Busch vice-president, worked as our bat boy. And we played well in St. Louis. So after we had lost the first two games, I called Mike and asked him to bring Sean to Los Angeles to work as our bat boy. He did, and we won the next four games.

The Cardinals heard about this and made him their bat boy for 1982. They won the world championship, giving Sean the incredible bat boy record of two world championships with two different clubs in two consecutive years.

The third game was the key to the entire Series. The incredible Fernando Valenzuela started for us. He gave up two runs in the second and two more in the third. I was on the verge of taking him out numerous times. I just couldn't. That was the year of Fernandomania. As the joke goes, Fernando did not know the meaning of the word "pressure" . . . he didn't speak English. A few years earlier, seventeen-year-old Fernando Valenzuela had been discovered pitching in the Mexican League by Dodger scouts. After one season in the minor leagues, during which Bobby Castillo taught him to throw the screwball, here he was, twenty years old, pitching the most important game of the season for the Dodgers.

Fernando was such a nice, sweet, happy, confident kid. He had pitched eighteen innings for us in 1980. In fact, I almost started him in the playoff game against Houston. If he had had one more day of rest since he had last pitched, I would've. Instead, I started Dave Goltz. So, Fernando pitched in our next game, opening day, six months later. He could do nothing wrong that season. If he had fallen in a river he would've found sunken treasure. Even in that abbreviated season he won 13 games, losing 7, with a 2.48 earned run average, leading the National League with 8 shutouts, 11 complete games, 192 innings pitched and 180 strikeouts. He also had the longest consecutive scoreless inning streak in the league that year, 36 innings. After the season he became the first player to win both the Rookie of the Year Award and the Cy Young Award as the best pitcher in the league. *The Sporting News* named him National League Pitcher of the Year, and he was the starting pitcher for the National League in the All-Star Game. It was the kind of season I didn't even have in my dreams.

I've never seen a city fall in love with an athlete the way Los Angeles fell in love with Fernando. Whenever he pitched Fernandomania took charge and people packed the ball park. I used to tell people he was really a three-thousand-year-old Inca chief sent to us from heaven by Walter O'Malley, who saw we needed help and convinced the Lord to send him down.

As much as we loved him, his impact was greatest on southern California's large Mexican community. He was the greatest hero they ever had. I remember I was jogging one day and a young Mexican boy started running with me. "Lasorda," he said, "my father is going out today to buy a radio so we can listen to Fernando pitch tonight." It's an amazing story, for only in this great country of ours, this land of opportunity, could this Mexican immigrant, a round-faced, chubby left-hander with a decent screwball, a boy from a family so poor that their alarm clock was a rooster, grow up to become the starting pitcher on the greatest team . . .

Because I spoke Spanish, I often interpreted for reporters. Once, for example, Fernando and I were on the "Today" show and Bryant Gumbel asked me to ask him how he felt about playing for Tom Lasorda. I did, he responded, and I interpreted. "Fernando feels that Tom Lasorda is the greatest man he has ever seen. He's the finest manager ever in the history of baseball. When he was a youngster all he ever hoped and prayed for was that he would grow up someday to play for Tom Lasorda."

"Wait a second," Bryant said, "he didn't say all that."

"Oh," I said, "I didn't tell you what he said, I was just telling you what he feels."

At a press conference at Dodger Stadium the day before the third game of the Series, Yankee manager Bob Lemon leaned over and said to me, "I don't know, he sure doesn't look like he's twenty years old to me."

"Lem," I said, "lemme tell you, sometimes when I see him out there on the mound, he looks like Robert Redford to me."

After that press conference, Tom Vallente of the baseball commissioner's office and I were walking on the fifth level of the stadium and he said, "Hey, Tommy, let's just sit down here for a second."

The auxiliary lights were on, casting a soft light over the empty field. An empty baseball field always makes me sad. We sat there, high above the field, behind third base. "It's tomorrow night," Tom said suddenly, "the ball park is filled with 56,000 people and you're a fan, sitting right here, right in this seat. The Dodgers have a one-run lead and Fernando Valenzuela is pitching. But the Yankees have loaded the bases with two outs, and Tommy Lasorda is walking out to the mound. Remember, you're a fan, what are you going to be doing?"

I cupped my hands around my mouth. "Leave him in, ya bum," I screamed. "Leave him in, he's pitching a good game."

Vallente continued, "Now you're the manager. You hear 56,000 fans shouting at you. What are you gonna do?"

"I guess, if he's pitching a good game, I'll leave him in."

The next night he gave up four runs in the first three innings. Leaving him in the game was one of the most difficult managerial decisions I've ever had to make. Traditional strategy called for me to take him out, but I just couldn't. I just couldn't. I knew he was throwing the ball well and . . . it was the year of Fernandomania. Sometimes you listen to your heart. He pitched into and got out of more jams than a snake charmer without his flute, but I just couldn't go out there and get him. We took a one-run lead into the ninth inning—and I heard the fans shouting exactly what I had been hollering the night before. And, in my heart, I was shouting with them. We came from behind to win 5–4.

In the fourth game I had exactly the opposite problem. Bobby Welch started for us, faced four batters and gave up three hits and a walk for two runs without getting anybody out. I took the long, slow walk to the pitcher's mound.

Bob Welch had been a hero in the '78 Series, but had suffered a sore arm in 1979. And just before spring training opened in 1980, he publicly admitted he was an alcoholic and entered a treatment center. This was long before so many athletes and entertainers began confessing alcohol and drug problems. In the three years he had been with the team I had never seen him drunk or unable to pitch, so this announcement came as a surprise to me. I thought it was a courageous thing to do, and admired him for facing his problems. In 1980, he had made an outstanding come-back in life and in baseball. So it was almost as difficult for me to take him out as it had been to leave Fernando in, but he obviously had nothing on his fastball that day.

I've had pitchers argue with me when I went to take them out. Jerry Reuss once ordered me off *his* pitcher's mound, for example. And I remember a game in which Hooton lost his composure and couldn't throw strikes. When I went to get him, he said, "That's the first time that's ever happened to me."

"Yeah," I told him, "that's the same thing Dillinger said when he was dying."

On one occasion I sent my pitching coach, Red Adams, out to talk to Charlie Hough. Charlie gave up a home run on the next pitch. When we came to bat we got two men on base, and their pitching coach went out to talk to their pitcher. Charlie yelled at him, "Tell him the same thing that Red told me!"

But most pitchers know when they don't have their best stuff. Welch didn't say a word when I took him out. Then Dave Goltz, Terry Forster, Tom Niedenfuer and Steve Howe combined to hold the Yankees to only 10 more hits, but Jay Johnstone pinch-hit a two-run homer as we overcame a 6–3 deficit to win game four 8–7, and even the Series at two games apiece.

Jerry Reuss, who had lasted only 2⅔ innings in game one, was my starter in game five. Now, I am not perfect. I sin. I use profanity. I get angry. I have an occasional drink. But I go to church and I apologize for my sins. I thought the Lord understood, but evidently he didn't. He sent me Jerry Reuss and Jerry Johnstone.

I've always believed a team needs one player with a sense of humor who is able to keep everyone happy. In the Pioneer League, for example, I had the amazing Gene "The Professor" Whillette. One day we were leading Caldwell by a run in the ninth inning, but they had loaded the bases with two outs. I had a left-hander and a right-hander warming up in the bullpen, and I took the long walk to the pitcher's mound. As I was standing there, waiting to see if Caldwell sent a left-handed or right-handed pinch-hitter to bat, I suddenly saw the Professor running as fast as he could from the bullpen to the pitcher's mound. "Skip," he was yelling, "Skip . . ."

I figured there was a problem with one of my players. "What is it, Professor?" I asked as he reached the mound.

He tried to control his breath, then said, "Did the clubhouse man remember to get soap for the shower for after the game?"

One player who can make a team laugh, *one* only. We had Reuss *and* Johnstone. Either one was one too many.

Someday, I believe, Steve Garvey will be the President of the United States. And he will be an outstanding President, too—unless he appoints either Reuss or Johnstone his Secretary of Defense. If that happens, I'm buying Russian war bonds.

When Reuss was pitching for the Pittsburgh Pirates, he once took his wife on a road trip against club rules, thereby becoming the first player in baseball history to be fined for sleeping with his wife.

Johnstone, on the other hand, used to fly with his wife's two toy poodles hidden in a carry-on case. When the dogs yelped within hearing distance of a stewardess, Jay would also yelp, then try to convince her he was working on a toy poodle imitation. Johnstone is also the player who, at the end of a serious team meeting with a drug counselor, sneezed, sending white talcum powder all over the room. About the best thing I could say about Johnstone is that he always thinks about other people. Whenever he forged my name on a dinner check, for example, he was always careful to leave a large tip so no one would think I was cheap.

Dealing with either one of them is difficult enough, dealing with both of them was a tough assignment for the Old Skipper. Once I looked up at the end of the sixth inning to see the two of them, dressed in coveralls, out on the field with the ground crew cleaning the infield. When they returned to the dugout, I fined both of them $250, then sent Johnstone up to pinch-hit. He hit a home run. When one of our announcers told the story on radio, fans began sending in donations to cover the fine. Reuss and Johnstone ended up making a small profit. I then insisted I had been responsible for these profits and made them take me out to dinner.

All of that kind of behavior was marginally acceptable. It was even acceptable when I introduced Reuss to Frank Sinatra and he said, "Pardon, I didn't catch the name?" It was just barely acceptable when they took the amplifier out of the telephone in my Dodgertown bungalow, then tied the front door to a tree so it could not be opened, trapping me in that room for an hour, saved only when our Latin American scout, Ralph Avila, heard my muffled cries for help.

All of that was marginally acceptable. But one day I walked into my Dodger Stadium office and was absolutely shocked to discover that every single photograph on the walls, all my autographed photographs of Sinatra and Rickles and President Reagan and Bob Newhart, Chuck Connors, Gregory Peck, John Beradino, Sandy Koufax, Jilly Rizzo, Don Drysdale, Walter O'Malley, Ted Williams, all 250 of them, had been taken down. And in their place hung three photographs; one of Jerry Reuss, one of Jay Johnstone, and one of pitcher Ken Brett, and a note reading, "How many games did these other guys win for you?" Now, that went beyond the boundaries of proper respect for an aging manager.

Fortunately, for them, they were outstanding players. Johnstone had the key hit in the fourth game and Reuss was my starting pitcher in game five. Reuss had won 10 games in the 1981 half-season and had been 18–6 in 1980. During that season he had pitched the Dodger's first no-hitter in a decade. "It couldn't have happened to a nicer guy," I said at first, but, after thinking about it, decided, "Yes, it could've, it could've happened to me. Reuss was tremendous in the fifth game, limiting the Yankees to five hits. Of course, Ron Guidry and Gossage held us to four hits—but two of them were home runs by Steve Yeager and Pedro Guerrero, leading us to a 2–1 victory. One more win, one more, and we would be world champions. We were so close I could taste it. It tasted like homemade lasagna.

Burt Hooton, the losing pitcher in the second game, started the sixth game for us. Tommy John, who'd pitched seven shutout innings to win that second game, started for the Yankees. With two out in the fourth inning, and the game tied 1–1, I decided to walk the Yankees' number eight hitter, Larry Milbourne, putting two men on base, but bringing Tommy John to bat. It was the third time in the Series I'd walked Milbourne to get to the pitcher. The first two times Yankee manager Bob Lemon reacted by sending up a pinch-hitter. I didn't know what he would do in this situation—John was pitching well but the Yankees hadn't been scoring many runs—but I felt I couldn't lose. If Lemon pinch-hit, John was out of the game, and he had been their best pitcher against us. If he batted, I was confident Hooton would get him out. Even if a pinch-hitter was successful, it was still early enough in the game for us to come back, particularly against the Yankees middle-inning relief pitching, which had been poor. George Frazier had been the losing pitcher in both the third and fourth games.

Lemon sent Bobby Murcer up to bat. I was glad I wasn't sitting in Lem's spikes. That was a tough decision to make, and if Murcer made out a lot of people would be questioning it. Murcer flew out to right field, and Lemon brought Frazier in to pitch.

We immediately scored three runs off him, eventually winning the game, 9–2, and the World Series.

A lot of people criticized Lemon for pinch-hitting for John so early in the game. But if Murcer had gotten a hit, the same people would have been praising Lem for his guts. Good strategy, I've learned, is whatever move you make that is successful. The best a manager can do is try to put the right player in the right place at the right time.

One night in Philadelphia, for example, I sent up left-handed batter Jorge Orta to pinch-hit for right-handed hitting Bill Russell, against the Phillies' right-handed pitcher. The Phillies brought in a left-hander to pitch, I sent right-handed hitter Jose Morales up to bat. The Phillies were stymied, because the rules make it mandatory that a pitcher face at least one batter. Morales knocked in the run, and I got credit for being a good strategic manager.

Soon afterwards, in Montreal, I sent up the right-handed hitting Morales to pinch-hit against a left-handed pitcher. The Expos brought a right-handed pitcher into the game and I countered by sending left-handed hitting Jay Johnstone up to bat. Johnstone popped out. That's what's known as being a bad strategic manager.

I knew we had the 1981 World Series won when, with two outs in the ninth inning, the Yankees trailing by seven runs, Bob Watson hit a routine fly ball to Kenny Landreaux. I just exploded out of our dugout. I was leaping in the air, I was flying. Finally, finally, we'd done it. At that moment I was the happiest man in the world. There might have been someone who could tie me, but no one could have been happier. It wasn't just winning the world championship, it was coming back from a two-game deficit to beat the New York Yankees. It wasn't just beating the Yankees, it was doing it with Garvey and Lopes, Russell, Cey, the people I'd been with for so long. We had started together in the lowest minor leagues, and together we had become world champions. The thousands of groundballs I'd hit to them, the countless hours of batting practice I'd thrown, the fights we'd had, the sad moments we'd shared, this was the culmination of it all, the crowning moment. In the clubhouse after the game I told my team that they had made the greatest comeback in baseball history, down two games to the Astros, trailing the Expos, down two games to the Yankees. I want to keep it going, I screamed as I nearly drowned in champagne, bring on the Tokyo Giants, the Japanese champions.

I was so elated that we had finally won the world championship that I spent the entire winter eating. Of course, had we lost, I would have been so unhappy I would have spent the entire winter eating.

Just before Christmas that year, Jo and I were invited to a party at the Gregory Pecks. When we walked into their home and saw Gregory and Veronica Peck, Kirk and Ann Douglas, Cary and Barbara Grant, Frank and Barbara Sinatra, Johnny and Joanna Carson, Dinah Shore, Lee Remick, Angie Dickinson, R. J. Wagner, Liza Minelli and so many other tremendous talented people, we felt like little kids. These were the people who had been providing America with so much enjoyment for so many years, and it was a tremendous honor to have been invited to the party.

After dinner, Gregory Peck stood up to say a few words. After thanking everyone for coming, as if anyone would have missed it, he said, "With all of you people here tonight, we probably could have a telethon. But there is one person to whom I want to pay a special tribute. This is a man we all respect, a man we're all very proud of . . ."

I looked across the table at Frank Sinatra.

Then Gregory Peck said, "Tommy Lasorda."

I couldn't believe it. To be singled out among all of these talented people was just . . . I couldn't believe it. I felt like pinching myself to make sure I wasn't dreaming. I stood up and thanked him. Everyone applauded. Although I was the person receiving the applause, I knew everyone was really thanking the entire Dodger organization for the year of thrills we had provided for our fans, and for the championship we had brought home to Los Angeles.

In the 1982 season, we again made the greatest comeback in baseball history. Joe Torre's Atlanta Braves opened the season with a 13-game winning streak, while we stumbled along, losing as many as we won. When we went to Atlanta on July 30 to begin a four-game series, we trailed the Braves by 10½ games. The day before, the Braves had removed the teepee of their team mascot, Chief Noc-A-Homa, from its place in the left-field stands to provide additional seats for spectators. I reminded my team that the baseball season was 162 games long, and that every team in the league, no matter how good it is, will lose at least one-third of those games, and every team, no matter how bad it is, will win at least one-third of those games. "All we've done," I said, "was get the losses out of the way first."

In the first game of a doubleheader on the thirtieth, the Braves were beating us 8–3 in the sixth inning. A loss would have put us 11½ games behind with two months remaining in the season. I like to tell people that next to General Custer, who told his cavalry troops when they were attacked by all the Indians in the world, "Don't take any prisoners," I am the world's greatest optimist. But even I had difficulty believing we could make up 11½ games in two months against a team playing as well as the Braves.

We came back to win that game, 10–9, then swept the remaining three games of the series, cutting Atlanta's lead to 6½ games. The following weekend the Braves came to Dodger Stadium for another four-game series. We won all four. By August 11, we were in first place, one-half game ahead of the Braves. We'd made up 11 games in twelve days. The greatest achievement since the Brinks robbery. Incredible. According to the record books, this was the most games made up by a team in the shortest time. It really was the greatest comeback in history. "It's like being given Last Rites," I told reporters, "taking your last breath and seeing them start to put you in the pine box—and suddenly waking up lying on a beach on a sunny day in Hawaii." By August 19, we were four games ahead of the Braves, a difference of 14½ games in twenty days. Unbelievable. The Braves finally succumbed to the demands of their fans and put back Chief Noc-A-Homa's teepee, this time adding a doll likeness of me, which was hung by its heels from the top of the teepee. Of course, I never believed in voodoo, but I did get the flu at the end of the season, and we did go on a losing streak.

The problem with streaks is that a team can have losing streaks just like it can have winning streaks. With 12 games to go in the season, we were leading the Braves by three games. We then lost eight games in a row. I tried everything I could to break that losing streak, everything. I screamed, I hollered, I tried the old sarcasm, "Who was that pitching out there against us, Walter Johnson?" or "How could you give up a hit to that guy? He couldn't hit the water if he fell out of a boat!" Although normally I'm not superstitious—I don't believe in any of that stuff unless it works—I tried sitting in different parts of the dugout, or sitting with my arms crossed, but nothing worked. I juggled the lineup, that didn't work. I held a team meeting, we lost our sixth in a row, dropping us into a first-place tie with the Braves. Finally, I did the only thing left, I threw a party.

A losing streak feeds upon itself. Each loss makes the next game that much more important, putting additional pressure on the players. They stop being aggressive because they're afraid to make a mistake, changing the way they normally play and making it even tougher to stop the losing streak. All a manager can really do as the losses pile up is try to control the way his players react. He has to prevent them from blaming each other, from blaming him, from blaming ownership, and throwing the situation into chaos. If a good team remains calm, it will eventually right itself. Once, in the minor leagues, I'd managed to relieve some of the pressure by locking my team in the clubhouse after another loss and ordering in beer and pizza. We'd partied all night and won the next day. The party I threw for the Dodgers in my office was brief, fun, and unsuccessful. The next day we lost our seventh straight. Finally, with four games remaining in the season, we started a winning streak, winning three in a row. With one game left, we were one game behind the Braves. We were playing the hated Giants, the Braves were playing San Diego. If we won and they lost we would be tied, and have a one-game playoff. I liked our chances to win—Fernando Valenzuela was my starting pitcher.

The game was tied 2–2 in the seventh inning. We loaded the bases and Fernando was the scheduled batter. I knew that if I let him hit and he made out, and we eventually lost the game, I would be criticized. Of course, if I pinch-hit for him and the relief pitcher lost the game, I would be criticized. I thought he was getting tired, so I sent up Jorge Orta to hit. Orta made an out.

The hated Giants' Joe Morgan hit a home run to beat us, 5–3, eliminating us from contention. "The defense of the '81 world championship ended Sunday afternoon," reported a Los Angeles newspaper, "not with a bang or a whimper or a one-game playoff or Fernando Valenzuela's twentieth victory. It ended with a last debate of a last Tommy Lasorda decision."

One of the things every manager must learn to deal with is second-guessing. Few people have the physical ability to come out of the bullpen with the bases loaded to strike out a good contact hitter like the Mets'

Keith Hernandez, but anybody can decide who they would call out of the bullpen to strike out Keith Hernandez. Everybody second-guesses a manager; his players, the fans, the announcers, his own family—and any manager who claims he doesn't second-guess himself isn't being truthful. I remember a game in which Tommy John was beating the Reds 7–2. Then they scored three times to make it 7–5. There were 56,000 people in the ball park telling me to take out John. Sitting in the dugout, I *almost* took him out. But I didn't, I didn't, and Ken Griffey hit a three-run shot to beat us, 8–7. After the game, Jo and I were driving home, and she asked, "Why didn't you take him out?"

In that car, knowing how the game turned out, I would have.

The hard part of managing is that you only get one guess. A manager probably makes more decisions in one game than most business executives make in a week. Some of these decisions are not going to turn out right. And when a manager makes a decision, he has to live with it. A manager can't allow his players, the crowd, the announcers, or even his wife to dictate strategy. One night, for example, Bobby Welch was pitching an outstanding game against the Pirates. With two outs in the ninth inning, he had given up only three hits and was winning, 1–0. Then Dave Parker got a hit, bringing Willie Stargell to the plate. Stargell was a left-handed hitter and I wanted a left-hander pitching to him. So I went out to the mound. "Bobby," I said, "I'm bringing in Howe to pitch to Stargell."

Bobby smiled. "There's 56,000 people in the stands, and every one of them is gonna boo you when you make that move, you know."

"Yeah, I know," I said, "but if I start managing the way they want me to, it won't be long before I'm sitting up in the stands with them."

"Let's walk off together," Bobby said, knowing the cheers for his performance would drown out the boos for my decision.

I shook my head. "Go get your applause." He walked off to a standing ovation. I walked off to a boo-shower. I sat in the dugout praying Steve Howe would retire Stargell. Willie hit an easy groundball and we won the game.

A good second guess is never wrong. First guessing is what's tough. I know that if I had a difficult decision to make in a ball game, and I could stop the game to ask each of the 56,000 people in the ball park what I should do, I would get maybe 25,000 different answers. But if I waited until after the play, every one of those people would be able to make the correct decision.

Only once have I challenged a second guess. I was managing Escogido in the Dominican, and we were tied with Santiago in the ninth inning. Santiago had the potential winning run on second base with two outs.

Right-hander Charlie Hough was pitching for us, switch-hitter Lou Camilli was the batter, and right-handed hitter Gene Clines was on deck. Do I pitch to Camilli, or do I walk him to set up a force at second and third and pitch to Clines? With a knuckleball pitcher, lefty-righty percentages don't really matter. I felt Clines was the much better hitter, so I told Charlie to pitch to Camilli. Camilli singled to right field to win the ball game.

The next day I was in our general manager's office, and he asked me why I hadn't walked Camilli. "Because Clines is the much better hitter," I explained.

"But Clines is a right-handed hitter, you would have been much better off having Hough pitch to him."

"That's not true," I said. "My job is to have my pitcher throwing to the inferior hitter."

"But it would have set up a force at second . . ."

That night we were playing in San Pedro. In the sixth inning Sandy Vance was beating them, 3–2, but they had a runner on second with two out. The batter was Cesar Cedeno, an outstanding hitter. Before Sandy got ready to pitch, I jumped out of our dugout and went over to the general manager's seat. "What do you want me to do?" I demanded. "Pitch to Cedeno or walk him?"

He jumped back. "I don't know," he said, "I don't know. You're the manager."

"That's right," I said, "I'm the manager. And I've got to make that decision before he gets to the plate. After Camilli got that hit last night, even my wife could have told me I should've walked him." He never again complained about a decision I made that season.

Do I make mistakes? Let me put it this way. One game, when I was managing Spokane, Ron Cey had hit three home runs against Eugene, but we still trailed by three runs in the ninth inning. With two outs, though, we had the bases loaded, bringing the Penguin to bat. Our runner at third base was Marv Galliher. I called time, and said to him, "Listen, I've got this feeling that Penguin's going to hit another home run to win the ball game. So even if the ball gets by the catcher, I don't want you running. Your run means nothing, so don't go under any circumstances, got it?"

On the next pitch, the very next pitch, the ball got by the catcher and Galliher took off. He was out by ten feet. In the clubhouse I was all over him, screaming, yelling, swearing, "How could you do that?" I yelled. "How could you do that? I told you, didn't I, even if the ball gets by the catcher, don't run. I told you that, right?"

"Well, Skip," he said softly, "you gotta remember one thing."

I wanted to hear this. "What's that?"

"Even the best of them make mistakes."

I think every man who has ever managed a baseball team would agree with that.

The first game of the 1982 season was the first game I'd managed in the big leagues without Davey Lopes on my team. And the last game of the season was the last game Steve Garvey and Ron Cey ever played for the Dodgers.

Jerry Reuss, who pitched for the Cardinals, Astros, and Pirates before becoming a real major leaguer and joining the Dodgers, once made a list of things a player could do to guarantee he will be traded: He could buy a house, order an extra-large box of address labels, buy a piece of jewelry for his wife with his uniform number on it, buy clothing accessories that match the team colors, or have the general manager tell him he plays out the remainder of his career in that city.

Of course, there are a few other ways in which a player can leave a team. He can have a couple of bad years in a row, he can play out his contract and choose to become a free agent, or he can grow old.

Seeing players traded, released, or deciding to leave a team is part of baseball. I know it is because I've told that to Jo many times. But when someone you've lived with, laughed with, cried with—someone you care about—leaves the team, it hurts. And in Jo's and my case, we didn't just lose a player, we lost his entire family. We were just as close to Sharon Hough and Mary Ann Russell and Ginger Hooton and Fran Cey and Harriet Baker and Yvonne Stephenson and their children as we were to the players. It hurt me to see Mad Dog Buckner be traded. It hurt me to see Wimpy Paciorek be traded. And Valentine and Vance and Fergy and Dave Stewart and all the rest of them. These weren't just people who had played for me, these were my close friends. They're still my close friends—everyplace but on the field.

Seeing Charlie Hough leave the Dodgers was as tough a moment as I've had in baseball. But Charlie was not pitching well for us anymore. The fans were booing him when he warmed up. "It wasn't all Charlie Hough's fault," a sportswriter wrote after he'd lost a game. "He didn't put himself in." I knew Charlie could still pitch, but I also realized it wasn't going to be in Los Angeles.

Al Campanis really tried to find another team that wanted him, but it was not a seller's market. General managers were not anxious to sign a knuckleball pitcher who was not pitching well. Paul Richards once said, "You just don't want a knuckleballer pitching for you. Of course, you don't want one pitching against you either." Finally, at the 1980 All-Star

Game held at Dodger Stadium, I ran into the Texas Rangers' general manager, Eddie Robinson. "Eddie," I told him, "you and I were teammates, you know I wouldn't try to fool you. Charlie Hough is available and nobody wants him. You take him, all it's gonna cost you is the waiver price. Please, I'm asking you, take him, because believe me, he can still pitch. I'll stake my reputation on it. He just needs a change of scenery."

"Tommy," Eddie said, "your word's good enough for me. I'll give him a shot." I wanted to kiss him, but he's 6'3" and probably didn't want to be kissed, so we shook hands instead. Since then, Charlie has been the Rangers' most effective pitcher, and in 1984 led their staff with 16 wins and was second in the American League with 266 innings pitched, one inning less than Toronto's Dave Steib.

Soon after the deal was announced, I was sitting on the floor at Charlie's house, playing with his daughter, Tracy. "Uncle Tommy," she said, looking up at me with the biggest, prettiest eyes I've ever seen, "I have to ask you a question."

"What is it, sweetheart?"

"You didn't trade my daddy away, did you?"

"No, I didn't trade your daddy," I said.

"Well, can you get him back then?"

Believe me, it hurts. But players do get older and they can't quite get the bat around on the good fastball or they're one step short of reaching the groundball up the middle. Mr. Rickey believed a player's peak years were from ages twenty-seven to thirty-four. He always said you'd rather send a player away a year too early than a year too late, because the level of ability drops off quickly.

Our infield—first baseman Steve Garvey, second baseman Davey Lopes, shortstop Bill Russell, and third baseman Ron Cey, the Penguin —played together nine years, longer than any infield in the history of baseball. It was a makeshift infield. Garvey had been moved from third to first, and Lopes and Russell moved in from center field, and as a group their defensive play received a lot of criticism. All they did was win the pennant in 1974, 1977, 1978, and 1981, and the World Series in 1981. They always did the job when it had to be done, and I was always proud of them, as a unit and as individuals. But they were getting older and we had to begin restructuring the team.

We didn't want to replace all of them at the same time. Davey Lopes, whose .831 base-stealing percentage as a Dodger was the best in baseball history, was the first to go. He was thirty-five years old and his batting average nosedived from .251 in 1980 to .206 in 1981. And we had two outstanding prospects, Steve Sax and Jack Perconte, waiting in the minor leagues. We had to make the move. We traded him to Billy Martin in Oakland. It hurt to see him go, and part of me went with him.

Steve Garvey's contract expired at the end of the 1982 season, making him a free agent. He had the option of signing with the Dodgers or any other club that selected him in the free agent draft. He had played twelve years for the Dodgers, 1,107 consecutive games, and there wasn't anything he couldn't do well, on or off the field. Once, for example, Tom Niedenfuer was having a post-game meal and something got caught in his throat. Garvey performed the Heimlich maneuver and possibly saved his life. The way I feel about Steve Garvey is this: If he were dating my daughter and came to the house to pick her up, as soon as he got inside I'd lock the doors and make sure he couldn't get out.

We were so close I'd let him take me out for dinner on Father's Day. I hoped he would re-sign with the Dodgers, but I was careful not to get involved. I knew he was going to make his decision very carefully, and I respected him enough to respect whatever decision he made. Before the final game of the 1982 season, in San Francisco, I went over to him and said, "I don't know which way you're going to go, but I want you to know how much I appreciate everything you've done for me and the Dodgers, and that whatever you do, my love is with you."

I felt that the Dodgers made him an excellent offer. I believe it was $4 million, plus options, for five years. But Steve wanted parity with the other top players in baseball. He wanted a Dave Winfield, Bruce Sutter-type contract. The Dodgers made their final offer before the free agent draft and when Steve and his agent turned it down, we did not retain rights to re-sign him. That is the Dodgers' philosophy. The reason behind that is simple. If the team cannot satisfy a player when no one else is bidding, there is little chance it will be able to do so after other teams get involved. Steve Garvey eventually signed with the San Diego Padres. Were we right to let him go? Without Steve Garvey, in 1983, we won the Western Division title. Of course, with Steve Garvey, in 1984, San Diego won the National League pennant. I know it hurt to see him go, and part of me went with him.

However, the following season I was sitting at the table we'd often shared in an Italian restaurant in St. Louis and I looked up to see a photograph of Garvey hanging above the table. And on the photograph he had written, "Tommy, I'm still watching over you!"

The Penguin was traded to the Chicago Cubs after the 1982 season. He had been the forty-fifth man to try to play third base for the Dodgers since the move to Los Angeles in 1958, and he only managed to last ten seasons. In that time he hit 228 home runs, the most ever by a Los Angeles

Dodger and fourth on the all-time Dodger list. He was also ninth among the Dodgers' all-time total-base leaders, eighth in extra-base hits, and ninth in runs batted in. But he never did manage to beat me in pool. Were we right to trade him? Without the Penguin, in 1983, we won the Western Division title. Of course, in 1984, with the Penguin and Lopes (for the last part of the season), the Cubs won the Eastern Division title, only to lose the league championship series by one game to Garvey's Padres. Did it hurt to see the Penguin go? Do you cry at the end of "Lassie"?

Someday, I realize, I'll have to go too. I'll sit in the clubhouse knowing I'm taking off the uniform I love so much for the final time. And it'll hurt to see me go most of all.

Actually, I've already started preparing for that day. The O'Malley family—Walter and Kay, when they ran the club, and now Peter and Annette—has always made sure that those people who have given of themselves to the Dodgers are well taken care of. They've quietly helped so many people in so many ways, among them Roy Campanella, Maury Wills, Goldie Holt, and Walter Alston. So, recently I gave an autographed photo of myself to Peter's children, Kevin, Brian and Katherine. "Hang this over your beds, where you can look up and see it every night," I told them, "because I'll be retired by the time you're ready to take over the club and I don't want you to forget me. I want you to be just like your dad and your grandfather, and take care of me." This is what is known as insurance.

So we opened the 1983 season without Garvey, Lopes, and Cey. Charlie Hough was gone. Terry Forster was gone. Reggie Smith was gone. Only Billy Russell and Steve Yeager remained from my minor league days. "Now we'll see how good a manager Lasorda really is," one sportswriter wrote. "Now he really has to manage." Just what did this man think I'd been doing for the past six years?

The transition period was a difficult one. We had a lot of problems trying to overcome the loss of so many outstanding players in such a brief period of time. I used more than 100 different starting lineups during the season as we scrambled to find the right combination. We suffered through an incredible throwing slump by Steve Sax, who had replaced Lopes at second base. We suffered through the disappointing debut of Greg Brock, a Rookie of the Year candidate who hit only .224 after hitting .310 at Albuquerque a year earlier, and a season-ending injury to catcher Mike Scioscia, and a prolonged batting slump that saw Dusty Baker's average drop from .300 in 1982 to .260 in 1983, and a pitching slump in which Jerry Reuss went ten weeks without winning a ball game, and the drug problems of our top reliever, Steve Howe, that resulted in him spending time in a rehabilitation center and later being suspended twice by the ball club, and the personal problems caused by the deaths of the fathers of three players on the team.

At one point during the September stretch run I fielded the youngest team I've managed since I had the kids in Ogden: twenty-three-year-old Steve Sax, in his third season, was at second base; twenty-three-year-old rookie Dave Anderson was the shortstop; twenty-four-year-old rookie R. J. Reynolds was the left fielder; Greg Brock, a twenty-six-year-old rookie, played first; twenty-three-year-old Mike Marshall in right field was in his second big league season; twenty-four-year-old rookie Jack Fimple was catching, and twenty-four-year-old Alejandro Pena, a third-year player, was pitching. Only center fielder Derrel Thomas, a thirty-two-year-old in his twelfth season, and twenty-eight-year-old Pete Guerrero, in his fifth major league season, but his first at third base, were really veterans. We lost that game in extra innings to Montreal, but as Expos broadcaster Duke Snider commented, "It took the Expos twelve innings to beat Albuquerque and San Antonio."

We were so young I called the team the Baby Blues. I knew we were going to make mistakes, and I was not disappointed. Our infield made 95 errors. We were like the four-year-old who one day can remember his ABCs and name the capital of Pennsylvania, and the next day cannot remember his ABCs, can't name the capital of Pennsylvania, and knocks over the filled ashtray onto the white carpeting.

I saw things happen that year that I had never even imagined possible. I remember playing the Mets one day. We had Greg Brock at third, Derrel Thomas on first, and Bobby Welch was the batter with one out. Welch hit a groundball to Mets shortstop Bob Bailor, who threw to catcher Ron Hodges. Instead of trying to score, Brock stopped halfway down the third base line and started retreating toward third. Hodges followed him. Meanwhile, Thomas, believing Brock would be tagged out, went all the way to third. Brock managed to get back to third safely, only to find Thomas standing there. Hodges tagged Brock—the wrong man to tag because Brock was entitled to the base—and Thomas took off for second. Thomas got back to second just as Bob Welch was arriving there. Welch turned around and took off for first. Hodges just stood near home plate holding the ball, and Welch made it back to first base. We had successfully run the bases backwards.

There were moments I really missed Garvey and Cey and Lopes.

Steve Sax then singled in two runs.

The strangest problem of the year, maybe of any year, was Sax's inability to make routine throws from second to first base. I don't mean difficult across-the-body throws, or double-play pivot throws, I mean the basic, simple, easy routine throw, toss, lob from second to first. His throws went over the first baseman's head, or wide of the base, or bounced on the ground. If he were in a throwing booth at a carnival, not only wouldn't he have won the kewpie doll, he would have been sued for personal injury by the manager of the next booth.

On the opening day of the season, Walt Alston was to have thrown out the ceremonial first ball, but he was sick and couldn't make it, so we chose a pre-school boy of about six to throw out the first ball. His throw went wild. Later, we began to think it must have been Sax's son.

Steve Sax is an outstanding young player and had a tremendous offensive season, leading the club with 94 runs scored, 175 hits, and 56 stolen bases, but his inability to make that easy throw drove me crazy. One day, after he'd thrown away a routine groundball to cost us the game, I told reporters that the only paper that could print what I was really thinking was the *National Enquirer.*

I had coaches Monty Basgall and Joey Amalfitano hitting him fifty grounders in pre-game practice every day, and before the game he was great. He made no errors before the game began. But as soon as the game started he'd field a groundball and throw it directly to a fan with a big glove sitting behind first base. If we had spent as much time studying to be doctors as we did working with Saxy on that throw, we would all be surgeons today.

Finally, one day in St. Louis, I told Sax, "Come on, take a walk around the field with me." As we strolled around the ball park, I said, "I want to ask you a question, Stevie. How many people do you think there are walking the streets of the United States who can hit .280 in the big leagues?"

"Not many," he said.

"That's right," I agreed, "and you're hitting .283. Now, lemme ask you, how many people are there walking the streets of the United States who could steal fifty bases in one season in the big leagues?"

He shook his head. "Very few."

"That's right, very few, and you've got thirty-seven already, so there's no question you're gonna reach fifty. But lemme ask you one more thing, how many people are there walking the streets of the United States who can throw the ball from second to first?" I didn't wait for his answer. *"Millions!"* I screamed. *"There are millions of them.* There are 10 million women who can do it and you're a big league ballplayer and you can't do it? I don't understand."

Obviously, it was a psychological problem. Like a team suffering through a losing streak, every bad throw made the next throw even more difficult. He began thinking instead of allowing his natural reactions to take control. Eventually, he overcame the problem himself, simply by convincing himself he would have no problems with the throw, and made only six errors the entire second half of the season.

Veterans Pedro Guerrero, Kenny Landreaux, Billy Russell, and second-year player Mike Marshall kept us in contention when the kids foundered. On August 9 we were 5½ games behind the Braves. I called a clubhouse meeting. Before I began, I sent our young batboys outside because I didn't want them to learn any new words. Some of our players were so young I considered sending them out of the room too, but they needed to hear what I had to say. Basically, in my own language, I told them that we were not playing up to our potential and needed to get some sort of streak going. Then the veterans interpreted for the younger players: He says, they explained, that we are not playing up to our potential and need to get some sort of streak going.

So we finally got a streak going, we lost two in a row. Naturally, this was not the type of streak I had in mind. I called another meeting. This time, I didn't hold back. "You people are playing like   ,
              ,   , and   .   and why you
         people   insist   !   believe   in   yourselves
because you're the   best team in the   league! . . ."
That speech lasted eleven minutes and veterans clocked me at 12 UWPM, unprintable words per minute, or 132 for the speech, a new record.

That same day we instituted the Mr. Potato Head Most Valuable Player Award. Obviously, as I have the clubhouse meal catered, I believe in keeping the clubhouse atmosphere loose and cheerful. I knew this would be particularly important this season because so many of our youngsters had never experienced the day-to-day pressure of a pennant race. Different teams will do different things to keep the clubhouse cheerful. One year, for example, we convened a kangaroo court after each victory, during which fines would be levied for things such as missing a sign; giving the wrong sign; saying the wrong thing; making a stupid play; putting chocolate brownies in Steve Garvey's glove when he was at bat so that when he stuck the glove under his arm and held it there with his elbow while putting on his sunglasses the brownies squashed, then blaming it on Jerry Reuss; or stealing the barbecued chicken out of the manager's office (considered a High Crime). The perpetrators of that last felony, Steve Howe and Fernando Valenzuela, got their just desserts thanks to fine work done by my attorney, F. Lee Boomer Yeager.

Mr. Potato Head is a children's toy in which plastic arms, legs, eyes, ears, nose, mouth and other body parts are stuck into a raw potato to create a face and body. Pitcher Joe Beckwith had created a Mr. Potato Head to look like our bald assistant trainer, Paul Padilla, and Rick Monday instituted the award. After every victory, Paul Padilla would put a smile on Mr. Potato Head's face, raise his arms triumphantly, and award him for safekeeping to that player who had contributed most to the win. After every loss, Paul would turn the smile upside-down, creating a frown, lower the arms, and stick Mr. Potato Head in the corner by himself.

No, I do not know why Joe Beckwith was playing with Mr. Potato Head.

As soon as the award was instituted we won 13 of 15 games, moving into first place. Naturally, the reporters wanted to publicize this outstanding contribution made by a potato, and interviewed him. Mr. Potato Head was quoted as saying he preferred to be called Spud, and he was worried that the strain of a pennant race was making his skin shrivel. Told that one solution might be for him to get out of the clubhouse and into the sun, he replied he would love to, but he was afraid of peeling.

We beat the Braves by three games to win our fourth title in seven years. The day we clinched the pennant, I was awarded Mr. Potato Head for the first time, the very thing he had been dreading all season. Unfortunately, we did not see eye-to-eyes and, when I was invited to a post-season celebrity roast, he disappeared.

During the pennant-clinching celebration Bobby Welch dumped an entire chocolate cake on my head. This is what is known as a dilemma. I did not want a chocolate cake dumped on my head. On the other hand, it *was* a chocolate cake.

We just didn't hit in the National League playoffs against Philadelphia, scoring only eight runs in four games, half of them in our only victory. The Phillies beat us three games to one for the championship. Besides receiving the prestigious Mr. Potato Head Most Valuable Player Award, I was also honored as the AP, UPI and Baseball Writers' Association Manager of the Year.

As usual, at the end of the season I went into Peter O'Malley's office to discuss my contract for the following year. I'm fortunate enough to be represented in these negotiations by the person who has my best interests at heart—me. I don't use an agent, but I don't see anything wrong with athletes being well represented. If I were going to buy a house, I'd use a qualified real estate agent; if I had to go to court, I'd hire a good attorney. But when it comes to knowing what makes me happy, I've got the expert.

Peter O'Malley has always been very fair to me. When he hired me to manage the Dodgers he gave me a very generous salary, more than I ever thought I'd make in baseball. Each year since then I've received a nice raise. I used to tell people I had an attendance clause—I had to attend every game. Peter and I have never had an argument about my contract. Whatever he wanted to give me, I took, and I was honored to get it. That might not be true if I were with another organization, but it was the Dodgers who gave me $500 to get married knowing I might never throw one major league pitch for them, and it was the Dodgers who gave me the chance to stay in baseball when my playing days were over.

At the end of the 1983 season stories began appearing in the media that George Steinbrenner was going to offer me a multiyear contract to manage the Yankees. That simply wasn't true. The media also reported that I was part of a group planning to buy the Chicago White Sox. Me buy a baseball team? "If it took a nickel to get around the world," I replied to that rumor, "I couldn't get out of sight."

The Dodgers had never given a manager more than a one-year contract, and that's what I expected to be offered and that's what I intended to sign. "I don't mind one-year contracts," I'd previously told reporters. "I don't like tying myself down to one organization for a long period of time."

"You did an excellent job this year," Peter O'Malley began as I sat in his office. We talked about the '83 season, what went right, what went wrong, and what we needed to do to prepare for the 1984 season. Then he simply offered me a three-year contract to manage the Los Angeles Dodgers and I accepted. I was extremely proud to have received the first multiyear contract in Dodger history and I said so. When I was managing in the Caribbean, instead of signing contracts, the owner of the club and I would each spit in our hands and shake. This time I grabbed a pen and signed as quickly as I could.

Naturally, I was thrilled at the big numbers on the contract. The Dodgers had made me one of the highest, if not the highest, paid manager in the game. The amount of money is nice, very nice, but it is not the most important thing to me. When I was playing for whatever salary they gave me, and there were times I did ask for more, I was the happiest man in the world. When I was scouting for $6,500 a year I was the happiest man in the world. When I was managing in the Pioneer League for $7,000 a year I was the happiest man in the world. When I was managing in Triple A for $9,000 a year I was the happiest man in the world. And when I was coaching for Walt Alston for $25,000 a year I was the happiest man in the world. Because I was doing the thing I really wanted to do. So getting a big contract to manage the Dodgers was not going to make me unhappy.

At the press conference announcing my deal I said, "If Peter had offered me a one-year contract that would have been fine because that's what I had for seven years. It doesn't make any difference. I love my job. The one thing that was impressive to me was that they showed me how much they love me."

Someone said that the multiyear contract represented security. "All I got," I said to that, "was a guarantee that they are going to pay me for three years. Security is something you have to find within yourself. I've been with the Dodgers thirty-five years, that's pretty good security."

Another reporter asked how I felt about the huge salaries players are receiving, compared to what managers are getting. "First of all," I said, "a fan has yet to be found who will buy a ticket to see a manager manage. And second, I've had my turn at earning more than my players. When I was managing them at Spokane, Davey Lopes, Ron Cey, Steve Garvey, and Bill Russell were making maybe $500 a month, while I was making $800. So you can't say I haven't had my inning."

Armed with my brand-new contract and a young team that had gained invaluable experience in 1983, I was really optimistic when the 1984 season began. But early in 1984 two men met on the street and the first guy asked, "How are things?"

"Not so good," the second man answered. "Business is just . . ." Did you ever have one of those years? Everything went wrong in 1984. At various times we had fourteen different players on the fifteen- or twenty-one-day disabled list, and that doesn't include less serious injuries. We had seven pitchers miss starting assignments. Steve Howe, our top reliever in '83, had been suspended from baseball for one year because of his drug problem, and Tom Niedenfuer, who we expected to take his place, missed 77 games because of various injuries. Our bullpen saved 13 fewer games in 1984 than it had the previous season, and we finished in fourth place, 13 games behind pennant-winning San Diego.

Things got so bad that one night in San Diego the Padres' ground crew cart ran out of gas as it cleaned the infield. Bill Russell hurt his back in batting practice. The only good news was that the many injuries gave us the opportunity to bring up some of our younger players from the minor leagues and evaluate them in big league competition. The bad news was that we found out most of them weren't ready for big league competition. We had to use so many young players that one day, when someone brought a seven-month-old baby into the clubhouse, I looked at him and asked, "Who's that? My new second baseman or my new shortstop?"

At one point in the season we recalled Jack Fimple, Gil Reyes, Larry White, and R. J. Reynolds from Albuquerque. Everybody arrived except Fimple; he had missed the flight to Los Angeles. I was furious. He showed up a few hours later and came walking slowly into my office. He knew I was going to blast him. "Before you say anything," he said, cutting me off, "read this." Then he handed me a note.

"Dear Mr. Lasorda," the note read, "I want to verify what happened to Jack Fimple. He was in my cab on the way to the airport, and we blew out the motor and I wanted you to know why he's late." It was signed, "A cabdriver."

I didn't say a word to Fimple. How did I know the note was really written by a cabdriver? I didn't. But in all the years I've been in baseball, that was the only time I'd ever heard of a player reporting late and bringing a note from his cabdriver. Even if it wasn't true, it was such an outstanding excuse, that it had to be worth something.

We couldn't even play a foul popup correctly. We were in Cincinnati, beating the Reds by a run with one out in the ninth inning. Cincinnati's Duane Walker was on second and Tom Foley hit a foul popup down the right-field line. Kenny Landreaux caught it and threw to second to try to catch Walker off the bag. His throw sailed past second baseman Steve Sax, past shortstop Dave Anderson, and rolled down the left-field foul line. This is when things really started to get interesting. Twenty-three-year-old rookie third baseman German Rivera and twenty-three-year-old second-year player Candy Maldonado collided going after the ball, and both were briefly knocked out. By the time twenty-three-year-old rookie pitcher Ken Howell, our second leading reliever with six saves, retrieved the ball, Walker had scored the tying run.

The question should not be Why do I have gray hair, but rather Why do I have any hair left at all?

Fortunately, we won *that* game in the tenth inning.

I wasn't sleeping, I was barely talking, I was only eating three meals a day, and I just couldn't take it anymore. I decided it was time to bid farewell to this outstanding world. I went to say good-bye to my coach, my friend Joey Amalfitano. "I just can't take it anymore, Joey," I told him, "I think it's come that time to end it all."

"Don't do that, Skip," he said, "there's always hope." Then he told me about an organization called Suicides Anonymous. Anyone who is contemplating suicide is supposed to call them up, and they will discuss your problems and attempt to talk you out of it. Joey gave me the number.

So I called. The counseler asked me what my problems were and I began to tell him about all our injuries, I told him about the mistakes our young players were making, I told him how ineffective our bullpen had been, I told him . . .

Finally, the counseler stopped me. "I think I understand what you're saying," he said, "and I want to tell you, after listening to your problems, I think you're doing the right thing."

The one thing we did prove in 1984 is that the Dodger fans are the most loyal in the sports world. Some 3,134,824 came to Dodger Stadium to suffer with me. That's the fifth-largest season attendance in baseball history, behind the 1980 Dodgers, the 1978 Dodgers, the 1983 Dodgers and baseball's all-time attendance leader, the 1982 Dodgers, who drew an outstanding 3,608,881. These are the only five teams to attract over 3 million fans in a season.

I spent part of the 1984 World Series in Detroit, watching the Tigers with my friend Lee Iacocca. One night he cooked a large spaghetti dinner at his house. As I sat there, I couldn't help thinking that I had come a long way from the days I couldn't afford a car to having the president of Chrysler cooking dinner for me.

Actually, losing doesn't bother me. Getting caught in a traffic jam bothers me. Going to the dentist bothers me. Losing kills me. It destroys me. If I'm not the world's worst loser, I would hate to get into a fight with the guy who is, because that's a fight that would never end. There are some managers who say they get over a loss before they leave the ball park. Not me. I take the pain home with me. I take it to church. I even take it to bed with me.

I can't sleep when we lose. One ball game in 1984, I remember, we had the winning run on third base with less than two outs in both the ninth and tenth innings, but couldn't score, and lost in the eleventh inning. There was no way I could sleep that night. I just lay there replaying the ninth and tenth innings, hoping that maybe I could get a sacrifice fly and score the run so I could get to sleep. But it always came out the same.

The entire 1984 season was tough, really tough, that's the lowest any team I've managed has ever finished—although we were only one game out of a second-place tie. But every loss, every season, is tough, and experience has not made me a better loser. I've been the losing manager in some very painful ball games. Losing that one-game playoff to Houston in 1980 made me sick. Losing the pennant on the last day of the 1982 season when Joe Morgan hit a home run killed me. Losing the World Series to the Yankees in 1977 and 1978 buried me. There have been many times in my career when we've been four yards offshore, and drowned. Is one loss tougher than another? They're all tough. Trying to pick out the most painful loss in a career is like trying to decide if I'd rather die from poison or in the electric chair.

Some people are able to keep it inside. Walt Alston was the same man win or lose. I can't do that. I shout, I holler, I jump up and down. I've never been shy about letting people know how I feel after a loss. Once, for example, I was so upset after Joe Ferguson (who shouldn't have been playing the outfield anyway) lost a fly ball in the sun in San Diego to cost us a ball game that I threw chairs around the clubhouse, stomped into the manager's office, and slammed the door shut behind me. I mean, I *slammed* that door. When I'm mad, and I'm always mad when we lose, I have to keep moving. I walk, I walk a lot. After walking around in circles in the manager's office, I turned to go back to the clubhouse. I couldn't get the door open. The door was jammed. That made me even angrier, but I couldn't scream because I didn't want my players to know. So I put one foot against the wall for leverage and tried to yank the door open, but it wouldn't budge. I was trapped in the room. Finally, I had no choice, I started hollering for help. My players responded immediately. An hour later the maintenance people got the door off its hinges so I could get out.

One of the very few things that has at least made losing survivable is the company of Dodger broadcaster Vin Scully. I call him Mr. Dodger. He adds so much to a ball game that Dodger fans began bringing their transistor radios to the stadium just to listen to the game they were watching. In Dodger Stadium, they say, a runner can slide into third base and the umpire can call him safe, but not one of the 56,000 people in the park really believe he is safe until Vinny tells them that he is.

When we've lost, when I'm down, he's one of the few people who can cheer me up. One night in Atlanta, I remember, Bob Watson beat us with a pinch-hit grand slam home run off Steve Howe. Blowing a three-run lead with my best relief pitcher in the game did not make me a happy man. After the game I was sitting in my hotel room with my good friend Dodger publicity director Steve Brener, and my good friend Dodger traveling secretary Billy De Lury when Scully came in to try to cheer us up. He called room service to order a bottle of champagne, but because of Georgia's blue laws they could not send a corked bottle to the room at that hour. "Okay," Vinny said without pausing, "send up twenty-four glasses of champagne, please."

After we lose a ball game, I'll often take a long, long walk. Sometimes, when we're on the road, I'll walk back to the hotel from the ball park. Scully has made many a long trek with me. Only once did he hesitate, in fact. We lost a game in Chicago and it was late and I was getting ready to walk to the hotel. Vinny stopped me. "As much as I love you," he said,

"I think we need more protection." So he recruited a few people, among them my 6'1" coach Mark Cresse, to lead the way. Cresse is another man who often walks with me. After a tough loss in Montreal in 1984, for example, we walked the entire seven miles back to our hotel. I don't talk too much during these excursions, except to ask directions when we get lost.

I'm no better when we lose at home, but it's tougher to walk on the freeways. Jo always waits for me after the game. More than once I've been so upset I've come out of the clubhouse and walked right past her without even realizing she's waiting there.

I've always been a bad loser, always. When I was pitching in the Dominican, I remember, a manager tried to take me out of a ball game after the third baseman had made two errors. I wouldn't leave the game. I walked around the infield, with the manager walking right behind me, demanding I give him the baseball. I refused. "Don't take me out," I screamed at him, "take out the third baseman, he's the one who made the errors."

One means I use to release my anger is through the careful use of those words in the English language not usually found in the dictionary. In the clubhouse, on the field, I curse. I swear. I use foul language. Profanity. And sometimes, when I'm angry, I say things I really don't mean, or things I do mean, but only when I say them. Sometimes I have to answer questions from the press when I don't even want to talk to my wife.

My use of profanity has attracted some attention. *Time* magazine, for example, once named George Washington and me as Americans known for cursing. Isn't that amazing, I thought when I read the story, to think that the son of an Italian immigrant, a runny-nosed little left-hander with a decent curveball, a player good enough only to be the third-string pitcher on his high school baseball team . . . could be compared to the Father of Our Country.

Because I try to be the best at anything I do, there is a certain amount of pride derived from being considered one of the nation's most colorful speakers, but it really is something I'm very careful about. I don't want young people thinking it is acceptable to use foul language in daily life. I absolutely, completely limit my use of profanity to the ball park. I do not curse when women or children are present, ever. Jo has never heard a foul word come out of my mouth. Billy Russell once told me he had been in and out of locker rooms with me for ten years and was amazed that I had never slipped and used profanity in front of my family or his family. He wanted to know how I was able to separate those two worlds so completely. I couldn't answer him. I don't know how I am able to do it, but I have never slipped, ever.

That doesn't mean I don't get angry at home. I do. I remember once, in Ogden, I brought Spunky to the ball park with me when he was about ten years old. Bobby Valentine had done something that day and I really gave it to him. I just peeled his skin back. Spunky really liked Bobby, so when I was finished, he went over to him and said, "Don't worry about it, Bobby, I'm the one who has to go home with him."

What has probably caused attention to be focused on my use of the language was a tape made by a radio reporter in the Dodger locker room after a ball game on Mother's Day, 1978, the same day I was to be honored by the Cystic Fibrosis Foundation as their Man of the Year. Dave Kingman, then with the Cubs, had hit three home runs and knocked in eight runs to beat us. His second home run had tied the score in the ninth inning and his third had won the game in the thirteenth inning. He had driven in all eight of the Cubs' runs. In the locker room after the game, a reporter stuck a microphone in my face and asked, "What's your opinion of Kingman's performance?"

Naturally, I proceeded to tell him. "What's my opinion of his performance? What the   you think is my opinion of his performance?   , he beat us with   three   home runs. What the   do you mean, what is my opinion of his performance? How could you ask me a question like that? What is my opinion of his performance?   , he hit three home runs.   . I mean, that's a tough question to ask me, isn't it? What is my opinion of his performance?"

"Yes, it is. I asked it and you gave me an answer."

"Well, I didn't give you a good answer because I'm mad, but I mean . . ."

"It wasn't a good question."

". . . That's a tough question to ask me right now, what is my opinion of his performance. I mean, you want me to tell you what my opinion of his performance is . . ."

"You just did."

"That's right.   . The guy hits three home runs against us. I mean, I don't want to . . . I don't mean to get   -off or anything like that, but I mean, you ask me my opinion. I mean, he put on a   show, he hit three home runs, he drove in eight runs, what the   more can I say about it? I didn't mean to get mad or anything like that, but   , you asked me my opinion of his performance."

That was not meant to be heard by anyone outside that locker room. The next day I was at the ball park and one of our regular sportswriters came over to me and said, "I almost ran off the freeway on the way to the ball park, listening to that interview you did yesterday."

I had done a number of interviews that day, including some at the cystic fibrosis dinner. "What was so different about this one?" I asked.

"This one was you giving your opinion of Kingman's performance."

I couldn't believe it. The profanity had been bleeped out and the tape had been played. Suddenly everybody seemed to have a copy of it. One radio station played it repeatedly. More people heard about it than actually heard it, and assumed it was much worse than it actually was. I did not feel good about it, because it was not intended for anyone but that reporter. And worse, I didn't have a royalty arrangement with him.

There is another tape that has been widely circulated, and that one really did bother me. When I went out to the mound to take out Doug Rau during the 1977 World Series, he did not want to come out, and we shouted at each other. That happens in the heat of a ball game. But I was wearing a microphone for the official World Series film, and that conversation was recorded. The tape of that conversation was circulated. It is one thing to record an answer I give to a reporter's question, that's fair, it is something else entirely to release a tape of a private conversation between me and one of my ballplayers. That should never have been done.

One Sunday I decided to do something about my use of profanity in the clubhouse. "Men," I told the team, "you're always hearing me use bad language, but today you're going to hear the real me." And I began quoting passages from the Bible about overcoming trials and tribulations. I had them in a reflective mood, thinking about overcoming adversity, when I concluded, ". . . and so now I want you to get out there on that field and   them!"

Surprisingly, considering my temper and my use of the language, I get along very well with umpires. At least, I think I get along very well with umpires. I'm not sure what umpires think. For some reason, people seem to believe I have a lot of arguments with umpires. Hey, I'm not an Angel, I'm a Dodger. I fight for my team, I scream at umpires. But I know they have a difficult job to do and I try not to make it any tougher than it already is. During my four years as Walt Alston's third base coach I got to know most of the National League umpires pretty well, and many of them took the time to tell me that they hoped that when Walt stepped down, I got the job. When I got the job I remembered that they had been on my side. Umpiring is a tough job. Half the people on the field are going to disagree with every decision they make on a close play.

During my first three years as Dodger manager I was ejected from a ball game only three times, and two of those were technical objections—according to the rulebook anyone arguing in these situations must be automatically ejected. On one occasion the umpire decided that my pitcher was throwing at a batter after he had received a warning not to, so both the pitcher and I were ejected. The second automatic ejection took place at the end of an inning in St. Louis. I went out to discuss what I considered a bad call on a pitch in the top half of the inning. Arguing a called strike is also an automatic ejection. "Where was that pitch?" I asked.

"Sorry, Tommy," the umpire said, "that's automatic. I gotta throw you out."

"What do you mean, automatic? I'm asking you a half inning later."

"It doesn't matter," he continued, "it's still automatic. It's in the rules."

I couldn't believe it. "In the rules? You mean to tell me if I came to you next week and asked, 'Where was that pitch?' you'd have to throw me out?"

"That's right."

"What about next spring? Would I have to go then?"

"Yep, you'd have to go. I'm telling you, it's in the rules."

Gee, I thought as I walked to the clubhouse, that's some great rule. But what I wanted to know was, if they can throw me out for arguing about a call six months after it happened, why can't they call Reggie Jackson out for interference in the fourth game of the 1978 World Series?

TEN

•

I Manage to Get to the Top

On April 10, 1984, Jo and I attended a State Department dinner at the White House honoring the President of the Dominican Republic, Jorge Blanco. Naturally, it was a tremendous honor to have been invited to the White House. When President Reagan and President Blanco arrived, Jo and I joined the long reception line. On a formal reception line the husband always precedes his wife, so I reached the two leaders first. And just as the Marine Corps officer announced stiffly, "Mr. and Mrs. Tom Lasorda," President Reagan smiled and said, "Oh, I know him," and gave me a big hug. We'd first met when he was governor of California at a birthday party for Frank Sinatra. Then he turned to President Blanco and said, "Mr. President, I'd like you to meet . . ."

"Me amigo, Tom!" President Blanco said, giving me a big hug. And we began discussing American and Dominican baseball in Spanish.

Two Presidents *and* a great meal in one evening. Only in this great country of ours, this land of opportunity, could the son of an Italian immigrant, a runny-nosed little left-handed pitcher . . .

Actually, I enjoy stopping by the White House any time I'm in the neighborhood—and I'm in the neighborhood any time I'm fortunate enough to be honored with an invitation.

My first visit to the White House was the day of a Kennedy Center gala honoring outstanding American artists, among them my friend Cary Grant. Jo and I had been invited by our good friend movie producer George Stevens, who was producing the show. On occasion, his sons

Michael and David will work as our bat boys. Coincidentally, Richard Schweiker, President Reagan's Secretary of Health and Human Services; Drew Lewis, the Secretary of Transportation; and I had known each other at Norristown High School, and when I flew to Washington for the Kennedy Center affair, they invited me to have lunch at the White House. Lunch? Naturally, I accepted. Before lunch they brought Jo and I into the Oval Office to spend a few moments with the President.

Standing in the Oval Office, the heart of our democracy, was one of the greatest thrills of my life. Presidential assistant Mike Deaver saw tears in Jo's eyes and asked what was wrong. "I'm just so honored to be here," she said. The only thing I was sorry about was that my mother and father had not lived to share the thrill with me. I'd brought Dodger jackets for the President and Nancy Reagan, and helped him put his on. "Now, Mr. President," I said, "right now you may not think this jacket is worth a great deal, but one day it might be very valuable. I'll tell you why. A few years ago I spoke at a sports banquet in Baton Rouge, Louisiana. After the dinner a man came up to me and introduced himself. 'Mr. Lasorda,' he said, 'I'm Dr. Leisner, and I'm on the staff here at Louisiana State University. I just want to tell you, I've been a Dodger fan all my life.'

"Naturally I told him how glad I was to hear that.

" '. . . and ever since I was eight years old,' he continued, 'the thing I've wanted more than anything else was a real Dodger cap.'

" 'Doctor,' I told him, 'I get a lot of requests like that, but I've enjoyed being here with you people tonight so I'll tell you what. You give me your name and address and hat size, and when I get back to Los Angeles, I'll send you a hat.'

"He was very excited. 'You'd do that for me?' he said. 'Well, that's tremendous. And I'd like to do something for you.'

"Hey, doc,' I told him, 'that's very kind of you, but it's not necessary.' But he insisted that he wanted to do something for me so, rather than insult him, I asked, 'What would you like to do for me?'

"He said, 'I'd like to give you a free gallbladder operation.' Now, Mr. President, think of it this way, if I could get a free gallbladder operation for a Dodger hat, just imagine what this Dodger jacket might be worth someday in the medical field!"

The whole visit was incredible to me. The runny-nosed little left-hander in the White House. If I had made it from Tom Rats's table to the Oval Office with just a decent curveball, imagine what I could've accomplished with a good fastball. As I stood there, watching President Reagan trying on his Dodger jacket, there was one thing I knew for sure. I wouldn't have been there if it hadn't been for baseball and the Dodgers. Everything I have I owe to baseball and the Dodgers. Because of the attention I've received on the field, my life off the field has been tremendously exciting. I've had opportunities I never even dreamed were possible when I started pitching in the Phillies organization in 1945. I've appeared on numerous television shows and I've even had small parts in a few movies. I've been asked to endorse products and I've made many commercials. I've covered the World Series as a newspaper reporter for *USA Today* and reported it as a broadcaster. I've spoken before more groups in more cities for more causes than baseball has baseballs, I've even had the honor of addressing 4,600 cadets at West Point and 3,000 at the Air Force Academy. I've received an honorary degree from Valpariso University and had a scholarship fund named after me. And I've been honored in my father's hometown of Tollo in the Abruzzi region of Italy, my adopted hometown of Los Angeles, and my real hometown of Norristown, Pennsylvania.

Nothing, of course, matches the thrill of meeting the President of the United States in the Oval Office, except winning the World Series.

My team has won only one World Series—so far—but I've been fortunate enough to have been invited to the White House a number of times. In October 1983, for example, I attended a luncheon honoring the Italian ambassador. After lunch, presidential press secretary Larry Speakes asked me to open his daily press briefing for the White House press corps. "They're tough," he said, "I'd like you to soften 'em up for me."

He introduced me as the Ambassador from Chavez Ravine, the location of Dodger Stadium. The first question was asked by ABC-TV reporter Sam Donaldson. Befitting his reputation, it was a difficult question, but fair. "I understand you sat next to the President at lunch today," he said. "Can you tell me what you and the President spoke about?"

I handled it deftly. "Economics, Mr. Donaldson," I said.

Naturally, he was surprised to hear this. What did he expect, nuclear energy? "You and the President spoke about economics?" he asked, and I must state that I detected a little disbelief in his voice.

"That's right," I said. "I told the President the story about the man who walked into the Chase Manhattan Bank in New York City and demanded to see Mr. Rockefeller. He was causing quite a commotion, so finally they took him to the twenty-eighth floor to meet Mr. Rockefeller. 'What can I do for you?' Mr. Rockefeller asked.

"This man said, 'I'd like to borrow $1,500.'

"Mr. Rockefeller said that could probably be arranged and sent him back downstairs to meet the chief loan officer. When the man again said he wanted to borrow $1,500, the chief loan officer asked what he could leave as collateral. 'This is the title to my brand-new Chrysler New

Yorker,' the man said, handing over the papers and the keys. 'It's parked right outside this bank. If I don't bring the money back in one week, you can keep the car.' So, this is a successful bank, they gave him the loan.

"One week later the man walked into the bank and returned the $1,500. The man asked, 'What's the interest on $1,500 for one week?' They totaled it up and it came to $17.50. The loan officer stopped him. 'Sir,' he said, 'we've run a thorough investigation on you and we've discovered that you're one of the wealthiest men in the United States. We just can't figure it out, why would you want to borrow $1,500?'

" 'Let me ask you a question,' the man said. 'Where else in New York City can a man park his car for a week for $17.50?' And that, Mr. Donaldson, is economics. Next question, please . . ."

There is one thing I can always depend on when attending an official government lunch or dinner. The food is going to be outstanding. After many years of hard work, I have earned a reputation as a big eater. I am proud of this. For example, in Lindsay, California, when they named a junior high school after Steve Garvey, they named the library after me. I told them that was a mistake—it should have been the cafeteria. Actually, I am not a big eater. This is a falsehood. I'm only 5'10". What I am is an endurance eater. I understand the importance of pacing when I eat. I learned early that slow but steady cleans the plate. My eating ability comes from my childhood, when my mother served us health food. If we didn't eat everything on our plate, she explained, it would be bad for our health.

Actually, food is the only weakness I have not been able to conquer. When I realized smoking was a weakness, I took a pack of cigarettes out of my pocket, stared at it, and asked aloud, "Who's stronger, me or this pack of cigarettes?" The answer was me. I never smoked another cigarette. Then I took a glass of vodka and said to it, "Who's stronger, you or me?" Again, the answer was me. I never had another glass of vodka. Then I took a plate of linguini with clam sauce, looked it right in the eye, and said, "Who's stronger, you or me?" And this little clam looked right back at me and said, "Linguini with clam sauce." I cannot beat the linguini habit.

Because of that, and because of my highly placed connections in Washington, D.C., I have started a campaign to make spaghetti our national dish. That way, at least, I'll feel a little better about not being able to resist it because I'll be doing something patriotic. It is incredible to me that this tremendous country does not have a national dish. I think spaghetti would be an outstanding selection. To begin with, it has curative powers. It makes you feel happy. Then, it is a social magnet—the family or friends that eat spaghetti together laugh together. And finally, when accompanied by the proper sauce, it has an outstanding taste.

Too much pasta has led to too much Lasorda. I have tried numerous ways of losing weight, and I have had help. Once, Steve Garvey had a uniform shirt made up by our outstanding clubhouse man, Nobe Kawano. The name "Lasorda" on the back had been replaced with the word "Lasagna." When that effort to embarrass me into a diet failed, our trainer, Bill Buhler, had T-shirts printed in English, Spanish, French, Italian, and Japanese reading: "Do Not Feed the Manager."

Now, that was a pretty good idea, but where he went wrong was not getting it printed in Chinese. Next to Italian food, Chinese food is very important in my life. In fact, in my office after the game, we do have the Chinese food right next to the Italian food. We usually serve Italian hard salami and pepperoni, and egg rolls supplied by my good friend Joe Tannenbaum. And I may be the only Italian honored by having a dinner named after him in a Chinese restaurant. The Tom Lasorda Special is available to the discriminating diner at Larry Wong's restaurant, Paul's Kitchen, on San Pedro Street in downtown Los Angeles. One night, when Charlie Hough and I were feasting there, Charlie warned me, "You'd better stop eating so much."

"Nothing to worry about," I told him, "everybody knows this food isn't fattening. Have you ever seen a fat Chinaman?"

"No," Charlie said, "but I have seen a lot of fat Italians eating in Chinese restaurants."

Frank Sinatra wanted me to try a behavior modification program. Why is it that thin people are always giving advice on how to lose weight? Taking advice from Frank Sinatra on how to lose weight is like taking hairstyling suggestions from Telly Savalas. Frank told me that a good way to lose weight was to eat only half of the portion on your plate. I told him I'd try it. The next time I saw him, maybe six months later, he asked, "How're you doing with your weight?"

"Not so good," I admitted, "I've gained three pounds."

He couldn't believe it. "You've gained three pounds! Have you been eating just a half of the portion on your plate?"

"I sure have," I said, but then I admitted, "but I've been ordering double portions."

I've tried various diets, but I haven't been able to stick to one. That's not completely my fault. Over the years I've made many outstanding friends in the eleven National League cities we visit. And wherever we are, either someone sends food into the clubhouse, or the clubhouse man sets out a terrific post-game spread. Am I supposed to insult a friend of mine, or a hard-working clubhouse man, who has gone to a tremendous amount of trouble, who has taken great pains to make sure my team does not go hungry, by not eating his food?

I've tried exercising. For a while, I jogged every morning. I was enjoying it until I began reading newspaper stories about joggers collapsing during their workouts. It was either stop jogging or stop reading, so I quit jogging. And since then I've come to understand what jogging has done to America. Our trainer, my good friend Bill Buhler, still jogs six miles every day. "Bill," I explained, "the difference between you and me is that you look better than I do. And when that heart attack hits you, and the people are filing by your coffin, they'll say to your wife, Barbara, 'Gee, Bill really looks good.'

"And Barbara will say, 'He oughta, he was running six miles every day.'

"And then, when the heart attack hits me, and I'm laying there, the people will file by and say to Jo, 'Gee, Tommy really looks bad.'

"And Jo will tell them, 'He oughta, he was staying up late every night and eating all the linguini in the country.' So, you see, Bill, the reason that I quit jogging is because, when I die, I want to have something wrong with me."

I still try to pitch batting practice as often as I can. When people try to convince me that pitching batting practice probably puts more strain on the heart than jogging, I remind them that they read about joggers having heart attacks all the time, but they never read about anyone having a heart attack while pitching batting practice.

My success in baseball has resulted in me being invited to appear on many of the most popular shows on television. I made my dramatic debut soon after I moved to Los Angeles, when I appeared on the top-rated "Red Skelton Show." He was doing a skit in which he was playing someone hiding out from a lawman at a carnival by pretending to work there. At one point in the skit he was supposed to stick his head through a hole in the canvas at a ball-throwing booth, and they needed someone who could throw a plastic ball and hit him in the head.

This is known as type-casting. Who could possibly have more practice at throwing a ball at someone than Thomas Charles Lasorda? In rehearsal, every time he'd stick his head through that hole, *bam!* I'd nail him. I was enjoying it, too. That was the same thing I once got fined for, and now they were paying me. That's what I call progress.

Once, as Red was rubbing his forehead, he asked me, "How come you never miss?" I explained that I was an ex-ballplayer currently scouting for the Dodgers. He eventually padded my part, giving me a few lines.

Naturally, the show was live, so there was a tremendous amount of pressure on me to hit him with every throw because if I missed, the point of the skit would have been lost. When we went on the air I was completely relaxed, because I knew what I was doing and had confidence in my ability to do it. And I nailed him every time.

Since that appearance, I've been on local and network news shows, quiz shows, sports shows, variety shows, and talk shows. Baseball is a tough game. After the 1978 World Series, Davey Lopes, the Penguin, and I represented the Dodgers on a quiz show called "Sports Challenge." We played the Yankees', Graig Nettles, Billy Martin, and, I believe, Lou Piniella. Just as in the Series, we won the early rounds, but when the game was on the line, Nettles came through for the Yankees. We were up something like forty points, and the first team to identify the "mystery guest" got fifty points. "This man . . ." host Dick Enberg began describing the mystery guest.

Blammmm! Nettles slammed down on his buzzer. "It's Rod Carew," he said correctly, winning the quiz for his team. I couldn't believe it, there was no way he could have figured out the mystery guest's identity from the clues. Later we found out that Nettles knew Carew's children, and had seen them backstage before the show.

After what he had just finished doing to us on the baseball diamond, I personally thought he could have shown a little more sympathy. Couldn't he at least have waited until Dick Enberg finished reading the question?

Naturally, after my appearance on the Skelton show, the offers began pouring in. So, fifteen years later I began appearing on such popular shows as "Chips," the quiz show "Tattle Tales" with Jo, my friend Robert Wagner's "Hart to Hart," "Police Squad" with Leslie Nielsen, and "Fantasy Island" with Ricardo Montalban. Usually I played myself. Does that make me a character actor? On "Fantasy Island" I was the manager of an All-Star team, as I have been three times in the National League. Gary "Radar" Burghoff's fantasy was to be a big league pitcher. So with the bases loaded and the game in jeopardy, I brought him in. He proceeded to strike out George Brett, Freddy Lynn, and Steve Garvey. That wasn't Fantasy Island, that was Mission: Impossible. Unfortunately, he also pitched to a ten-year-old girl, who hit a tremendous home run off him. Well, that's show business baseball.

Proving that the manager of the Dodgers can get away with assault with a deadly weapon—in this case, my voice—I sang "Strangers in the Night" on the "Mike Douglas Show" and "Gimme That Old Dodger Blue" on "Hee Haw." I've been on all the daily shows, "Today," with my good friend Bryant Gumbel, and "Good Morning America," with my good

friend David Hartman and "CBS Morning News" with my good friend
Diane Sawyer. In the afternoon, I've been on my friend John Davidson's
show, my friend Merv Griffin's show and my friend Mike Douglas's show.
I've sat between Johnny and Ed on the "Tonight" show, I've answered
questions from Ted Koppel on "Nightline," discussed the World Series
with Charlie Rose on "Nightwatch" and I've talked about baseball with
Tom Snyder when there was a "Tomorrow." That is a full day of television.

I also appear regularly as the "baseball wizard" on "The Baseball
Bunch" starring Johnny Bench and the Chicken. I usually appear in the
last segment of the show, emerging from a cloud of smoke, dressed in a
turban and cape. The outfit I usually wear when I go to the ball park. My
job is to give the young viewers an instructional and inspirational message.
I might tell them, for example, how important it is for them to get along
with their teammates, or why they should listen to their coaches. One
Saturday morning, which I will never forget, they broadcast a show in
which I carefully explained to young players why they should not lose their
tempers on the field, and why it is wrong to argue with umpires.

In the game that afternoon, umpire Frank Pulli ejected me for refusing
to leave the field after a heated argument over a call at second base. After
that, I was afraid the producers might make me turn in my turban.

Product endorsements have become as much a part of baseball as
exploding scoreboards, and I have had the opportunity to endorse quite
a few of them. I can definitely state that I would buy any product I
endorse, because I wouldn't put my name on anything I don't believe in
or haven't tried. For example, I am a spokesman for Yoplait yogurt,
Chicago Brothers frozen pizza, Diet Coke and, to top it off, Rolaids
antacid tablets, as well as Datsun and Colgate shaving cream.

The first commercial for which I auditioned was for a well-known car
rental agency. A week after the audition the producer called me and said,
"Congratulations, you finished second."

Congratulations? For finishing second? "That means I didn't get it,"
I said.

"That's right," he explained, "you didn't get it. But you should be very
proud. You beat out . . ." and then he read a list of all the other people
who also didn't get it.

That did not make me feel any better. I was quite upset, and I asked
him who had been selected. He named a talented television character
actor then playing an important supporting role in a hit series.

"Him? Are you kidding me? Why'd they pick him over me?"

"Because he's much better known than you are."

What an excuse! "Of course he is today," I said, "but he won't be soon." And if they had given me that commercial, I would be writing about the rental car company right next to that outstanding, delicious yogart, Yoplait, and that outstanding frozen pizza, Chicago Brothers, and that outstanding antacid table, Rolaids.

The most difficult commercial I've ever done was for Swanson's Hungry Man TV dinners. I pride myself on being able to get my lines right on the first take, but on this commercial they stuck me with Steve Garvey. Now, Garvey may be like a son to me, he may be a decent, caring human being, but between you and me, he's no Cary Grant in the acting department. On this job I had to carry the kid. It wasn't easy, because every time he'd flub a line I'd be forced to eat another one of those delicious dinners. Admittedly, the producer might have accepted a few of his readings, but I wasn't satisfied, so I kept him at it all afternoon until he got it just right. I felt that was a reasonable sacrifice to make for one of my players.

One product I believe in and have tried, and tried again just to make sure I believed in it, was Natural Light beer from Budweiser. I did a Natural Light commercial with my good friend Norm Crosby, in which a bartender tells me my wife has called and warned me I'd better get right home. I respond by telling him I rule my own roost, then order a round of beer for everyone in the place . . . and "one for the road," I scream as I dash out.

Naturally, because of these appearances, I am often recognized off the field. No matter where I go people are always stopping me to say hello and offer advice on how to run the ball club. One day, for example, I was being given a tour of the New York Stock Exchange, and I was standing on the balcony, looking down on this incredible, hectic scene, when somebody on the floor noticed me and shouted, "Hey, Lasorda, you made a bad trade when you traded Garvey to San Diego." I didn't want to tell him we hadn't traded Steve, he had left as a free agent, so when the laughter died down, I shouted back, "Listen, you make more bad trades in one day than I've made in a lifetime!" Then I was invited onto the floor and signed autographs. The whole place practically came to a standstill.

The next day a headline on the *New York Times* financial page read: STOCK EXCHANGE STALLS, I realized it was a good thing I hadn't tripped, otherwise that headline would've read: STOCK EXCHANGE CRASHES.

Actually, Jo rarely complains about the hours I spend away from home in the off-season. Only once in our entire marriage do I remember her getting upset about my being away too long or coming home too late. In 1982, I spoke at a dinner honoring FBI agents, and after the dinner we had a few drinks and told a few stories, and by the time I got home, it was almost 3 o'clock in the morning. I couldn't believe it. So I just eased the car into our driveway with its motor and lights off, then quietly got out and quietly walked into the house and quietly started taking off my shoes—and there was Jo waiting up for me. "Just where have you been?" she said. "Don't you realize it's 3 o'clock in the morning. I don't believe you, you're out every night having a good time while I have to sit here."

"Now wait a second," I said. "Just hold the phone a minute here." Then I took a bottle of vodka out of the liquor cabinet and poured some in a glass. "Drink this," I told her.

"You know I don't drink," she said. "Get that stuff away from me." "Drink it," I insisted.

Finally, she took a small sip. "Ugghh," she said, "this is awful." "That's right," I agreed, "it is. And I have to drink it while you think I'm out enjoying myself."

In fact, Jo had been right, I had been out having a good time. A few years ago, Justin Dedeaux, Rod Dedeaux's son, asked me if I really believed in free speech. "Of course I do," I replied. "Free speech is one of the most important liberties we enjoy in this great country of ours. Free speech is the foundation of our democracy."

"Good," he said, "because you're going to make one."

If I can't be on a baseball field, I like to talk about being on a baseball field. And I get many opportunities to do so. Many, many opportunities. I speak to corporations and conventions, civic organizations, schools and universities, military and civilian uniformed service groups, religious groups, and charity benefits. I speak at breakfasts, lunches, and dinners. I've spoken to forty-five hundred cadets in the Great Hall at West Point and I've spoken to seven salesmen in a room in San Diego. I've spoken on land and on cruises. I've spoken to computer experts, Little Leaguers, students in graduate business programs, police and firemen, fertilizer salesmen, doctors, and just about everybody in between.

From the end of the 1984 season to the opening of spring training in 1985, I made between 100 and 125 speeches. I spoke at the University of Nevada at Reno, Brigham Young, Miami Dade North Junior College, Southwest Louisiana University, Fresno State, the University of North Carolina at Charlotte, I spoke at Notre Dame and I helped dedicate the new athletic center at Valpariso University. I spoke to the Boy Scouts in Ontario, California, and the Boys Town of Greenville, South Carolina, the Westwood, California, Shriners, a scholarship fund dinner in Niles, Ohio, Jim Brewer's golf tournament for retarded children in Tulsa, Oklahoma, I spoke at the air force base at El Segundo, California, St. Pancratius Church in Lakewood, California, and Father Osborne of Our Lady of Pillar in St. Louis even invited me to give the sermon. I was honored as Man of the Year by the City of Hope in Los Angeles, and Steve Brener and I spent one entire night in New York City going from subway station to subway station meeting members of the Transit Police Force and signing autographs. And this was just the beginning.

I'm thrilled at every invitation. There have been many years in my life when nobody wanted to listen to me for me to pass up an opportunity to speak. And I do believe in free speech—I've never accepted a fee from a religious group, school, charity, or civic organization that can benefit from my appearance. One night, for example, my friends Stu Nahan and Jim Hill and I spoke at a dinner and afterwards were given envelopes with cash in them. I immediately donated mine to the charity, and felt tremendous being able to do so—and I felt even better later that night when Stu called to tell me that we had been given each other's envelope and I had donated his money while he still had mine.

I particularly enjoy speaking to firemen, policemen, and military organizations because these are men and women who literally put their life on the line for other people, and I love, respect, and admire them.

I make all these appearances to help spread the gospel of baseball and the Dodgers, of putting something back into that big pot from which I have received so much. I love being Baseball's Goodwill Ambassador because I never get tired of promoting baseball and the Dodgers. Could a man ever get tired of kissing a pretty girl?

I don't use notes when I speak because I have tremendous confidence in myself as a public speaker, but it wasn't always that way. I first began making speeches when I was an active player. Believe me, in those days I was nervous. I'd forget what I wanted to say, I'd mix up names, I'd give away the punch line of a joke in the middle. The only reason I made speeches was that I felt I had an obligation as a player to help the ball club any way I could. I certainly didn't enjoy it. Once, in fact, I was so nervous before I spoke to a fans' group in Montreal that somebody told me I had so many wrinkles in my forehead I'd have to screw on my uniform cap that night. But I realized I could be an effective speaker one night in 1964, when I was working as a Dodger scout. I was invited to be one of the speakers at a dinner at the Huntington Hartford Hotel in Pasadena honoring all the Eagle Scouts in the San Gabriel Valley, and, since I never passed up a chance to go places where I might meet young ballplayers, I accepted.

As I sat on the dais in front of the huge ballroom, looking out at the room jammed with Eagle Scouts, their families, friends, and Scout masters, I thought to myself, What am I doing here? It was by far the largest group I'd ever spoken before. I really had no idea what I was going to say. I'd been a Scout in Norristown, mainly because the troop had a sports program that included boxing and they served meals at the meetings, but that had been a long time ago.

The master of ceremonies stood up and began introducing the first scheduled speaker, a judge. And then he continued introducing him, and continued . . . This judge had a list of credits and accomplishments that took ten minutes to recite.

Whew, I thought, even if they stretch, it'll take them thirty seconds to introduce me.

The next speaker to be introduced was a retired admiral who was on the board of directors of General Dynamics. It took even longer to read his impressive biography.

Unfortunately, I had picked that day to give up smoking. It turned out to be a bad choice. I was dying for a cigarette.

Finally, the emcee stood up to introduce me. He managed to take a full thirty seconds, but that included a pause to sip some water. The audience applauded politely as I walked to the podium. The judge had been an impressive speaker. The retired admiral had been even better. I was in serious trouble.

I stood there and looked out at these people waiting for me to say something worthwhile. So I said some of the most worthwhile words I'd ever learned. "On my honor," I began, "I will do my best to do my duty to God and my country, to obey the Scout laws, to help other people at all times, to keep myself physically strong, mentally awake, and morally straight. A Scout is trustworthy, loyal . . . brave, clean, and reverent." When I finished you could hear a pin drop in that room. I told those people I couldn't remember my army serial number, but I remembered the Scout oath and the Scout laws because I knew those things would help me throughout my life. When I finished speaking I received a standing ovation. I was never again nervous about making a speech.

The thing I enjoy most about public speaking is that it gives me a chance to spend time with baseball fans. I'm very fortunate my work is baseball, because I happen to be as big a baseball fan as anyone in the world. It's tremendous to be able to get out and meet people who feel the same way, and who feel good about seeing me. And, on occasion, there are additional benefits.

In 1978, I spoke to the graduating class of the Houston, Texas, police academy. While I was there I met the commander, Captain Leroy Michna, and his son, Willie. Five years later Willie had an accident and was in a coma. His doctors continually asked him questions, but he didn't respond. Then his father shouted at him, "Willie! Who's the manager of the Dodgers?" He opened his eyes, the first time he had responded to anything since the accident.

Coincidentally, the Dodgers were playing in Houston that day. I received a call in my hotel room telling me about the accident and Willie's response, and went over to the hospital to visit him. From that day on, every time we were in town, I'd see him.

Eventually, he got out of the hospital into a wheelchair. He'd come down to the clubhouse in that chair, and the players all got to know him. One day, I took him out for lunch. Between courses, I said, "Willie, you really love the Dodgers, don't you?"

He nodded.

"All right, I'm gonna tell you what I'm gonna do. The next time we play the Astros, if you can walk into the clubhouse without a wheelchair and without crutches, I'll put you in a Dodger uniform, and you'll sit in the dugout with me during the game."

About three months after that we returned to Houston. All the players were sitting around before the game when the clubhouse door opened, and Willie *walked* in. The players stood up and gave him an ovation. That was one of the most touching and gratifying things I have ever seen. Now, if I can be a part of something like that, I'll speak to any group, anywhere, anytime.

When I make a speech I usually tell a few jokes, then stress an inspirational and motivational message. I believe that if I can make a roomful of people happy for forty minutes, and maybe leave them with a little reminder of what can be accomplished if they believe in themselves and are willing to pay the price to achieve their goals, then I've been successful.

A speech I gave at the UCLA Graduate School of Management in 1981 is representative of the many other speeches I've given. "I'm extremely honored that I was asked to be part of your program," I began, and I *was* honored to be there. I thought it was pretty impressive that a man who left high school in eleventh grade to pursue a career as a left-handed pitcher—although I later got my equivalency degree—would be asked to give advice to graduate students in business school. Although the speech is too long to reproduce in its entirety, and besides, I may find use for it again, this abbreviated version will give some idea of what has made me one of the most popular public speakers in my entire household. "Recently I had dinner in Houston with the great golf star Doug Sanders, and we got into a big argument. I told him that the toughest thing to do in the world of sports was to hit a baseball. He said that it was much more difficult to hit a golf ball. So I told him about a man I knew, a blind golfer. This blind golfer went up to Jack Nicklaus and challenged him to a $10,000 winner-take-all golf match. Nicklaus couldn't believe it. 'You're blind,' he pointed out. 'I don't want to take your money.' The man insisted that they play, and finally Nicklaus agreed, because he didn't want to hurt this man's feelings. 'Okay,' he said, 'when do you want to play?'

" 'Eleven o'clock tonight,' the blind man said.

" 'So you see,' I told Sanders, 'a blind man can hit a golf ball, but he couldn't hit a baseball.'

"But I'm not here to tell you about hitting a baseball. I'm here to tell you that you are soon to be embarking on a career that you hope to follow for the rest of your lives. But everything we do in baseball relates to the things you are going to be learning in these classrooms and in your offices. There is no difference, believe me. In baseball, and in business, there are three types of people. There are those who make it happen. There are those who watch it happen. And there are those who wonder what happened. And I find that to be true in baseball just as you'll find it to be true in whatever business you go into. And there is only one way you're gonna make it happen, and it's the same way a man becomes an outstanding baseball player. When Steve Garvey and Billy Russell and Joe Ferguson and all the rest of them played for me in the rookie league I had to get them prepared. So I worked with them for endless hours getting them ready to play the best competition in the world. I told them the story of the man in New York City who was going to see the opera. And he got lost, and found a policeman, and asked, 'How do I get to Carnegie Hall?'

"And the policeman told him, 'Practice, young man, practice.' That's the way my players made it to Dodger Stadium, through endless hours of practice, practice, and more practice. And through those hours of practice they learned to do things instinctively. For example, I had to teach Tom Paciorek to hit the ball to right field. I told him, 'You've got to have your hands out in front of the barrel of the bat in order to hit the ball over there. You have to drag the bat around. But when the ball is coming at you ninety miles an hour, you can't stop to think, I've got to have my hands out in front of the barrel, because the ball will be by you. You have to practice it over and over and over so when the time comes you'll be able to do it . . .'

". . . and that is what it is going to take for each and every one of you sitting here today, you have to have the preparation because when you go out in the business world and meet your competitors head on, the one who is going to get the sale is the one who is better prepared, who has the desire and the preparation. You've seen it. Two people are in the same business on the same street. One of them prospers and the other does not. Why is that? Because one of them wants it more than the other one. Because it is not always the strongest man who wins the fight, or the fastest man who wins the race, or the best team that wins the game. In most cases it is the one who wants it the most, the one who has gone out and prepared himself, who has paid the price . . .

"Right now, I am preparing myself to go to spring training. I want to get the team prepared mentally and physically to meet our competitors head on. I want them to believe that by the end of this year the pennant flag will be flying over Dodger Stadium. And if I can get those twenty-five players believing that, along with the preparation it takes to get physically prepared, there is no question that we will win the pennant this year. I believe that and I want them to believe that. And I want you to believe that whatever you want to be, you can be. You can do it, but I'm gonna tell you something, there is nobody who is going to hand it to you. You have to fight, you have to prepare yourself, and you have to work . . .

"Let me give you an example of what a man will do to win a baseball game. We were playing in Cincinnati one weekend last season and Sunday morning I got up to go to Mass. I was sitting in a pew, and who comes in and sits right next to me but John McNamara, the manager of the Reds. Now, I know why he's in church, he knows why I'm there. When Mass is over, as we are leaving through the center aisle; as we approach the front door, John McNamara says to me, 'Wait for me outside, I'll be right out.' I said, 'Okay,' but I thought it was a little strange. I began wondering what he was going to do and I stopped and I watched him. He went over to the right side of the church and he knelt down and he lit a candle. When I saw that, I walked up the left aisle, and when he left I went over to the right side and I blew out his candle. And all during the game, I kept hollering to McNamara, 'It ain't gonna work, John, I blew out the candle.' The point is that you have to do anything you can to win, because your competitor is going to be doing everything he can, he's gonna be lighting candles all day if he thinks that'll give him an advantage . . .

"I guarantee you one thing. When you're my age, you're gonna look at yourself in the mirror and you will say to yourself one of two things: How far could I have gone if I had really given it all I had? And you'll never know the answer to that question. Or you'll look in the mirror and say, I did the best I could, every day, I gave it all I had. And if you can say that, you will have no regrets . . .

"There are four things in my life that I have never regretted for one day, and I can say this as sure as I'm breathing. Number one is the love

I have for God. I go to church and I say my prayers and I'm thankful for everything I have. Number two, I have never regretted the family that I have. They are the best family a man could possibly have. Number three, I have never regretted for one day that I am a citizen of this great nation. I have been to other countries and I have seen the way they operate, and when I get home I want to get down and kiss the ground because I am so proud to be an American. And number four, I have never regretted one day I've spent with the Dodgers. I love this organization, and they have shown that they love me too . . .

"In closing, I would like to say that I hope that something I've said here today may inspire you or motivate you to achieve some of the goals you have set for yourself."

Of all the speeches I've ever given, the one that stands out most in my mind was the day I addressed three thousand cadets in General Hap Arnold Hall at the Air Force Academy. That day I remembered my father, sitting at the head of the table in our house, telling his sons, "You are living in the greatest country in the world, and you should do everything you can to keep it that way, even if you have to fight for it, even if you have to give your life for it." And every one of us served in the armed forces. My brother Morris, for example, put in twenty years in the air force. So being asked to speak to these young men was a special honor for me, and for my father.

"I'll be very honest with you," I started, "I don't even know how to spell bombardier, I don't even know where the doors are on the planes you fly. But I'll tell you something I do know, I do know what it's going to take for you to make it. You are the future leaders of this country. You can be anything you want to be, all you have to do is be willing to pay the price. There is only one route to success, and that is the avenue of hard work . . .

"In everyone's lifetime, there comes a moment when one door will close, and if you are so concerned with the door that closes, you may never find the one that has opened . . .

"The difference between the possible and the impossible lies in a man's determination. Set your goals in life, and go after them with all the drive, self-confidence, and determination that you possess . . ."

I spoke for forty minutes, and received a standing ovation. I looked out at these bright young men, standing and applauding me, and thought how far I'd traveled since I was busy being Van Lingle Mungo back in Norristown.

Not that far, as it turned out. Of all the affairs I've attended, one that stands out took place on December 15, 1981, at Norristown's Westover

Inn and Golf Club, where I was honored by my friends. Well, maybe "honored" is not exactly the correct word. Red McCarthy said I was "the only guy who can follow you into a revolving door and come out ahead of you," and the master of ceremonies complimented my eighth grade teacher, who was there, by saying "Tommy often says those were the four years that really molded him."

Being honored by my friends in my hometown was an outstanding feeling, but being honored in my father's hometown, Tollo, Abruzzo, Italy, was perhaps the greatest thing that has ever happened to me off a baseball field, except for meeting Jo. In 1976 I received a call from Dr. Maximo Ciceotte, head of the Italian Federation of Baseball, asking me how much I would charge to come over to conduct clinics for Italian coaches. Baseball is about as well known in Italy as bocci is here. "You're calling from Italy?" I asked. He was. "And you're Italian?" I didn't want to take anything for granted. He was. "Then it won't cost you anything," I said, "because you've already given me the greatest gift I've ever received, my father." So I flew to Italy and traveled around the country conducting clinics, in Italian, naturally. When I returned, I told my *interbase* man, Bill Russell, that I didn't want him trying to hit *fuori campis*, home runs, I wanted him to concentrate on *rubatas*, steals. "*Si,*" he said, and I had never known he spoke Italian.

Four years later I became the first Italian-American to be invited to return to Italy to be honored in the hometown of his family. My father had left Tollo in 1920, and Jo and I assumed there would be few people there who remembered him. But as we entered the city of Tollo on Tom Lasorda Day we were met by the city band, town officials and school children. A banner had been strung across the street reading *"Benvenuto Tomas Lasorda, Figlio de Sabatino Lasorda,"* or "Welcome Tom Lasorda, Son of Sam Lasorda." When I saw my father's name up there I began to cry, and a very old woman came up to me and took my hand. "I used to dance with your father," she said, "before he went to America."

As I looked around this town, as I met these people, I could almost see my father, a young man, dancing in the town square. It was a little difficult to believe that had led to 56,000 people screaming as loudly as they could in packed Dodger Stadium.

The Big Dodger in the Sky has been so good to me. Once, after I'd pitched an hour of batting practice, and the sweat was pouring off me, an elderly fan said he had been watching me and wondered if my energy came from taking vitamins. "Vitamins!"I said. "This baseball that I'm holding is my vitamin A; the uniform I'm wearing is my vitamin B; the sun, wind, and rain out here on the mound are my vitamin C; and the paychecks I get on the first and fifteenth of each month are my multiple vitamins. That's why I'm a healthy man!"

Once, I used to tell people that when I died I wanted to be buried under the pitcher's mound at Dodger Stadium, so that someday, when a young pitcher is struggling, I'll be able to whisper to him to slow down and maintain his composure. But after the Dodgers' executive vice-president, Fred Claire, told me I couldn't be buried there, I decided to settle for a epitaph on my tombstone reading "Tommy Lasorda, Dodger Stadium was his address, but every ball park was his home."

One day in spring training Peter O'Malley called me into his office and surprised me with a tombstone with these lines written on it, and Dodger Blue blood dripping from it.

Naturally, I was overwhelmed by this outstanding present. After accepting it, I said, "Mr. O'Malley, I want to tell you that I love the Dodgers so much that I want to keep working for you even after I'm dead and gone."

He knew I no longer planned on being buried beneath the pitcher's mound, so he asked how I intended to do that.

"Well," I explained, "every season I want you to send someone out to the cemetery with a copy of the Dodger schedule and have them tape it to this tombstone. That way, when people are out at the cemetery seeing their loved ones, they can stop off at my grave to see if the team is home or on the road!"

Being able to spend my life in baseball is like being given a sugar cone; being able to spend it with the Dodgers is like being given the ice cream. As I've often said, if someone came up to me and said he's with the Padres, I would say "When did you become a priest?" If someone came up to me and said he was with the Indians, I'd ask what reservation he came from; if he said he was a Twin, I'd ask, "Where's your brother?" If he said he was a Cardinal, I'd pat him on the back and say, "Work hard, the next step is to be pope. But if someone comes up to you and says he's a Dodger, you know he's in major league baseball.

I want the whole world to know that I think I'm the luckiest man on the face of the earth. I'm a Dodger.

Acknowledgments

Walter Alston, Bobby Bragan, Lou Brock, Jocko Collins, Andy Golce, Wally Fiala, Tom Gorman, Mickey Houston, Sid Korshak, Sid Luckman, Billy Martin, Lee MacPhail, Reds Picard, George Randazzo, Branch Rickey, Robert Schuller, Aaron Spelling, Barbara and Frank Sinatra, Ray Travaglini, Tom Villante, John Weibusch, Ken and Bob Aspermonte, Matt Byrnes, Lou Brock, Norm Crosby, Johnny Carson, Rod and Justin Dedeaux, Chub Feeney, Andy Granatelli, Bob Hope, Bill Fugazy, Kenny Kondo, Andy McKenna, Stan Musial, Joe Phillips, Coach Eddie Robinson of Grambling College, Marty Russo, Chuck Tanner, Ted Williams, Bud Wilkinson, Johnny Werhas, Bill Walsh, Donny Soffer of Turnberry Isle, Jerry Weintraub, Bob Smith, Chuck Stevens, Frank Rothman, Jim Nabors, Eddie Minasian, Tony LoBianco, Bob Kurlan, Fred Hartley, George Green, Cary Grant, Marvin Davis, J. J. McMahon, Ed McMahon, Jim Campanis, Jim Bacon, Charlie Blaney, Cy Berger, Jerry Bellgard, Dutch Belnap, Edward DeBartolo, Sr., and Jr., Buzzy Bavasi, Peter Bavasi, Blake Cullen, Leo Durocher, Danny Goodman, Florence Henderson, Ed Hookstratten, Chuck Knox, Mel Levine, Sonny Monastero, Gabe Paul, Jilly Rizzo, Pete Rozelle, Peter Rouselle, Danny Schwartz, Larry Speakes, Andy Spagnola, my old roomie Tim Thompson, Billy Weinberger, Bob Walker, Zack Samuels, Bert Wells, R. J. Wagner, Joe Tannenbaum, Cy Sussman, Frank Sinatra, Jr., Harvey Silbert, Sugar Ray Robinson, Dwight Patterson, Tom Mulcahy, Rabbi Magnin, Danny Kaye, Lee Iacocca, Alan Hirschfield, Charlie Gritto, Joe DiMaggio, Senator William Cohen, Perry Como, Mayor Tom Bradley and his wife, Ethel, Lou Boudreau, Vic Damone, Joe Garagiola, Dr. Frank Jobe, Bowie Kuhn, Boom Boom Mancini, Ron Masak, Sandy Petruso, Ken Shanzer, Grant Tinker, Dorothy Uhleman, Larry Wong, Fred Wilpon, Tom Flores, Matt Burns, Mike Fratello, Rollie Massamino, Lou Carnesca, John Robinson, Jerry West, Jerry Buss, Joe DiCarlo, Art Watson, Pete Rose, Hal Evans, Lew Wasserman, Tony Hamilton, Mark Burnett, Gary Nardino, Ernest Borgnine, Tony Orlando, Sheriff Block, Pat Cooper, David Gerber, Irv Schecter, Sam Lovello, Cliff Schmilling, Giuseppe Bellisario, Ricardo Montalban, Marino Nibbi, Mike Shannon, Jack Buck, Jerry Vale, Bill Thomas, Ed Nalbandian, Ed Vrdolyak, Marty Klein, Bill Walsh, Dominic Moceri, Bob Walker, Chuck Young, A. C. Lyles, Dick Pelletire, and last of all, Don Rickles and his wife, Barbara.

Fresco Thompson, Don Drysdale, Carl Furillo, Wes Parker, Tom Paciorek, Pee Wee Reese, Bill Schweppe, Bobby Valentine, Sandy Koufax, Don Zimmer, Johnny Podres, Tony Zweickel, Billy Buckner, Steve Garvey, Barry Stockhammer, Hoyt Wilhelm, Don Sutton, Rick Rhoden, Rick Sutcliffe, Tommy John, Tony John, Charlie Hough, Jerry Stephenson, Mike Garman, Joe Beckwith, Ed Liberatore, Ben Wade, Fred Claire, Ken Brett, Willie Crawford, Bruce Ellingsen, Joe Ferguson, Terry Forster, Ed Goodson, Von Joshua, Jay Johnstone, Danny Ozark, Ron Perronaski, Dick McLaughlin, Mark Cresse, Red Adams, Monte Basgall, Jim Gilliam, Joey Amalfitano, John McNamara, Manny Mota, Roy Campanella, Bill Buhler, Rick Honeycutt, Bert Hooton, Doug Rau, Jerry Reuss, Oral Hershiser, Fernando Valenzuela, Alejandro Pena, Bobby Welch, Sid Bream, Nobe Kawano, Jim Muhe, Jerry Turner, Ike Ikuhara, Merrit Willey, Sam Fernandez, Jerry Royster, Ron Roenicke, Pat Zachary, Geoff Zahn, Bill Russell, Steve Yeager, Mike Scioscia, Jerry Grote, Johnny Oates, Bobby Stinson, Greg Brock, Davey Lopes, Ron Cey, Dusty Baker, Rick Monday, Reggie Smith, Mike Marshall (the outfielder), Ken Landreaux, Dave Anderson, Pedro Guerrero, Steve Howe, Kenny Howell, Tom Niedenfuer, Dave Stewart, Jack Fimple, Candy Maldonado, Terry Whitfield, Boog Powell, Lee Lacy, Mickey Hatcher, Darrell Thomas, Juan Marichal, Andy Messersmith, Jose Morales, Billy North, Jorge Orta, Boyd Bartley, Bob Bishop, Bob Bodet, Bobby Darwin, Paul Duval, Tommy Johnson, John Keenan, Jim Garland, Dick Hanlon, Denny Haren, Gail Henley, Ron King, Steve Lembo, Carl Loewenstine, Dale McRaynolds, Tommy Nixon, Reggie Otero, Bill Pleis, Dick Teed, Corito Varona, Raphael Avila, Mike Brito, Mel Didier, Frank Lucchesi, Frank Rossi, Harry Bardt, Terry and Rollie Seidler, Paul Padillo, Guy Wellman, Jackie Robinson, Gil Hodges, Rube Walker, Preacher Roe, Carl Furillo, Guy

Wellman, Gil Hodges, Rube Walker, Carl Erskine, Clem Labine, Don Newcombe, Bill DeLury, Bill Shumard, Preston Gomez, Ted Sizemore.

Jerome Holtzman, Jim Hill, Stu Nathan, Mel Durslag, Jack Lang, Dick Young, Al Malamud, Arthur and Milton Richman, Doug Kerkourian, Gordy Verrell, Joe Reichler, Dave Anderson, Bill Madden, Ken Gurnick, Gordon Eddes, John Lowe, Ed Pope, Dan Foster, Furman Bisher, Tom McEwen, Jessie Outlar, Scott Ostler, Earl Lawson, Hal McCoy, Paul Meyer, Phil Hersh, Cy Burick, Blackie Sherrod, Mark Purdy, Randy Gallaway, Chris Mortinson, Dave Kindred, Harry Caray, Phil Pepe, George Vecsey, Art Spander, Randy Youngman, Harry Shattuck, Murray Chass, Joe Donnelly, Henry Hecht, Moss Klein, Buzz Saidt, Mike Lupica, Kenny Hand, Terry Johnson, Francis Dale, publisher of the *Los Angeles Herald-Examiner*, Tom Johnson, publisher of the *Los Angeles Times*, Ross Newhan, Peter Schmuk, Mitch Chortkoff, Lowell Schrader, Jim McCormack, Mike Waldner, Ed Arnold, Tony Hernandez, Roy Firestone, Tom Kelly, Fred Roggin, Tommy Hawkins, Lisa Bowman, Tracy Ringolsby, Sid Hartman, Maury Allen, Joe Falls, Jock Beauchamp, John Striege, Jeff Rimer, Tony Kubek, Frank Dolson, Bill Conlin, Ross Porter, Jaime Jarron, Rene Cardenas, Joe Durso, Bill Dwyre, Howard Cosell, Hal Bodley, Larry Keith, Ron Fimrite, Dick Kaegel, Al Michaels, Brent Musburger, Lou Palmer, Tom Boswell, Peter Gammons, Tom Singer, Joe Goddard, Steve Daley, Ron Rappoport, Bob Verdi, Jerry Green, Chuck Howard, Harry Coyle, Chet Forte, Roone Arledge, George Finkle, Keith Jackson, Jerry Doggett.

Johnny, Breck, Timothy, Allison, and Gladys Reeves, Lee and Orell Miller, Fran Redick, Meb Redick, Kim and Alan Vaughan, Lee Miller, Jr., Billy Miller, Jean and Dean Kennett, Charles Kennett, Buster Kennett, Beth Kennett, Mrs. Sue Miller, Eddie and Betty Lasorda, Carmella and Aurelio Soriano, Harry and Virginia Lasorda, Sammy and Sandy Lasorda, Joey Lasorda, Eddie Lasorda, Michele Lasorda, Morris and Joan Lasorda, David Lasorda, Tony Cavatto.

My coauthor would like to acknowledge the assistance of Rosemary Rogers and Nell Rogers, Dave Aust, Glenn Deutsch, Clorinda Marie Cardillo, Andy and Matt Glenn, and Jill Boniske.

We would both like to sincerely thank Bill Thompson and Fred Chase of Arbor House, for their perseverance, and Basil Kane and David Burns of the Burns Sports Literary Agency, for their efforts.